A Consummate Lawyer

A CONSUMMATE LAWYER

William Reece Smith, Jr.

Michael I. Swygert

CAROLINA ACADEMIC PRESS

Durham, North Carolina

ISBN 978-1-59460-806-3
LCCN: 2009936352

CAROLINA ACADEMIC PRESS
700 Kent Street
Durham, North Carolina 27701
Telephone (919) 489-7486
Fax (919) 493-5668
www.cap-press.com

Printed in the United States of America

To Dianne in celebration of our approaching 50th wedding anniversary.

CONTENTS

FOREWORD: A LIVING LEGEND

A "living legend" generally refers to a person who has achieved a sustained and enduring level of accomplishment that not only exceed the ordinary, but also exceeds the extraordinary. Reece Smith is a living legend. One cannot find a precedent for his life in the law. He is *sui generis*—a scholar-athlete, Rhodes Scholar, lawyer, teacher and leader of bar organizations as well as civic/community organizations. But above all, he is a tireless, passionate advocate of measures that will assure access by all to legal counsel and equal justice under the law.

By his conspicuous example, he has taught our profession that the practice of law is more than the billable hour, more than a means to wealth—it is a means of gaining great satisfaction in using the privilege we have to practice law to help those in need have access to the legal system. Reece Smith has been doing that now for over half a century in Florida, the United States, and across the world. Even today, in his 80s, he continues to work towards the goal of access to justice for all those in need of legal counsel.

Reece Smith has not only led our profession, he has made an impact on many individual lawyers. His influence on his law firm to hire minorities (starting with me, over 45 years ago) long before that was politically correct, was courageous but he thought it was the "right thing to do." His emphasis upon professionalism has had a lasting impact upon scores of law students, including one who is now a shareholder of our firm and applied to our firm having taken Reece's ethics course and concluding: "I want to practice law in this man's firm." Those of us who have been so influenced by Reece Smith owe him much, as does the profession at large.

This book about this remarkable professional—this "living legend"—should be required reading in every ethics class in every law school. But it will also be fascinating to those already in the profession, as it provides a riveting story of a life well-lived in the law. Enjoy, and let us all commit to follow Reece Smith's stellar example of true and rewarding professionalism.

Sylvia Hardaway Walbolt
Shareholder, Carlton Fields, Tampa, Florida

Acknowledgments

This book is the result of the work of many people, indeed, a team effort. I owe each a debt of gratitude, but none more so than Reece Smith, the subject of this biography. Mr. Smith and I spent scores of hours together over the last three years, for the most part in his office at Carlton Fields in Tampa. Throughout, he was generous with his time and patient with my repeated requests for explanation and information. I thank Mr. Smith's administrative assistant, Sandra Kinley, for her help in tracking down legal materials, speeches, and other documents I requested.

A key contributor throughout has been Sylvia Walbolt, a shareholder and former chair of Carlton Fields. Not only did she furnish fascinating "Reece" stories, she graciously volunteered to read and to edit the manuscript—not once, but several times—a task she has performed superbly. In addition, Ms. Walbolt's husband, Dan Walbolt, an administrator at the University of South Florida when Mr. Smith was the University's interim-president, provided valuable insights and information and also read the manuscript.

In terms of total time, no one surpassed the effort of Carol Ann Ransone, my research associate for two years. A graduate of the Stetson University College of Law, she searched records and files covering the eighty-four years to date of Mr. Smith's life and career, locating, organizing, and distilling relevant information. I extend to Carol Ann my sincerest gratitude as I also do to Ms. Sharon Gisclair, an incredibly talented person who has helped me produce three books. Sharon has served as the administrative assistant to a federal judge, a practice group administrator at Fowler White Boggs, a Tampa law firm and, presently, a business coordinator for the firm of Banker Lopez Gassler. Sharon went beyond the call of duty, working many evenings and weekends at home on this project. Roberta Kemp Flowers, the William Reece Smith Jr., Distinguished Professor of Law at Stetson University College of Law, has encouraged me from the the time I conceived of the idea of writing this biography and I sincerely thank her for her support.

There are others deserving mention. Among them are Ruth Ann Schmitt, an administrative assistant to Mr. Smith when he was President of the American Bar Association, and Harriet Ellis, who had worked for the Legal Services Corporation. Ms. Schmitt and Ms. Ellis met with Mr. Smith and myself over a two-day period in the Chicago area to discuss in detail his work as ABA President. Meanwhile, Dan Perez, a senior office staff member at Carlton Fields, assisted in the digitalizing and editing of the photographs in this volume. Throughout, Louise Petren, head of faculty-support services at Stetson Law School, provided needed services. I give special thanks to Dean Darby Dickerson of the Stetson College of Law for providing me with an office while working on this book..

Most of all, I thank my wife Dianne for her love, support, encouragement, and patience in my undertaking this project and for her critical reading of portions of the manuscript.

Michael Swygert
St. Petersburg, Florida
June 7, 2009

A Consummate Lawyer

CHAPTER ONE

EQUAL JUSTICE

*In the service of the principle of equal justice, William Reece Smith, Jr.,
has always been at the forefront. When president of the ABA ... [he] had
projects and ideas. And, as I was soon to learn, many of the items on this
president's agenda had to do with protecting the rights of poor people.*

So said Peter R. Bonavich, a former American Bar Association official, in a
speech in April 1993 on what he called "the public service of one of America's
great lawyers." The occasion was a surprise dinner in honor of William Reece
Smith, Jr., of Tampa, Florida. Bonavich commented that the way people talked
about Smith seemed inconsistent with the image that Bonavich had of other
ABA presidents. "Everybody at the ABA seemed to know this guy personally
[and] people spoke of him like he was a member of the family."

Reece Smith had been a small-town boy who became a recognized and respected leader of lawyers and bar organizations around the world. Throughout his long career, he has worked persistently to improve the legal profession
and to further the mandate of equal justice under the law. Smith is an extraordinarily humble, friendly and gracious person, with a courteous and re-
spectful demeanor and distinguished appearance. Those he has met or worked
with overwhelmingly like him and recognize him to be an ethical, professional,
and skilled lawyer.

Throughout the course of his career, Smith has put the public's interests
and those of his clients first. Seeking neither to maximize his income nor to wield
political power for self-aggrandizement, he is a lawyer committed to using his
knowledge for the benefit of clients, the profession, and the public. By doing
so, he has become a world-renowned and respected lawyer. His world exposure came as a result of being elected—the only American to have been so—
president of the International Bar Association, an umbrella body that includes
bar associations and law societies around the world representing over two million lawyers. Previously he had headed his local county (Hillsborough), state
(Florida), and national (American) bar associations. While president of the
American Bar Association and later the International Bar Association, Smith

visited over eighty countries and traveled more than 300,000 miles—not bad for a small-town boy born in Tennessee who once sacked potatoes for twelve cents an hour.

In addition to telling the story of Smith's bar service to lawyers around world, this book chronicles his childhood in Florida; service in the U.S. Navy; playing football at the University of South Carolina; three years as a Rhodes Scholar at Oxford University; practicing law at his Tampa law firm, including taking four cases to the United States Supreme Court; service as City Attorney for Tampa; bettering race relations in the Tampa Bay area; working on behalf of higher education; serving as interim president of a major research university; advising mayors, legislators, and governors; teaching on law school faculties; sitting on boards of universities and law schools; rendering community service on behalf of civic and philanthropic organizations; working to remove gender, racial, and national origin barriers; and, above all, continually working to make *pro bono* legal services more available for poor people—not only in America—but in countries around the world.

Smith's core beliefs are best summarized in three sayings he often recites in his speeches:

> *We must always remember that a right lost to one is lost to all;*
> *Meeting the legal needs of the poor is not a race for the short winded;*
> *If we are to keep our democracy, there must be one commandment:*
> *Thou shall not ration Justice.*

The first two our Smith's own while the third comes from legendary jurist, Learned Hand. Judge Hand's commandment is orthodoxy for Smith. He has striven throughout his career to change peoples' biased attitudes regarding race, gender and national origin. He has worked to increase jobs for people of color, and to ease tensions and resolve differences among ethnic and racial groups. Reece Smith indeed is a consummate lawyer.

* * *

CHAPTER TWO

WILLIAM REECE SMITH, JR.— AN OVERVIEW

Born and raised in modest circumstances, Smith was fortunate in having caring parents as well as a cultured and college-educated grandmother living in his household. The grandson of a farmer and son of an insurance agent, he grew up to become a Rhodes Scholar at Oxford University. Smith was selected on the bases of his character and integrity, military and public service, educational record in college and law school, and athletic success in college. Ultimately, Smith headed one of the largest and most respected law firms in the Southeast and became a nationally and internationally known lawyer.

In 1949, when twenty-three years old, Smith was admitted to law practice. When thirty-four, he was elected president of the Junior Bar Conference of the American Bar Association (ABA) and, two years later, president of the Hillsborough County Bar. When he was forty-six, he was named president of The Florida Bar and seven years later was elected president of the American Bar Association. Then in 1980, Smith became the first *elected* American president of the International Bar Association.

Today, in 2009, sixty years later, he goes to his law office at Carlton Fields on most days where he is chair *emeritus* of the 300 member law firm. He enjoys talking with young lawyers regarding nuances of the law, but even more he is passionate about the professional responsibilities consequent to the privilege of practicing law. He always encourages the firm's new lawyers to become involved in civic and charitable activities as well as bar association work.

The beneficiaries of Smith's legal talents extend far beyond his firm's clients and bar associations. He once served fourteen months as interim president of the University of South Florida (USF). Although he was urged to stay on as the permanent president, his run for the presidency of the ABA prevented him from doing so. Nonetheless, the cause of higher education was, and remains, one of Smith's top priorities. Smith chaired for several years USF's Council of Advisors, an influential policy body concerned with the university's academic and financial well being. Besides USF, Smith has endeavored to advance the interests of several other universities and colleges. He has served on the boards of Bethune-Cookman College (vice-chair), Stetson University (trustee), University of Tampa (advisory board), and the New College Foundation (vice-chair), and as a member of law school oversight committees or boards at Florida State, Stetson, and Miami.

Smith turned 84 years old in 2009. He claims he is retired, but don't believe it! He continues to maintain a demanding schedule, speaking at law schools, universities, and bar and civic functions across the country. He rarely misses either mid-year or annual meetings of the ABA, or those of the American Law Institute, The Florida Bar, and the American Bar Foundation. The list goes on.

Young in energy and spirit, Smith continues to participate in lawyers' programs involving legal aid and the *pro bono* representation of poor people, either as a speaker or a participant. In one recent year, he spoke to faculties and students at three law schools, various meetings of Inns of Court (organizations of judges, lawyers, and legal academicians), conclaves of local, state, and national bar organizations and conferences on lawyer professionalism. As if these demanding activities are not enough for this unique octogenarian lawyer, he teaches courses in legal ethics and professional responsibility to law students at Stetson University College of Law.

Today, Smith routinely is honored at state and national functions. Several universities (eleven) have awarded him honorary doctor degrees. He has scores of other citations, awards, metals, testimonials, and plaques. In 2005, a new courtroom on the Tampa campus of the Stetson College of Law was named in his honor. Not only do Stetson law students use the facility, so does the Tampa division of Florida's Second District Court of Appeal.

* * *

CHAPTER THREE

Lineage and Family

Coming to America

In the 1600s, Rebecca Rhys, a Quaker, left Wales along with other Quakers because of religious persecution. Over the next two-hundred years, the spelling of "Rhys" went through several permutations before "Reece." After coming to the New World, Smith's ancestors settled mainly in Maryland where Rebecca Rhys met and married Moses Bowen. They journeyed down the valley of Virginia to the French Broad River region of Tennessee and Kentucky. Several years ago, Reece Smith, Jr., and his son, William Reece Smith, III, traveled to Wales and found records identifying Quakers who left Wales in the 1600s. One was Smith's ancestor, Rebecca Rhys Bowen. In time the Bowen line merged with the Pickens line through marriage.

Robert Pickens was born in 1747 in South Carolina. He was a son of Robert Pike Pickens, who left Ireland to relocate in Colonial America. Robert Bowen was a descendant of Rebecca and Moses Bowen. Robert Bowen fought in America's War for Independence in the 1770s as did Robert Pickens. Both were captains in the Colonial Army. In 1775, Robert Pickens and his wife Dorcus Hallum had a son named John Pickens while, that same year, Robert Bowen and his wife Mary Gillespie (also from Ireland) had a daughter they named Nancy.

John Pickens and Nancy Bowen married in 1799 in South Carolina. They had ten children, including Mary Bowen Pickens, one of Reece Smith's great-great grandmothers. She was born in 1800 on Three and Twenty Creek in northwestern South Carolina. When eighteen years old, she married John Smith. They had a son they named William Reece Smith, born in McMinn County, Tennessee, the first of what would be five Smiths in the lineage having the same name.

"William" and "Reece" were chosen because "William" was the first name of John Smith's father, William Smith, (born in 1770), while "Reece" was the name of Mary Pickens's uncle, Hugh Reece Bowen (the brother of Mary Bowen Pickens' mother, Nancy Bowen). The first William Reece Smith was born in 1825, exactly 100 years before William Reece Smith, Jr., was born. In between, another William Reece Smith came into the world in 1894—Smith's father, William Reece Smith (who in this book is referred to as William Reece Smith, Sr., to avoid confusion with William Reece Smith, Jr.)

The 1825-born William Reece Smith married Frances Jane Wilson in 1848. Of their ten children, Israel Jefferson Smith, was born in 1857. Israel is Reece Smith's fraternal grandfather who farmed in McMinn County. In 1890, Israel Smith married Dollie Mae Lee of Tellico Plains, Tennessee, one of Reece's fraternal grandmothers. They had seven children, including William Reece Smith, Sr., (Reece's father) who in 1922 married Gladys Elizabeth Moody (Reece's mother). The senior Smith and Gladys had one child—William Reece Smith, Jr.

In 1963, Smith (the lawyer and subject of this biography) married Marlene Medina. They have one son—William Reece Smith, III, born in 1966, in Tampa, and one grandson, William Reece Smith, IV, born in 2008, also in Tampa. If the usual numerical order had been maintained, Smith Sr. would have been William Reece II, and Smith Jr. would have been William Reece Smith III, whose son would be William Reece Smith, IV, and his grandson, William Reece Smith, V.

Smith's mother, Gladys Elizabeth Moody, was born on August 4, 1894, in Athens, McMinn County, Tennessee. She was the daughter of Mary Noel Estes and Thomas Edwin Moody. The Moody and Estes lineages, like that of the Smith family, have deep Southern roots. The Moody ancestors came to America before the American Revolution, initially residing near Williamsburg in eastern Virginia. One of the early Moodys in Virginia was Marshall Moody, who married Elizabeth Shelton in 1823. Soon afterwards, they migrated through the Shenandoah Valley of western Virginia to western North Carolina and eastern Tennessee. In 1830, Marshall and Elizabeth had a child they named Henry Shelton Moody (Smith's great grandfather). Later, another relative, also with the name of Henry Shelton Moody, married Elizabeth Minor Noel.

Their son Thomas Edwin Moody (Smith's maternal grandfather) married Mary Noel Estes (Smith's maternal grandmother). They had eight children, three of whom died in infancy. The five survivors included two daughters—Gladys Moody (Smith's mother) born in Athens in 1894, and Gray Estes Moody (Smith's aunt) and three sons—Thomas Edwin Moody, Jr., Henry Shelton Moody, and Patrick Mann Moody (Smith's three uncles). For several generations, the Moody clan lived in eastern and central Tennessee. Then, in 1885, Moreau Estes Moody—a Tennessee druggist (and brother of Smith's maternal grandfather) moved to Mango, Florida, where he opened a pharmacy. Moreau relocated the drug store in 1891 to the promising new town of Plant City, Florida.

After Moreau Moody moved to Florida, Smith's grandmother, Mary Noel Estes Moody, and her husband, Thomas Edwin Moody, relocated to Lakeland,

Florida for health reasons. After living there two years, they decided to move back to Tennessee where Thomas Edwin died. In 1901, several years later, Thomas Edwin Moody, Jr., moved to Plant City to form with his uncle, Moreau Estes Moody, "the Moody & Moody" insurance agency.

Plant City had no bank at that time. Moreau Moody, however, maintained a secure safe at his pharmacy, in which he allowed the town's business proprietors and area farmers to deposit money. Recognizing that the small community needed a bank as well as a drug store, Moreau Moody, his cousin Edwin, and C.T. Young established Plant City's first financial institution in 1902—the Hillsboro State Bank (today, the Sun Trust Bank of Plant City.) Young was its first president. Following his death, Moreau Moody became president. Later still, Thomas Edwin Moody became the president of the Hillsboro State Bank.

In time, Patrick Mann Moody, the youngest of Mary Noel's other two sone also relocated to Florida—Patrick Mann Moody and Henry Sheldon Moody. The latter became president of the Manatee Bank and a respected and citizen and business leader of Manatee County. Among the Moody descendants, James Shelton Moody was appointed a judge on Florida's Thirteenth Judicial Circuit Court in Tampa. One of his sons, James Sheldon Moody, Jr., was appointed by President William Clinton to the U.S. District Court for the Middle District of Florida in 2000. Smith proudly spoke at his investiture.

Throughout the past century, the Moodys of east Hillsborough County have been high achievers and active in community affairs. As historians Bruton and Bailey put it: "The Moodys ... have contributed substantially to the development of East Hillsborough County and have established an admirable record for exemplary citizenship and useful public service." One of Smith's Moody relatives, Frank Moody, not only worked for the desegregation of the local public schools, he also assisted in successfully bringing higher education to Plant City. On October 6, 1976, as chair of the East Hillsborough County Chamber of Commerce, Moody joined other leaders in breaking ground for the first permanent building for Hillsborough Community College's Plant City Campus.

In addition to the Moody line, the second dominant lineage on Smith's maternal side is that of "Estes." The surname Estes and its prior spellings—Est, Este, d'Este, Esis, and Esteuse—go back nine centuries. The most distant Estes ancestors in Smith's family have been traced back to Ferrara, Italy. From there, one branch migrated to France, while another went to England and later relocated to Wales before coming to America in the seventeenth century. In 1704, Abraham Estes owned 200 acres in King County, Virginia. Benjamin Estes, a grandson of Abraham, was born in 1753, and his son Joel was born in 1780. Joel was Smith's great-great-great grandfather.

Joel Estes fought in the War of 1812 as Captain of the Riflemen of the 43rd Regiment of the Virginia Militia. After he migrated to western Tennessee, he ran for the U.S. Congress in 1829 against the incumbent—the legendary Davy Crockett. In a three-man contest, candidates Joel Estes and Adam Alexander opposed Crockett. "Campaigning from the stump," Crockett easily won with 8,525 votes, compared to roughly 5,000 for Estes and Alexander combined.

During the campaign, Davy Crockett referred to Joel as "the aristocrat," with some justification. Estes was a prominent and prosperous plantation owner who built a grand home he named Estes Hall in the Big Hatchie area of Haywood County, Tennessee. Joel and his wife, Sarah Bates, were the first of three Estes generations to reside in Estes Hall. Joel and Sarah had nine children, including Moreau Pinckney Estes (Smith's *great, great* grandfather). In 1836, Moreau married Mary Quarles Noel and they in turn had ten children. Tragically, on July 22, 1864, two of their sons—Moreau Pinckney Estes and Thomas Ewell Estes—were killed in the same charge in the Battle of Atlanta during Sherman's March through Georgia. One of the brothers who survived the Civil War was Joel Henry Estes (Smith's *great* grandfather). In 1882, Joel married Martha Ann Mann and their first child, Mary Noel Estes (Smith's grandmother), was born one year later.

At one point, the Estes clan and another Tennessee family—the Kefauvers— intermarried. As a result, Smith is related to several Kefauvers including Estes Kefauver, a U.S. Senator from Tennessee. He became nationally known for heading the "Kefauver Committee," a U.S. Senate committee that investigated organized crime and political corruption in America. During his time in the Senate, Estes Kefauver ran unsuccessfully for the vice-presidency of the United States.

Another Estes, Patrick Mann Estes, a brother of Smith's grandmother, was a lawyer who became a successful and wealthy businessman in Nashville, Tennessee. As a lawyer, he helped organize and acquired substantial stock holdings in the Life & Casualty Insurance Company. The Tennessee company grew into a nationally prominent insurance provider. Smith's "Uncle Pat" built a large home near Nashville named Grayswood after his wife, Gray Estes. Smith remembers staying in the stately residence where Uncle Pat once gave him a dollar to zip up a golf bag. Smith was thrilled because a dollar was a considerable amount of money in the Great Depression.

Family

William Reece Smith, Jr., was born on September 19, 1925. That year Babe Ruth was at the peak of his career with the Yankees; the Four Horsemen of

Notre Dame dominated college football; flappers were dancing the Charleston; President Calvin Coolidge was in the White House; and Clarence Darrow and William Jennings Bryan battled in the Scopes Monkey Trial over the teaching of evolution.

Though born in the hills of eastern Tennessee, Smith and his parents relocated to Plant City, Florida, three months after his birth. Smith's father was a veteran of the First World War who returned to his Tennessee home to find his former job in a textile mill no longer existed. Unable to find suitable employment in McMinn County, the senior Smith decided to move to Plant City where two of his wife's brothers resided. Smith and his mother took a train to Florida, while Smith's father drove the family car from Athens to Plant City, over largely unpaved, dusty roads through Georgia.

Smith's parents found Plant City hospitable. Moreover, they stood on firmer ground economically than they had in Athens. Shortly after coming to Florida, Smith's father began working with his brother-in-law in the family insurance business and the two soon became partners. During their years in Plant City, the family resided in three homes, the last being a large, two-story frame house on Reynolds Street, where Smith spent most of his childhood.

Though neither Smith's father nor grandfathers went to college, Smith's mother, Gladys, attended Richmond College. She was a nurturing, sympathetic, and caring parent, as well as a dedicated housewife and a responsible citizen in the community. Active in Plant City's Baptist Church, she rarely missed Sunday services. When Smith played football and basketball for Plant City High School, she often attended the games. Similarly, when Smith played football for the University of South Carolina, she went to those games whenever possible, though South Carolina was a good distance from Florida. She was pleased by her son's achievements in school, both on and off the gridiron. Gladys Elizabeth Smith died on the anniversary of Pearl Harbor, December 7, 1974, in the family home in Plant City.

Smith's father was born in McMinn County, Tennessee, his ancestors having migrated in the early 1800s from the Anderson District of South Carolina, traveling across the Smokey Mountains of the Appalachian Range to the Piedmont and foothills of southeastern Tennessee. There they homesteaded and farmed the land. Smith's father, however, chose not to be a farmer but took a job at the Eureka Textile Mills of Englewood, a few miles north of Athens. Besides work, he enthusiastically pursued a number of hobbies, including astronomy (he built his own telescopes), collecting stamps, and collecting rare coins. Smith chuckles over his father's dry sense of humor. One example: Smith's father, upon learning that his son had been nominated for presidency of the ABA, told a reporter for the *Plant City Courier*:

Reece was an average student [pause]. Oh yes, he was chosen for membership in *Phi Beta Kappa*; was first in his class in law school, elected to the University of Florida Blue Key Honorary Society, and was a Rhodes Scholar at Oxford.

His father did much more than make Smith laugh. He helped him with his arithmetic homework, the subject the young boy found most challenging in school.

Smith's father died at the age of eight-eight on September 9, 1982. He is buried along side his wife in Plant City. Smith says: "My father, William Reece Smith, Sr., though a quiet man, was very bright and friendly, one of Plant City's most popular figures."

Mother Mary

Mary Noel Estes (Moody, after marriage), Smith's maternal grandmother, was born in 1863 at Estes Hall in Haywood County, Tennessee. Smith refers to her as "Mother Mary" and says that she may have been the most important person in his upbringing. He describes her as "a daughter of the old South, a woman far ahead of her time." He adds that "a whole volume could be written about her."

Mary Noel's father — Joel Henry Estes — fought for the Confederacy in the War Between the States along with seven of her uncles. Her parents encouraged her to go to college. She did and earned a bachelor of arts degree at age sixteen from Brownsville Female College in Tennessee. Later, she earned an advanced degree in literature from Hollins College in Virginia. After raising eight children, she spent several summers at Harvard University, where she studied classical literature.

In 1928, Mary authored a book titled *Trails of Two Travelers,* under her married name, Mary Noel Moody. The book relates the details of an eleven-week trip though Europe in the summer of 1927 that Mary took with her daughter, Grey Estes. Tragically, Grey died not long after their journey ended. In remembrance, Mary authored *Trails of Two Travelers.* On its acknowledgment page, she credits Harvard Summer Schools and Hollins College "for giving me a love of good books."

In 1941, the New York House of Field published *Trails of Two Travelers.* On virtually every page she refers to classical poets and authors. Examples include Shakespeare, Horace, Virgil, Byron, Shelly, Gray, Dante, Dryden, Voltaire, Tennyson, Longfellow, Fielding, Goldsmith, Pope, Balzac, George Bernard Shaw, George Eliot, and Jane Porter. Of all the referenced authors, Mary Noel mentions most often Elizabeth Barrett Browning and her husband, Robert Browning (the two poets she most admired) and quotes verses authored by Elizabeth ("The Court Lady") and by Robert ("The Statue and the Bust"). She also cites passages from George Eliot ("Romola"), Lord Byron ("Prisoner of Chillon"), and Gray ("Elegy in a Country Churchyard"). In their travels through England, Ireland, Scotland, France, Italy, Belgium, Germany, Holland, and Switzerland, mother and daughter visited places where renowned men and women of letters were born, wrote, or died.

Smith underscores that his grandmother possessed a deep love for literature, a fondness she manifested throughout her adult life. Her devotion to good books was infectious. When living in Athens, she organized a literary club called the Browning Circle (in honor of Elizabeth and Robert Browning), which she led for thirty-two years. Smith believes that the Browning Circle "sustained intellectual thought" within the Athens community. After moving from Athens to Plant City, Mary formed another Browning literary club. When Reece turned one year old in 1926, Mother Mary gave him a leather-bound book on Homer, written in both English and Greek. She inscribed it to her "grandson Reece," who has prized the book for over eight decades.

Smith's grandmother not only loved classical poetry and literature, she also had a fondness for history—especially of the South—about which she read extensively. In addition, she studied classical music, played both the piano and the pipe organ, and had a strong appreciation for art.

When the Smith family moved to Plant City, "Mother Mary" came with them. Her husband Thomas Moody had died in Athens six years earlier, and she desired to be with family.

In the Smith household, Mary served as the family matriarch and from Smith's infancy, until he left for college, she resided in the family home. This educated and cultured lady profoundly impacted Smith's view of the world. She motivated him to be the best he could be at whatever he undertook, to work hard, to develop a love for literature, and to take education seriously. She persistently stressed the importance of honesty and honor, telling Smith that he must deal with every person he would meet with integrity, respect, and sense of duty. To this day, he remembers Mother Mary's moral edict: "*A good name is rather to be had than great riches.*"

Mother Mary was a leader of Plant City's Women's Christian Temperance Union (WCTU). The WCTU has been called the "moderate" wing of the prohibition movement, one that arose in America during the 1840s and 1850s. After prohibition failed, the WCTU turned its attention to lobbying individuals to cease consuming alcoholic beverages. From the late 1920s through the '30s, Mary worked with the WCTU chapter in Plant City to publicize the evils of alcohol. For four years, young Smith was a member of the Loyal Temperance Legion (LTL), a group consisting of sons and daughters of active WCTU members. They participated in activities to discourage drinking alcohol and smoking cigarettes. Smith remembers chanting verses calling out for the demise of alcohol such as "Down with booze! Down with booze! We want clothes! We want shoes!"

Though he has not remained rigidly faithful to his maternal grandmother's temperance way of life, Smith has followed her example in seeking social change for a better society. Mother Mary was not satisfied with the *status quo*, especially when it came to women not having the right to vote. She was only thirty when she began to campaign for women's suffrage in McMinn County, Tennessee, a cause she continued after moving to Plant City. In addition to organizing women to push for the right to vote, she encouraged them to develop their "God-given intelligence" by reading literature and history, by becoming knowledgeable about political and civic affairs, and by pursuing an education beyond high school. She extolled women to express their opinions openly on public issues, a practice quite aberrational under the societal norms and stereotypical thinking of the times. She herself wrote articles and commentaries for the local newspaper.

As a molder of changing attitudes, she taught not only through words, but even more so by example. She became the first woman in Tennessee to hold statewide public office, having been appointed a member of the Tennessee State Health Commission. In that position she worked to improve the circumstances of mountain folk, mill workers, and inmates of mental institutions. She participated in both the Daughters of the American Revolution and the United Daughters of the Confederacy, and in time became president of the Florida United Daughters of the Confederacy.

In addition, she served as president of the Plant City Women's Club. In that capacity, she and the club members worked relentlessly for the creation of the city's public library. That happened, Smith says, because of Mother Mary's efforts to promote literacy. She volunteered for many hours working in the library after it opened, coming most weekday afternoons to run the library when no one else was willing to do so. For several years, she purchased most of the library's books, often revealing her preferences for titles pertaining to history and literature.

After her death in 1948 (at the age of eighty-five), Smith and other descendants donated funds for a conference room in the Plant City Public Library to be named the "Mary Noel Estes Moody Room" in recognition of her work in establishing and developing the library. Today, her portrait and a plaque describing her dedication and service to the library hangs on its walls.

Following her death, the *Plant City Courier* described her as "one of the most talented and gracious persons in Plant City." Observing that the city's public library seemed closest to Mary's heart, the *Courier* noted: "Without the efforts of Mrs. Moody, Plant City might not have had a library."

Mother Mary took her religion — Baptist — seriously, donating much time on behalf of the town's First Baptist Church. She played the organ at Sunday services and founded the Women's Christian Missionary Union. Members of the congregation called her "the pastor without salary."

When Mary Noel Moody died, Smith was twenty-two and a second-year student at the University of Florida law school. The day of her funeral, the public schools of East Hillsborough County were dismissed in her honor. Today, Smith still admires his Mother Mary, saying "she was a woman of great warmth, charm and amazing vitality; a friend to all regardless of religion, race, or circumstances." Mother Mary's counsel was that Smith should always be the best he could be regardless the endeavor. That moral edict has stayed with him through this day.

Decades after Mother Mary's death, Smith recalls a train tour of the Midwest and West with her as a young boy. They traveled to Chicago where they went to the Planetarium and visited Chicago's world-famous stock yards. Smith was dazzled by the skyscrapers. Of course, he could not imagine that one day he would return and have an office in one of them as president of the American Bar Association.

From Chicago, they took a train through the Badlands of the Dakotas in traveling to Yellowstone National Park in Wyoming and Montana. In a frightening experience, Smith and his grandmother encountered a bear as they were returning after dark to their cottage in the park. "My fearless grandmother curtsied to the bear and said to me 'come along Reece.'" The bear turned and went his way, and grandmother and grandson went theirs.

From Yellowstone, they traveled to Emmet, Idaho, near Boise and the Snake River. One of his grandmother's sisters lived there with her husband, Paul Kefauver (Smith's great uncle). Kefauver owned a fruit ranch on which he grew peaches, apples, and plums. At the ranch, Smith swam in an irrigation ditch and, as a result, developed an infection in his left ear. A doctor came to the home and poured hot oil into Smith's ear, a customary procedure for ear infections at the time. But the oil did not help and the infection worsened, causing Smith's left ear not to heal properly. He remains partially deaf in that ear today.

* * *

CHAPTER FOUR

Childhood

Family Occasions

When Reece Smith was a youngster, America was in the deepest depression in its history. Yet life in the Smith household went on with little direct impact from the economic disaster. Smith's father worked in the Moody & Moody Insurance Agency throughout, providing for the family's needs. At home, all family members contributed to making sure the household chores were done.

Smith spent much of his childhood in a large, two story green and white wooden-frame house at 608 West Reynolds Street, a major tree-lined thoroughfare in Plant City. The home was a fine setting for family get-togethers, when many of Smith's aunts, uncles, and cousins joined his mother, father, and grandmother for the festivities. There were so many that they could not all be seated at the large dining room table. Consequently, Smith and his cousins sat at smaller card tables, but close enough to the food path where overflowing platters of food with delectable aromas were brought from the kitchen. Smith liked to sit near an older cousin, James Moody, who at that time was in college and a football player, something Smith wanted to do when he went to college. Years later, Smith's hope came true when he was a starting quarterback at the University of South Carolina.

Plant City Strawberry Festival

When Smith was five years old, F. Scott Fitzgerald's *The Great Gatsby* had just been published, Herbert Hoover was attempting to right the country's economy after the year-earlier stock market crash, and the Lone Ranger was a radio favorite and prime source of entertainment in the pre-television era. That year, Smith made his first "public appearance" in a parade for Plant City's Second Annual Strawberry Festival. He rode on the Festival's Queen's Float as a page to her Majesty. His mother, father and grandmother Moody were among the observers. The young Smith's photograph on the float appeared in the *Plant City Courier.*

He had another important duty to perform later that evening. During the Coronation of the Festival's Queen, he was delegated the job (or given the honor, depending on one's point of view) of holding up the Queen's train of "long fine silk." The local newspaper account read: "Master Reece Smith, Jr., carrying the train, was attired in a white satin suit and cap."

Grammar School

When Smith attended grammar school, Plant City's public schools were segregated by race. Not until 1971 did Hillsborough County end school segregation. As discussed in more detail later, Smith later worked with other community leaders to ease race relations in the local area, never thinking they would see an African-American President of the United States in their lifetime.

From kindergarten through eighth grade, Smith attended three grammar schools: Stonewall Jackson School for first grade, Mary L. Tomlin School for second and third grades, and William Jennings Bryan School for fourth through sixth. An early grammar-school mentor—Mabel Hillsman—was his first grade teacher at Jackson. Smith respected her, and perhaps a bit more. "Miss Mabel," he says, "was one of my favorites. I had a crush on her." Smith found a note his mother had saved written by Miss Mabel to Smith in September 1931. It reads: "Dear Reece, We missed you so much from school today. Take good care of that bad cold so you will be able to come to school Monday. Miss Mabel."

One year later when Smith was in second grade, he entered a department store contest. The contest was for the best essay on the topic: "Why every boy and girl should wear Polly Parrot shoes." The winner would get a live pony. The seven-year-old Smith submitted his essay but did not win the pony. The department store wrote him saying: "You came mighty near winning the pony, for you wrote a dandy essay." The letter continued: "Bring in this letter and select a Polly Parrot set of shoes and the store will make you a present of them." A pair of Polly Parrot shoes in lieu of a pony?

The following year the now eight-year-old again had high expectations, this time from Santa Claus. He wrote Saint Nick telling him what he wanted for Christmas: "A football, a baseball, a baseball bat, an indoor basketball, a bicycle, a cowboy suit—the name of it is Stage Coach Dan." Smith signed the letter "Your dearest friend, W. Reece Smith, Jr.," and then added to underscore his number one wish: "My bicycle size is twenty-six inches."

At an early age Smith thought he might like being a forest ranger, perhaps due to the trip with Mother Mary to Yellowstone Park and the mountains of Idaho. In junior-high and high school, there was the more immediate problem of pocket money. Smith's part-time jobs included delivering newspapers for both the *Tampa Times* and the *Plant City Courier* At one point, Smith worked at the Plant City A&P store for twelve cents an hour, during which he spent what seemed endless hours sorting potatoes by size into large, medium and small groupings. The routine was excruciatingly boring; it was not the work he wished to pursue.

Summers in Tennessee

The grammar school academic year was short by today's standards—only six months, primarily because the school district could not afford a longer term during the Great Depression. The short year enabled Smith to spend extended summers in eastern Tennessee, alternating between his maternal grandmother's (Mary Estes Moody's) home in Athens, and his fraternal grandfather's (Israel Jefferson Smith's) small farm on the outskirts of Englewood, six miles from Athens. A clay road connected the two communities. Besides playing with his cousin Edward Lee and other children, Smith helped his grandfather on the farm.

He alternated his summer times between Athens and Englewood and sensed a difference between "city life" of Athens and the "rural life" of the farm. By the time he had reached puberty, and from his junior high school days forward, he spent a greater portion of his summers in Athens, residing in Mother Mary's home. He liked to play tennis at a well-to-do neighbor's tennis court, and to socialize among the town's teenagers. The attractions of the farm had become less important than the "charm" of the young ladies of Athens.

Nonetheless, in the summer of 1940, when Smith was fourteen, he worked on Cyril Jones' farm not far from Athens in a small community named Niota. Jones was a friend of Smith's parents. Though not related, Smith called Jones " Uncle Cyril." Smith's motivation to work on the farm was to "beef up" for the upcoming football season at Plant City High School. The work involved much physical labor, and that was what Reece wanted, thinking ahead to the Fall's football games. Uncle Cyril paid him 75 cents a day and room and board.

Uncle Cyril not only owned the farm where Smith worked, he also was the postmaster of the Athens Post Office. During the summer of 1940, acting in his capacity as postmaster, Uncle Cyril played a prank on Smith. He claimed that one time when Smith went hunting, he mistakenly shot a carrier pigeon belonging to an Athens resident. Jones said he had posted a reward notice on the wall of the Athens Post Office, seeking information leading to the arrest and the conviction of the culprit who had felled the winged carrier. The poster read:

> Know ye all that I will pay $500,000 reward for the arrest and conviction of one young man, name unknown, formerly of somewhere in Florida, who did willfully shoot, kill, eradicate, eliminate, and otherwise destroy one carrier pigeon, marked with leg banding showing plainly said "pidgeon" was my property.... While this party's name is unknown, he was known under the following alias, i.e., farmer boy.

In an accompanying letter to Smith's father and mother, Jones wrote: "I am putting the notice in the darkest corner of the Post Office lobby and behind the notices of other famous wanted persons...." In a more serious vein, Jones praised young Smith for his work on the farm, writing that the teenage boy had put in long hours and that he had enjoyed working with him. The following summer Smith returned to work at Uncle Cyril's farm.

Diversion: The Battle of Athens

Years later, Smith returned to visit the family home in Athens in the summer of 1946, shortly after being released from the Navy. There Smith witnessed an aberrational historic event in American history. What transpired was a one-day *county* civil war or sorts when citizens of McMinn County, Tennessee battled each other in a gun fight in what historians have labeled "the Battle of Athens."

During World War II, the county's government was controlled by politicians who were considered to be corrupt and who arbitrarily exercised authority over the county's citizens. Following the end of the war, the veterans who returned to McMinn County became increasing intolerant of the apparent crookedness of county officials. The vets decided to run their own slate of candidates for public office. When the voting had finished, but before the votes had been counted, the incumbents took the ballot boxes to the Athens jailhouse. There they refused to allow anyone—including the veterans—to help count the votes or even to oversee the incumbent office holders tally the votes.

Outraged by what they felt was a carnage of democratic principles, several veterans hurried to their homes, returning with rifles and shotguns. Soon shots were fired and the confrontation escalated into a raging gun battle. At the time, Smith was standing behind a large oak tree a few blocks from the battle's epicenter witnessing the event. The battle ended only after troops from the Tennessee National Guard rolled into town.

Plant City High School

When Smith enrolled in Plant City High School, the war in Europe was in full swing. Germany had invaded several of its neighboring countries. Then, the Japanese bombed the American fleet at Pearl Harbor. Smith had turned sixteen some two months before the December 7, 1941, attack. America soon was drawn into World War II. At Plant City High School, Smith and other classmates joined the "Victory Corps" to prepare for what they assumed would be military service following graduation. An ROTC instructor from the University of Florida directed the Plant City High School's Victory Corps unit. Smith rose to the Corps' highest rank, Battalion Commander.

Despite deep anxieties about the future caused by the war, Smith took part in typical high school activities over and above studying, including, in his own words, "courting girls and participating in sports." He bought a used 1934 Ford for $75 so he "could get around." Smith and several friends played football in the yard of his family home. One of the players later started for Georgia Tech a few years after Smith had been the starting quarterback at the University of South Carolina.

At Plant City High School, Smith participated in football, basketball, and track. Of the three, playing football was without question Smith's most enjoyable sports activity. "Every male at Plant City High, Smith went out for football if he could walk," Smith says.

Smith's benefits from playing football included the guidance and influence of another key person in his life—Plant City High football coach, Denton L. Cook. Not only did Cook "toughen us up physically," Smith notes, "Cook taught us to respect learning and to be multi-dimensional." Smith continues: "He was a unique guy, the American ideal of the constructive influence that teachers can have on their students." Coach Cook knew how to handle people. When two teammates who considered themselves "tough guys" ignored Coach Cook's instructions, he wrestled them both in a single match and won. Thereafter, they obeyed and respected the coach.

Cook not only coached football, he also taught history, and did so in a manner that impressed Smith. The good impression was reciprocal. Cook wrote in Smith's yearbook: "I enjoyed having you both in athletics and in the classroom, Reece."

Cook also influenced Plant City High School students in molding character. Smith believes that "Coach Cook did a lot to help us mature and prepare for the experience of going to war." The 1943 Plant City High School Yearbook was dedicated "to classmates in the Armed Forces." Two of Smith's classmates lost their lives in the war: Hillard Hunley (who died in France in 1944) and Robert West (who died in pilot training in 1945).

In addition to Cook, Smith mentions another one of his high school teachers, Francis Hull, who taught English literature. "She was," he says, "one of my favorites." Years later in 1979, when the Plant City community learned that Smith was a finalist for the presidency of the American Bar Association, Hull told the *Plant City Courier* that Smith was up to the task: "He is very bright; capable in every way."

* * *

CHAPTER FIVE

College, Navy, Law School

University of South Carolina

Following graduation from high school, Smith spent the Summer of 1943 attending The Citadel in South Carolina while waiting to enter the Navy's V-12 officer training program. He entered the program at the Georgia Institute of Technology that Fall. Less than a year later, Smith was directed by the Navy to transfer to the Naval ROTC program at the University of South Carolina (USC) where he enrolled in the University's liberal arts college.

At USC, Smith played varsity athletics. His favorite was football in which he was a starting quarterback on the USC football team. Back then, quarterbacks, besides running, passing also blocked for the running backs. According to newspaper accounts, Smith excelled as a blocker and also was an aggressive defensive player. Smith's most satisfying gridiron experience was playing in the *first* New Year's Day Gator Bowl in Jacksonville against Wake Forest. Though the Gamecocks lost, Smith intercepted a pass, a play recorded for posterity by a photograph on the front page of a Jacksonville newspaper.

Years after leaving USC, Smith returned to his *alma mater* in 1991 to receive the University of South Carolina's "Distinguished Alumni Award." He used his acceptance speech to reminisce about what he had learned at USC, beginning with the opening stanza of the university's *alma mater*: "*We hail thee Carolina and sing thy high praise with loyal devotion remembering the days.*" Smith then spoke:

> Remembering the days … How happily we recall those halcyon days of youth! Days when yesterday's broken dream was only a prelude to a new romance. Days when we little appreciated that our light-hearted parties were but a joyful part of the lessons of responsibility we were learning. Days when our disappointments in the classroom, or on the playing field, taught us to take heart and to try again. Days when our teachers enhanced our knowledge and inspired our lives.… Days of fun and promise and inspiration. Days we shall always remember and cherish.

Concluding his address, Smith said that he would never forget how greatly the University enriched students' lives, "and enhanced our capacity to respond to the challenges of life." He believes this to be one of the best speeches he ever gave.

During his time at USC, Smith admired many of his teachers, including Havilah Babcock who, Smith says, "gave me a love for literature and taught me the word *sesquipedalian* even though I still don't know how best to use it." And there was Dean Joe Norwood, who (as related below) suggested that Smith apply for a Rhodes Scholarship, a seminal experience in his life.

Service in the United States Navy

Smith received his undergraduate degree from USC in 1945 and simultaneously received a Naval commission as Ensign in the United States Naval Reserve. The ROTC program he had completed at USC was modeled along the lines of the curriculum at the United States Naval Academy in Maryland. The program was designed to provide enhanced officer training for what the military anticipated would be a long war.

Smith subsequently was sent to Newport, Rhode Island for further training following which he was assigned to sea duty, including a short stint aboard a submarine. But he spent the majority of his time on a light cruiser—the USS *Columbia*. He had assumed the ship would be sent to the Pacific where the United States had been preparing for an invasion of Japan. But, as it turned out, America dropped two atomic bombs on Japan resulting in Japan's surrender.

Ensign Smith remained aboard the USS *Columbia* for several months. Damaged in a battle in the Pacific during the war, it had returned to the states for repairs. The USS *Columbia* subsequently was "rededicated" in a ceremony in Charleston, South Carolina. Smith was on board the ship and listened to testimonials by the governor of South Carolina, the mayor of Charleston, and the ship's commander. Thereafter, the USS *Columbia* traveled to Bermuda where the Captain assigned Smith to be the Navy's official escort for the twin daughters of Arthur Murray (who sold dance studio franchises throughout the country). By then Smith had become—to quote him—"an aide of sorts to the ship's captain."

After cruising up the east coast of North America and down the St. Lawrence River, the USS *Columbia* docked in Philadelphia where, on July 12, 1946, the Navy released Ensign Smith from active duty. He believes his Navy experience was time well spent.

University of Florida Law School

During his Naval service, Smith began to ponder what he might do afterwards. Prior to the war and through most of his undergraduate work at South Carolina, he assumed engineering or science would be his career. While serving aboard the USS *Columbia*, however, Smith read widely in his spare time. He says his readings raised his consciousness on issues such as racism and poverty in America. By the time he was honorably discharged from the Navy, Smith had changed his mind about his career. He knew he did not do particularly well in engineering and science courses. On the other hand, at the University of South Carolina he found that he liked history and English literature (the specialities his Mother Mary had been proficient in). Both disciplines required prodigious reading, an undertaking he had come to enjoy in the Navy. Accordingly, after his discharge from service and a summer of travel—including a return to his birthplace, Athens, Tennessee—Smith enrolled the following fall at USC seeking a graduate degree in the liberal arts. At that point he had not thought seriously about law school. But that soon changed.

During the 1946 fall semester, Smith dated a woman whose father was a South Carolina state senator and prominent lawyer. For the first time in his life, Smith began to think seriously about changing direction from pursuing a masters of arts degree to seeking a law degree. He considered applying to the USC law school but, before doing so, he and his girlfriend broke up. No longer having her nearby, Smith applied to the University of Florida (UF) law school. Though apprehensive about the work that law study would demand, he was optimistic, perhaps because his mother had once told him: "Reece, you would make a good lawyer because you argue so much." Smith was accepted at the UF law school in Gainesville and matriculated in January 1947.

As a veteran and now a law student, Smith was a member of what has been hailed as "the greatest generation." Like all veterans of World War II, Smith was ecstatic over America's success in the war. But he and the million-plus veterans were anxious to get on with their lives. Tom Brokaw, former anchor of NBC News and author of the best selling book, *The Greatest Generation*, wrote:

> Many of the [veterans] had been born in the 1920s in a time of national promise, optimism, and prosperity, when all things seemed possible as the United States was swiftly taking its place in the world.... When the war was over, [they] joined in joyous and short-lived celebrations then immediately began the task of rebuilding. They left campuses with degrees and determination to make up lost time.... As veterans,

they came to understand the need for social change in the country, including the need for civil rights legislation.

One Floridian who served in World War II was Sam Gibbons, later a powerful U.S. Congressman. A few years older than Smith, Gibbons studied law at UF after the war, around the same time as did Chesterfield Smith of Arcadia, Florida (who had also served in the armed forces). Brokaw writes that Chesterfield Smith was "eager to start anew" after the war ended. And so too was Reece Smith. The two became life-long friends, though for several decades they were staunch competitors, each heading what were two of the largest law firms in Florida at that time. Reece Smith became chairman of Carlton Fields while Chesterfield Smith became head of Holland and Knight. Each served as president of The Florida Bar and the ABA.

Brokaw writes that another prominent personage from Florida with service in World War II was Mary McLeod Bethune, who once served as president of the National Council of Negro Women. According to Brokaw, Bethune was one of "forty black women" in the United State Army's Women's Auxiliary Corps, a group best know by its acronym — the WACs. After the war, Bethune founded and became president of what was later called Bethune-Cookman College. Later, Smith was appointed a member of its board.

When Smith entered the UF law school, the students were older than students of earlier eras because of their military service in World War II. Years later in 1995, Smith spoke to 400 veterans who graduated from UF law school during the period of 1946 through 1951. Smith said: "We were eager to get a decent education and then earn a decent living." With tongue in cheek, he added: "And at least half of us were planning to be Governor of Florida." The UF law graduates of that era had indeed distinguished themselves. They included: a U.S. ambassador; an assistant and a deputy U.S. secretary of state; three members of Congress; four U.S. district court judges; a U.S. bankruptcy judge; a U.S. Army general; three Army and Marine colonels; and two Naval commanders. In addition, there were two chief justices of the Florida Supreme Court; a dozen members of the Florida legislature; a state attorney general; twelve district court of appeals judges; four state attorneys; two ABA presidents (one being Smith); seven Florida Bar presidents (again, Smith included); four state university presidents (one was Smith); several law professors (Smith being one); and a mayor of a major city — all UF Law School graduates who were veterans of World War II.

During his address to the graduates in 1995, Smith reminded them: "We came to law school with great trepidation." He talked about the faculty, noting that a retired Wisconsin prosecutor named Professor Clarence Teselle "terrified us." In evidence class, Teselle required students to stand when reciting, and on occasion responded sarcastically to what a student said. In many instances, Teselle told students their classroom responses to his questions were like "heifer dust," a reference to the haze that heifers caused while running aimlessly around a barnyard. Some claimed Teselle evaluated student exams by throwing them down steps, but nobody took the assertion seriously.

The anxious moments notwithstanding, Smith found law school intellectually invigorating. "My classmates and I were captivated by the faculty," he says. Smith describes James Day "as a true gentleman ... and *the* authority on real property." One of Professor Day's students—Harold Crosby—used shorthand skills acquired as a railroad telegrapher in recording the professor's every utterance in the property class. Crosby then sold transcripts to class members. Upon learning this fact, Professor Day was not angered; rather, "he simply acquired a copy of the Crosby transcript and incorporated it into his teaching."

Another professor Smith remembers was Professor Clifford W. "Pop" Crandall who, Smith recalls, "always found time to talk with students." Smith points out that Crandall was Florida's principal authority on pleading, having authored the definitive treatise on the subject at that time. Smith describes Crandall as "an affable man with a bald head, goatee, and commanding presence."

In recalling his law school days, Smith also mentions George Miller, who had left the Wall Street law firm of Davis Polk to join the Florida law faculty. Professor Miller became an authority on state constitutional law and authored the first article published in Volume One of the *University of Florida Law Review*. As Smith was to become, Miller had been a Rhodes Scholar. Still other faculty members Smith remembers are Karl Krastin (who held "fireside chats" with students); Robert Mautz (later, Chancellor of Florida's University System); Frank Mahoney who Smith notes, "devoted his career to the law school and became one of its most distinguished deans"; Richard Stevens, who established UF's graduate program in taxation (one of the nation's finest); Dexter Deloney, who taught bills and notes (*not* Smith's favorite course); Henry Fenn (who succeeded Trusler as dean); and Professor Slagle, whom students affectionately called "Sloogie."

During law school, Smith compiled an exemplary record, graduating number one in his class and the only class member to earn the LL.B. degree "*with high honors.*" Moreover, he did so in only two years by taking heavy course loads and attending two summer sessions. Besides his academic success, Smith was active in the Cockrell Inn, the law school's chapter of the national law fraternity *Phi Delta Phi*; during his last year he was elected the chapter's president. He also was elected president of the law school Student Bar Association. In addition, Smith represented law school students on the University's Student Council. His high grades caused him to be invited to join the editorial staff of the initial volume of the *University of Florida Law Review*. He was soon selected the *Review's* editor-in-chief.

But before that happened, Smith authored an article published in volume one of the *Florida Law Review*, titled *"Constitutional Law: The Right of the Negro to Legal Education."* He presented an interesting and insightful argument, especially coming from a law student in his second year of law school. It revealed that the young man from Plant City had an analytic mind, a flair for research, and a creative thinking capacity—all harbingers of his future as a lawyer.

Smith's article analyzed the 1948 United States Supreme Court case of *Fisher v. Hurst*, a decision handed down only weeks before he began his research. In *Fisher*, the Supreme Court reaffirmed its 1895 precedent of *Plessy v. Ferguson* that established the "separate but equal" doctrine, thereby allowing the continuation of segregated public schools so long as the segregated facilities for blacks supposedly were substantially equal to those available to whites. This form of segregation, the Court had held in *Plessy*, did not violate the Equal Protection Clause of the Fourteenth Amendment of the Constitution.

Over fifty years had passed since *Plessy* had been decided, and its doctrine of separate but equal was now challenged by an African-American denied admission to the Oklahoma's public, white-only law school. In *Fisher*, the Court adhered to *Plessy*, holding that a law program for minorities—provided it was "substantially similar" to the one available to white-only students—was permissible under the equal protection clause of the Constitution.

Carefully studying the *Fisher* opinion, Smith was not persuaded that the case had to be decided the way it was. After researching relevant substantive and procedural laws, he turned to the *Fisher* opinion and analyzed the case authorities the Court had cited. After summarizing these cases, Smith began his analysis. He pointed out that the Supreme Court decided the issue in *Fisher* solely under the *Plessy* doctrine—i.e., that separate but equal schooling was constitutionally permissible. Smith pointed out, however, there was no discussion of key factual issues—most notably, whether Oklahoma's Board of Regents had complied with the fundamental requirements of *Plessy*, that is, whether the state had facilities for black students that were substantially similar to those provided to white students. If the facilities were not substantially equal, then the state had not abided by the Court's mandate and stood to be held in contempt. Smith suggested the petitioner might have prevailed had her attorney timely raised this pivotal factual issue in the lower court.

The Right of the Negro to a Legal Education was Smith's first published article. Underlying his analytic reasoning was a core belief that segregation of public education was unjust. In 1954, seven years after Smith's article appeared, the U.S. Supreme Court reversed both *Plessy* and *Fisher* in the seminal case of

Brown v. Board of Education of Topeka, Kansas. The Court now held unanimously and unequivocally that separate facilities based on race were inherently unequal.

* * *

CHAPTER SIX

RHODES SCHOLARSHIP; OXFORD

Applying for the Scholarship

While at USC, Smith was told about Rhodes Scholarships and encouraged to apply. He did so in the Fall of 1946, though he knew the competition would be intense. Smith, however, was not selected and was disappointed, though not surprised given the odds. But a few years later the story had a different ending.

One of Smith's favorite law professors at UF's law school was George John Miller who was the faculty advisor to the law review. During Smith's tenure as editor-in-chief, Miller often came to the law review's office to see how the current issue was progressing. On one occasion, Smith was reading a flyer about how to apply for a Rhodes Scholarship and casually mentioned he had applied earlier for a Rhodes, but had not been selected. Miller, himself a former Rhodes Scholar, told Smith he should apply again.

Smith did so and the University of Florida selected him, along with two others, to be the University's Rhodes nominees. In the state-wide competition, Smith and one other Florida applicant were selected for the Southeastern District finals. A seven-member committee that included former Rhodes Scholars would consider the two finalists from Florida as well as candidates from six other states.

In December 1948, Smith again went through the rigorous interview process with the other finalists. Soon he learned he had been selected to be one of the two Rhodes Scholars representing the Southeastern District of the United States. He had made it! The news of Smith's selection quickly appeared in stories and editorials throughout Florida and Georgia, including The *Atlanta Journal*, the *Florida Times Union*, the *Tampa Tribune*, and the *Plant City Courier*. Smith received official notice of his scholarship from the American Secretary of the Rhodes Foundation:

Dear Smith: It gives me great pleasure to inform you that the Rhodes Trustees have formally confirmed your selection to a Rhodes Scholarship to go into residence in October 1949.

Before replying, Smith first had to clear up one situation. During his last year in law school he had accepted an offer to join the Tampa law firm of Fowler, White, Gillen, Humpkey, and Trenam. After learning he had been selected as a Rhodes Scholar, Smith went to the firm's two principal partners—Cody Fowler and Morris White—and asked them what he should do. Fowler told Smith: "Don't miss the chance to study overseas." Morris White, on the other hand, said: "If you want to be a lawyer, get to it." Nonetheless, both Fowler and White each told Smith that if he chose to accept the Rhodes, they would support his decision. In short order, Smith chose Oxford.

After receiving his law degree from Florida in the Spring of 1949, Smith was admitted to the practice of law by Circuit Judge Harry Sandler, under Florida's then-in-effect diploma privilege. Smith opened a temporary law office in Plant City, temporary because he would be off to Oxford in three months. As a new, unknown sole practitioner, paying clients did not flock to his office. One client, however, did pay him a $300 fee, about the extent of his compensation that summer.

Still, Smith kept busy. He sought appointments to represent indigent clients from judges of the U.S. District Court for the Middle District of Florida and from jurists on Florida's Thirteenth Judicial Circuit. He tried several cases and gained significant trial experience as well as being sensitized to the difficulties poor people had in obtaining lawyers to represent them. But when the summer ended, Smith closed his law office and prepared for his journey to England as a Rhodes Scholar.

Origin of the Scholarships

The Rhodes Scholarship program was established in 1902 following the death of Cecil John Rhodes. Rhodes wanted to bring to Oxford University each year what he called "the best men for the world's fight." Rhodes dreamed of improving the world through the diffusion of future leaders who would "serve their contemporaries, trained in the contemplative life of the mind, and broadened by their acquaintance with one another and by exposure to cultures different from their own." In furtherance of that vision, Rhodes wanted extraordinarily well-rounded applicants for the program. As English historian Lord Elton explains, "the Scholars were to be selected not merely like all other scholars, for scholastic attainments—they must not be "merely bookworms'—but also for qualities of character."

In a letter to his barrister in 1899, Rhodes wrote: "In awarding the scholarships, great consideration shall be given to those who have shown during school days that they have instincts to lead and take an interest in their schoolmates, which attributes will likely guide them to esteem performance of public duties as their highest aim." In addition to "literary and scholastic attainments and social and character qualities," they must have a "moderate fondness for outdoor sports such as cricket, football, and the like." Above all, Rhodes wanted his scholars to become national and world leaders following their two or three years at Oxford University.

In his 1902 will, Cecil Rhodes created the Rhodes Trust and bequeathed the bulk of his enormous fortune for its perpetual implementation. The terms of the trust require the trustees to select each year a limited number of applicants from designated countries, applicants "who possessed excellent academic prowess, top physical fitness, impeccable character, and high standards of personal morality" from designated countries, including the British Colonies, United States and Germany. Rhodes included Germany because learning English was then compulsory in the German schools and because he believed that Germany someday would become a powerful ally of England. Within a year of Rhode's death, his program for awarding scholarships was in place. Today, thousands of Rhodes Scholars have attended Oxford. His expectations came to pass, as Rhodes scholars over the years have become leaders in their respective professions throughout the world.

American Rhodes Scholars have included: President William Clinton; U.S. Supreme Court Associate Justices John Marshall Harlan, Byron White, and David Souter; Attorney General Nicholas Katzenbach; Secretary of State Dean Rusk; Speaker of the U.S. House of Representatives, Carl Albert (and at least eleven other House members); U.S. Senators William Fulbright, Richard Luger, Paul Sarbanes, Russell Feingold, David Boren, Bill Bradley and Robert Reich; Librarians of Congress, Daniel Boorstin, and James Billington; Supreme Allied Commanders General Wesley Clark and General Bernard Roger; and two Secretaries of the Navy, a Director of the Central Intelligence Agency, and several members of Presidential cabinets.

Others have included over fifty university and college presidents, including Harvard, Princeton, Virginia, New York University (two), Florida (two), Swarthmore (three),Vanderbilt, North Carolina, Connecticut, Johns Hopkins, Alabama, West Virginia, Oklahoma, Oregon, Louisiana, Oberlin, Pomona, and the University of South Florida (where Smith served as interim-president). Several became deans of law schools. including Harvard, Yale, Howard, South Carolina and Wisconsin. In addition, the list of American Rhodes extends to best-selling authors, including Robert Warren, James Atlas, Michael Kinsley, Naomi Wolf, Paul Blustein, Nicholas Kristof, Rachel Simmons, James Fellows and Noah Feldman.

Aboard the *Isle de France*

In September 1949, Smith and a dozen other American Rhodes Scholars embarked on the French liner *Isle de France* from New York City and began a five-day trans-Atlantic crossing to South Hampton. The voyage allowed them to get to know each other. *Life Magazine* documented the crossing in its October 11, 1949, edition with a two-page photograph of twelve Rhodes Scholars standing on a deck of the *Isle de France*. After Oxford, each became a high achiever as noted in the list below). (The *Life Magazine* picture appears in the middle of this volume). In the front row left to right are: Thad Marsh, provost, University of the South (Suwanee); William Barber, general secretary, American Committee for the Rhodes Scholarship Trust and professor at Wesleyan; Steven Muller, president of Johns Hopkins; Frank King, economist, journalist and author; Robert Kirkpatrick, professor, Missouri Valley College; Smith; and Nelson Taylor, president and later chancellor at University of North Carolina. In the second row left to right are: Barney Childs, composer and musician; Herbert Cahn, an entrepreneur who had fled Germany with his family to escape the Nazis; and Clyde Anderson, a physician who later headed the U.S. Air Force Hospital in England. In the top row, left to right are: Richard Wiley, a lawyer and general counsel of the U.S. Department of Defense and later trustee of the World Peace Foundation; Walter Frank, economist, author, and corporation president.

Arriving in Oxford

> *On an eminence of scarcely perceptible elevation, at the confluence of the rivers Isis and Cherwell, in the bosom of a delightful valley, surrounded by luxuriant meadows, and, at greater distance, environed by gently swelling hills, which smile in all the pride of cultivated beauty, and are richly diversified by hanging woods, stands the fair city of Oxford.*

Both Oxford University and the town have medieval origins. The town dates back at least to the ninth century. No historical indicators suggest, however, that scholars were there until the latter half of the twelfth century, when townsmen erected a *stadium generale* (hall for general studies). In time, the stadium became a learning center for upper-class English students. Around 1249, some 250 years after the town was first settled, a group of scholars established University College. Soon other colleges opened. Historian Professor V.H.H. Green describes the thirteenth century colleges as the "foundations of Oxford University."

University College continues to stand today at the corner of High Street and Logic Lane. Historian Christopher Hibbert of Oxford University describes it as "the oldest English-speaking university in the world." In 1949, when Smith arrived at Oxford, the university was celebrating its seven-hundredth anniversary.

Prior to setting foot on English soil, Smith wondered where he would stay. He knew the University consisted of residential colleges. One of the oldest and best known was Christ Church. Two former Rhodes scholars from Florida—George John Miller and William A. McRae—had told Smith to apply for residency at Christ Church, in which they had resided. Each wrote the Warden of Rhodes House recommending Smith be admitted to Christ Church. In due course, Smith learned that his application for residence had been approved. Thus, when he disembarked from the *Ile de France* in Southampton, Smith knew his final destination. He took a train to London, and then another to Oxford. Leaving the train, he saw the quintessence English countryside of rolling green hills. Bags in hand, he took a cab to the center of the town, exiting on High Street, Oxford's main road, (residents call it "The High"). It has its admirers. William Wordsworth loved "the stream-like winding of that glorious street." Historian Sir William Hayter described it as "one of the most beautiful streets in the world."

Walking down The High, Smith saw a panorama of edifices like none he had seen before. Sir Hayter paints the picture: "Lining each side of the High are the noblest of buildings of varying dates and yet all living harmoniously together." Poet Matthew Arnold described the panorama in a poem: "That sweet City with the dreaming spires; she needs not June for beauty's heightening." Smith seemed to be in a medieval city, though the streets bustled with modern activity—red double decker buses, black cabs, pedestrians and, more than all the others combined, bicyclists. With map in hand, he located Christ Church, his residential college.

Upon arrival at the college for the first time, Smith entered through a huge wooden gate that was swung open. The gate stands below a tall tower called "Tom" in honor of Thomas Becket, which was designed in 1681 by Christ Church alumnus Christopher Wren. It is an excellent example of an architectural style known as English-Baroque Gothic. At the top of the tower is a large ornate clock, suitably called "Great Tom."

When Smith attended Oxford, the Tom Tower gate was the main gate in and out of the college, but there were others, all of which closed in the early evening. The Tom gate, however, remained open until 10:20 p.m. each evening, when it too was closed. Within its massive front was a small door through which late entrants came through. If they did so, however, they were under scrutiny. Residents were expected to be inside the Tom gate before 10:20 p.m., and those who entered later were reported to the College's "censor" who was the College' disciplinarian. For most students, being tardy required meeting with the censor who imposed a fine for violating the rule. Older students, including returning vets and Rhodes Scholars, were not required to pay fines, though they still had to meet with the censor if they returned after 10:20 p.m. Smith learned there was a way to bypass Tom gate, thereby avoiding a trip to the censor. He would climb over a wall though it was risky to do so. The stone fences were topped with steel spikes and broken glass set in concrete.

Christ Church

Sir John Hayter calls Christ Church "the largest and grandest of all the Oxford colleges." Among its magnificent structures is a chapel that serves as the cathedral for Oxfordshire and is officially named the "Cathedral Church of Christ in Oxford." Though the smallest cathedral in Britain, some claim it is the most beautiful. The college named Christ Church commonly is referred to as "The House," based on the Latin phrase *Aedes Christi* meaning "House of Christ."

The modern era of Christ Church by that name began in 1546, when King Henry VIII opened its doors. But historians believe that the site of Christ Church has been occupied since the eighth century when a monasterium, or nunnery, was founded by a princess known as Saint Frideswide (circa, 600–750). According to legend, Saint Frideswide performed miracles. Her story is told in brilliant colors on a stained glass window in Christ Church Cathedral. At some point, the monastery became known as Saint Frideswide' Abbey.

In 1524, Cardinal Wolsey, then Lord Chancellor of England, took over the site of St. Frideswide Abbey. There he established a college with the intention "to give it a grandeur and magnificence equaled by no other college." He hoped its magnificence would surpass his royal house at Hampton Court near London. Wolsey, whose ecclesiastical designation was the Cardinal of York, named it Cardinal College. When it opened, sixty Augustinian canons, forty junior canons and one dean resided there—a total of 101, a number that is significant at the college even today. Each evening, the College's clock in Tom Tower strikes 101 times in remembrance of those who attended when the College was founded by Wolsey. In 1529, five years after Wolsey opened Cardinal College, England's King Henry VIII took it over and renamed it after himself. Later in 1546, the King renamed it again—this time Christ Church, the name it has had for four and one half centuries.

Smith in his inimitable way, summarizes the founding of Christ Church as *"a distinguished Oxford college which had been rudely stolen by Henry VIII from a nice guy named Wolsey who didn't believe in divorces and beheadings."*

Over the centuries, graduates of Christ Church became renowned leaders, including several kings, philosophers, revered authors, and academicians. Among these are King Edward VII, philosopher John Locke (whose theories of the social contract served as an intellectual justification for the American Revolution), William Penn, John Wesley; W. H. Auden, Charles Dodgson (Lewis Carroll, of *Alice in Wonderland*), Lord Halifax, and *thirteen* British Prime Ministers including Sir Alec Douglas Home, Sir Anthony Eden, and the legendary William E. Gladstone.

The Hall

Portraits of some 300 graduates hang in the College's grand dining room, which is known as "the Hall." Built in 1529, the spacious room with massive beams and vaulted ceiling has been described as "the most splendid and largest of the ancient dining halls at either Oxford or Cambridge." The Hall is 115 feet long, 40 feet wide, and has a 50 feet tall ceiling "crowned with a richly ornamented roof." For those who have seen the Harry Potter movies based on the books of J.K. Rowling, the film's set for the "Hogwarts School for Wizardry" is the Hall of Christ Church.

Students take most of their meals in the Hall during term. Smith remembers frequent servings of "brussel sprouts accompanying either whale meat pie or jugged hare." The students sit at long solid oak tables below the "high table," which stands about three feet higher on a raised floor. The college dons (faculty), professors (the top faculty scholars), college officials and invited guests sit at the high table during the meal. All diners wear academic gowns.

For centuries, each dinner begins with a Latin grace that never varies. Today, fifty odd years later, Smith can recite verbatim the opening grace. Some years ago, he took his law partner Sylvia Walbolt and her family to Oxford to show them where he had spent three years. (Walbolt and Smith at the time were attending a meeting of the ABA in London). After entering the Christ Church

Hall, Smith walked up to the lectern, looked at his friends, and in Latin re-cited the grace. Sylvia Walbolt remembers: "My young son's jaw dropped open."

Oxford's Academic Pedagogy

When Smith entered Christ Church, he became part of a university/college system very different from America. Each college was self governing, raised it own money, had its own budget, appointed its own administration, and hired its own staff. This included the college faculty, typically consisting of instruc-tors called dons, only a small percentage of whom attained the rank of "pro-fessor." ("Don" is a shortened version of the Latin term "*dominus*," meaning a master in learning.)

Most of the individual colleges have no specific academic focus, and welcome students who pursue any course of study they choose from a broad range of subjects, including social and physical sciences, languages and linguistics, en-gineering, and medicine. Unlike in the United States, undergraduate students at Oxford who want eventually to practice law may "read law," somewhat anal-ogous to "majoring" in a subject. In contrast to more vocationally-oriented American law schools, the emphases at Oxford are on the historical, jurispru-dential, and theoretical aspects of law. Those who wish to become either so-licitors or barristers after Oxford go for vocational training at either the Colleges of Law (various locations) to become solicitors, or to one of the four London-located Inns of Court—Inner Temple, Middle Temple, Lincoln's Inn, and Gray's Inn—to become barristers.

Oxford and Cambridge universities and their colleges do not offer tradi-tional, large classes for students. Rather, the most utilized teaching pedagogy is tutorials. When Smith was attending Oxford, a tutorial session consisted of tutor (a don) and one or, at most, two students. Today, due to the high costs of the required small tutor-student ratio, tutorials involve a don and a group of students. Typically, a tutor meets in college quarters each week with stu-dents, and typically requires them to write essays on assigned topics, which they are to research. Later, the tutor makes critical comments, but does not give specific grades to the essays.

The tutorial method has been described as Oxford's *forte*. But the Ameri-can Secretary of the Rhodes Trust noted that tutorials created some problems for Americans:

> Many Rhodes Scholars at first find their tutors niggling and fussy crit-ics, but they soon learn that what is in question is not mere minutiae

of form but coherence of thought; if they reap nothing else from Oxford, they will be in her debt if they have learned to weigh their words before committing them to speech or paper.

Smith chose to study private international law as a graduate student. His tutors Sir Zelman Cowen (later, the Governor-General of Australia) and Peter Carter of Wadham College (later to become internationally recognized as an esteemed scholar.). In addition to participating in tutorials, Smith took advantage of the other leading educational experience available to Oxford students—lectures by renowned specialists in various academic disciplines. At university lectures (open to all Oxford students), attendance was not required. Nonetheless, Smith made it a point to attend all the lectures on international law given by Professor A.L. Goodhart.

Besides law and jurisprudence, Smith also attended lectures on other subjects. He recalls certain of the topics and lecturers: Keynesian economics by Professor Roy Harrod, Shakespeare by Lord David Cecil, and the history of art by Sir E.H. Gombrich. The latter's treatise—*The Story of Art*—had sales in excess of six millions copies by 2006, according to *U.S. News & World Report*, which described the work as the "world's best selling art book."

Smith understood that his learning at Oxford would not be "practical" training for a profession. But rooted in the Jeffersonian tradition of American education, he was cognizant of the benefits of a liberal education that went far beyond preparation for a specific trade or profession. A friend who was studying ancient civilizations told Smith that, though he intended to go into banking after his studies at Oxford, "I never will have the same chance to learn about people and about great civilizations of the world as I have here," adding that he would later learn "banking on the job." Smith took the lesson to heart. Years later, in a speech in Virginia, Smith said:

> I take issue with the vocational emphasis on learning. It is more important to learn the lessons of these disciplines that teach about life, its values and how to live it more abundantly ... We must make discriminating decisions about what we read and listen to, and even what we choose to talk about with others.... [B]e selective in what you choose to learn, whether your goal is to become book smart, world smart, or both.

Because Oxford students do not attend classes as such, they spend much of their time on their own. Cardinal Newman observed over a century ago that Oxford students educate themselves. They still do. Students typically research and read books and other sources related to their specialized course of study.

At Oxford, Smith studied in four libraries: Bodleian, the 600-year old library located near the city center, Codrington, All Souls College (which has an extensive law and history collection), and the Rhodes House Library to which Rhodes Scholars have access.

These libraries notwithstanding, an Oxford student is expected to search out needed sources, whether available locally or not. Once Smith needed to consult the American Law Institute's *Restatements of the Law*. The Oxford libraries did not have the *Restatements*, requiring Reece to go to London to locate copies in one of the Inns of Court.

Going Up; Coming into Residence

Prior to Smiths "going up"—matriculating—and "coming into residence"—moving into college—he received a list of things to bring, including tea crockery and an eiderdown blanket, the latter being more important than the former. He was advised to have a "good supply of socks because it is difficult to get mending done in the college." He was further advised:

> The usual Oxford wear is a tweed jacket and flannel or corduroy trousers, warm scarves, and gloves. Old [military] service dress is often worn. Dinner jackets are useful for parties, but not absolutely essential. Full evening dress is rarely worn, but a white bow tie is required for certain University ceremonies.

The rules applicable to students dress included the requirement that they wear "common" academic gowns to university ceremonies, sermons, examinations, meals in the Hall, and when appearing formally before all University officers. On a few occasions, students also had to wear mortarboard caps. In addition, both the University and the colleges held formal occasions each term where "gentlemen's attire" was the norm. Usually, however, clothes were less formal, consisting of tweed jackets, shirts, ties, and slacks, wool sweaters and, of course, bad weather gear.

Upon arriving at Oxford, Smith was assigned a suite in the Meadow Building, so named because it faced an expansive field named "the Meadows," which ran from the College fence down to the Isis River. In earlier times and in accordance with an ancient college statute, every undergraduate at Christ Church kept a cow in the Meadows to provide the student with daily fresh milk. Though not having his own cow, Smith enjoyed seeing the cattle grazing in the fields and the students and visitors walking on the Meadows' paths beneath his window. For centuries strollers had walked these grounds, including Samuel Johnson, John Rubin Drew, and John Locke. Smith loved the Meadows, especially in Spring when they become ablaze with lady's mantle, columbine, butter cups, and moneywort, and other varieties of wild flowers. (John Locke reportedly gathered flowers in the gardens while in residence at Christ Church). Smith still can visualize the view out his window, declaring "it was magnificent."

Smith lived on the third floor of the Meadow Building, one of the college's more "modern" structures (the circa 1865 built Venetian-Gothic edifice was approaching its centennial). To access his quarters, he entered a passageway that led to a three-flight stairwell. On each floor were two suites of rooms facing each other. A single student resided in each suite. The student's quarters consisted of a living room with a small fireplace and an adjacent bedroom. There were neither *en suite* toilet facilities, baths, showers, nor hot water, though the six suites shared a common bathroom having one water closet (toilet)—nothing else. When Smith took a shower, he walked down a chilly staircase, through a cold passageway, and into an even colder outdoors to get to a "nearby facility." Oh, to remember the Florida beaches.

Smith found the English climate and weather strikingly different from Florida's, as Oxford lies close to the latitude traversing Hudson Bay, Canada. Consequently, he experienced long periods of penetrating chills and dampness, often accompanied by persistent rains. Prior to going to bed, he routinely put on gloves, socks (sometimes two pairs) and heavy pajamas and then pulled up a thick eiderdown blanket. In spite of these efforts, Smith often found himself uncomfortably cold. This unhappy situation prompted him to purchase an electric heater for his bedroom. It did what it was supposed to do and his chills lessened, but not for long.

The college's head porter learned Smith was using an electric heater and shot off a note: "Dear Sir: It has been reported that you have an electric heating device in your rooms. Use of these activities is prohibited. The College's Regulations make it clear that the light circuit may not be used for heating." So the college's inadequate electrical capacity trumped Smith's comfort, forcing him to again rely on intermittent heat from his small coal-burning fireplace. Fortunately, the college's head porter took pity, informing Smith that because he "was from the tropics," he would be allocated an additional ration of coal for his fireplace.

On the first floor, a "scout," a college staff member who served the six student suites, had a small office. A 2005 brochure published by Lincoln College at Oxford University describes what an Oxford college scout does: "He is [the] one who is responsible for cleaning and maintaining the students' room and for serving at table. The scout is usually a cheery soul that wakes you up and *could* keep a file on your private life." When Smith was at Oxford, scouts provided wake-up calls, brought hot water to the rooms, cleaned and tidied up the suites, shined shoes, made fires in the fireplaces, and ran errands. Smith found his scout—Alec Clarke—to be courteous, helpful and very friendly. Contrary to the Oxford norm, Smith befriended Clarke, sometimes staying with him and his wife in their small home during vacations.

In 1989, Smith returned to Oxford and went to Christ Church to find his old friend. As he approached the Meadow Building, Smith called out: "Alec." Though not yet seeing Smith, Clarke promptly replied: "Coming Mr. Smith." Neither man had seen each other for years but their friendship had survived the years apart.

Alec began working at Oxford University when he was fourteen. By 1989 he had given more than fifty years of service to the University. In recognition, Christ Church named Alec a "Senior in Service" and immortalized him as a gargoyle affixed to an outside wall of the college's Great Hall. Smith took pride in his Oxford scout. Clearly the feeling was mutual.

The use of "scouts" in the university's colleges was a lingering characteristic of the old English hierarchical class. For centuries, Oxford and Cambridge were institutions for "gentlemen." Their students for the most part came from elite, all-male preparatory schools where academic training was rigorous and social and family backgrounds, not to mention peerage, were very important. Certainly, no American university today has staff who runs errands, brings hot water or other needed items, or shines shoes for students.

The administrative organization of an Oxford college has a dean—often called "master"—while each school has its own porters, censors, and scouts. The porters at Christ Church wore bowlers when Smith was there, and were in charge of the college's keys. They also kept watch over the premises, manned the gates, and handled the mail. Meanwhile, the college censor handled minor disciplinary matters, though the proctor had the real power, including the authority "to rusticate" a student. To be "rusticated" was to be suspended from the university for a specified period. The word "rusticate" comes from the Latin word *rusticare*, meaning "to live on the land" (rather than living at Oxford). In contrast, to be permanently expelled was to be "sent down."

By 1949 when Smith came up to Oxford, the long existing English class divisions were less noticeable than before World War II. When he matriculated, Oxford had broken the gender barrier as a few women-only colleges now existed. More than any other factor, the war had altered previously entrenched class and social perceptions, as rich and poor fought side by side. But there is also another factor that affected attitudes on social stratification at Oxford—the changing manner in which it was funded. Joseph A. Soares, an historian of Oxford University explains:

After [the war], shifts in the sources of funding available for British universities made Oxford's metamorphosis possible. Before the war, Oxford was a private liberal arts university with an exceptionally privileged social class ethos and composition. By the end of 1950, Oxford was effectively a state institution with a middle-class constituency and a meritocractic ethos.

Friends, Travels, Princes, Princesses, and Royal Happenings

During his time at Oxford, Smith became acquainted with most of his American Rhodes classmates, many who entered in 1947, 1948 and 1950. They included (with future positions): James Hester, presidents of the Guggenheim Foundation and New York University; U.S. Attorney General Nicholas Katzenbach; Spencer Kimball, dean at the University of Wisconsin Law School and law professor, University of Chicago; Charles Merdinger, naval officer, civil engineer and college president; Richard Nolte, U.S. Ambassador and chair of the U.S. Geological Society; Bernard Rogers, Supreme Allied Commander in Europe; Edgar Shannon, president, University of Virginia; Stansfield Turner, head of CIA; Leslie Youngblood, Senior White House Advisor under President Eisenhower; Ewell Murphy, chair, Fulbright Scholarship Board and partner in Houston law firm of Baker & Botts; Wesley Posvar, chancellor, University of Pittsburgh; William Slesnick, professor, Dartmouth College and Consultant for American Council on Education; Bruce Rosier, an Australian priest and later Bishop of Willochra; John Turner, Prime Minister of Canada; and Harvey Poe, lawyer, educator and corporation president and Smith's long-time friend.

On many evenings Smith and his friends would meet before dinner in the Christ Church Buttery, a lounge that served beer, ale and other refreshments. Located atop a spiral staircase in the entranceway leading into the Hall, the Buttery offered a pleasant place to relax after the day's activities. Smith claims students consumed the alcoholic beverages at the Buttery so they would be able to eat whale meat pie and brussels sprouts.

It was at the Buttery where Smith first met a man from Texas and a Prince from Yugoslavia. The Texan—Dan Lockwood McGurk—first crossed paths with Reece over half-pints (or pints) of beer. Born in Alabama, McGurk grew up in several places, ending up in Texas. He graduated from the U.S. Military Academy at West Point. Shortly afterward he was commissioned an Air Force officer. Later, McGurk became a Rhodes Scholar, entering Oxford in the Fall of 1949. After leaving Oxford, McGurk taught at both West Point and the U.S. Air Force Academy, and then entered business, becoming president of several companies, including Xerox Data Systems Corporation and Southland Title Corporation.

When Smith first met McGurk at the Buttery, he was wearing civilian attire with a solid blue U.S. Air Force tie. Smith too had a tie, his having red and blue stripes. While they were chatting, a well-dressed, dignified, and urbane gentleman approached and introduced himself as "Nick." Looking at Smith and McGurk, he declared: "Gentlemen, you need to know that you're not properly attired." He pointed to McGurk, telling him that he was wearing an Oxford blue tie, one *only* worn by Oxford lettermen. Turning to Smith, Nick noted that he was wearing a Grenadier Guards tie, one *only* worn by members of the Grenadier Guards. In short, the Americans' ties were "in poor form."

It turned out that the debonaire and handsome stranger was Prince Nicholas of Yugoslavia, who was related to the British Royal Family and was a nephew of the Duchess of Kent of the House of Windsor. Clearly, the Prince had standing to be critical of their attire, and Smith and McGurk were nonplused until the Prince smiled. A lively conversation over beer followed, and the two Americans and the Yugoslavian Prince (who drank wine and spirits) soon became close friends.

Smith traveled with his friends on the European continent during his Oxford years. The first such trip was in December 1949 with Pat Murphy (Rhodes Scholar from Texas), Greeley McGowen (student at Pembroke College from Alabama), and David Schwayder (a Rhodes Scholar from California). The three climbed into Schwayder's Volkswagen and headed off to Italy "to get warm." Once there, Smith saw Naples, Pompeii, Rome and the Vatican for the first time.

On another trip—this one to Spain—Smith became exasperated when, "to save a little money," his friend Pat Murphy purchased two *third-class* tickets for a bus trip from Grenada to Madrid. Third-class tickets meant they had to sit on hard wooden planks in the back of the bus. In mid-journey, a member of the Spanish police—the *Guardia Civil*—came aboard, walked to the back, sat down next to Murphy, and, intentionally or not, stuck the end of his rifle barrel next to Murphy's left ear, causing him great concern. Smith told his friend the discomfort was just punishment for a false sense of economy.

One journey was especially memorable. Smith and his girlfriend at the time, Jane Hartley, whose family owned an English marmalade and jam company, along with McGurk, his wife Frannie, and Prince Nicholas piled into McGurk's Chevrolet convertible. After taking a ferry across the English Channel, they drove to Paris. The car was having difficulties and McGurk took it to a Parisian mechanic to have it fixed. Instead, the mechanic broke another part of McGurk's car. Unfortunately, Prince Nicholas—the only one of the five who spoke French—was elsewhere in Paris. Neither McGurk nor Smith were able to explain in their broken French that the part had to be repaired. With a sense of desperation, Smith turned to English and asserted: "You break 'em; you fix 'em." In short order, the mechanic restored the vehicle to its *status quo ante* condition, allowing Smith and his friends to leave Paris and head for the Cote d'Azur. (His friends never forgot Smith's instructions to the mechanic.)

Although Smith did not have his own car in Oxford, he used McGurk's on occasion, including to pass the English test to obtain a driving license. Smith learned how to navigate roundabouts, driving on the left side, and that a car's "bonnet" is the hood, the "boot" is the trunk, the "windscreen" is the windshield, and "tyre" is how the English erroneously spell "tire."

Smith's mother once sailed aboard an ocean liner to Portsmouth where Smith picked her up, having borrowed Prince Nicholas's car. Being a Prince, the car had a special license tag. Realizing it could be embarrassing if the police stopped Smith, the Prince wrote a note for Smith that read: "This is to certify that Mr. W. R. Smith has my full permission to drive and be in control of my Vanguard LLP405. [signed] Nicholas, Prince of Yugoslavia." (Later, Smith's father flew to England and the family toured various European destinations.)

Smith's friendships with Prince Nicholas and McGurk led to some unique opportunities. The Prince occasionally dated H.R.H. Princess Margaret, the sister of the future Queen of England. During an evening he will never forget, Smith joined the Yugoslavian Prince Nicholas and the English Princess Margaret on a double date, after the Prince had paired Smith with one of Princess Margaret's ladies-in-waiting.

Smith's contacts with royalty did not stop there. Dan McGurk was a member of the Oxford University Polo Club, as he had played polo before coming to Oxford and was an experienced equestrian. The Club sometimes practiced on the estate of Lord Cowdrey, an acquaintance of Prince Phillip (later the Duke of Edinburgh). Prince Phillip was a highly skilled and admired polo player who on occasions attended the Oxford Polo Club's matches. Often his wife would accompany the Prince—H.R.H. Princess Elizabeth (who later became H.R.H. Queen Elizabeth.)

On one occasion, Lord Cowdrey, an owner of a grand estate, held a formal dinner. The guests included Prince Phillip and Princess Elizabeth as well as a few Oxford polo players including McGurk. McGurk had been told that "black-tie" attire was required, including, as McGurk knew, "brilliantly" shined black shoes. To his surprise, he discovered he had left his black shoes back in Oxford. But not one to miss a once-in a-lifetime opportunity, McGurk walked into the midst of royalty, head held high, adorned in black tie, a well-pressed tuxedo, and bottomed off with cowboy boots straight from Texas.

The future Duke of Edinburgh and Queen of England were present at the dinner and took notice. Some time later, Prince Phillip and Princess Elizabeth were watching an Oxford Polo Club match within a "royal tent" next to the playing field. The Royals invited the Club's members and some of their friends to tea after the match, including McGurk and Smith. When the future Queen saw McGurk, she laughingly told the story of his coming to the formal dinner wearing his Texas cowboy boots.

Oxford Clubs

Though instances of intermingling with royalty were rare, that was not the case when it came to Smith's participation in Oxford's social, political, and debate clubs, including the Bryce Club. It had forty-eight members, sixteen from Great Britain, sixteen from the British Commonwealth, and sixteen from other countries, including the United States. The club typified the Oxfordian norm—a somewhat elitist group of students had to be elected into a club that supposedly had a serious purpose. In Bryce's case, it was to afford "periodic opportunities for discussion of Anglo-American relations and foreign affairs." Smith, however, has no recollection of such serious discussions. This may be explained by a passage appearing in the 1949 Oxford University Student Handbook, which describes the Club's meetings as beginning with members giving toasts while sipping Der Weltburger.

The Bryce Club was not the only organization Smith participated in at Oxford. Another was the *Twenty Club* of Christ Church. The club consisted of *nineteen* elected student members, two being Smith and McGurk. The twentieth member was *not* elected; rather, "it" was a goldfish that the members selected before each meeting from the Mercury Pool located in the College's Tom Quad.

The *Twenty Club* was a debating society but one with an interesting twist: all the topics were purposefully farcical, though the debates were serious. Subjects included: *History Is a Thing of the Past*; *Work Is the Curse of the Drinking Class*; *Trespassers Will*; *Indiscretion Is the Better Part of Valor*; *Better a Dog's Life Than a Cat's Pajamas*; and, *A Woman Is Only a Woman, but a Good Cigar is a Smoke*. The *Twenty Club's* constitution mandated that the organization hold a minimum of three debates per term. Smith enjoyed the debates, as the participants were bright and articulate. He attended all the club's meetings, each of which was numbered in succession. At the 853rd meeting of the Club on October 13, 1951, Smith was one of the debaters (though he does not recall the topic). At Oxford, he also participated in several other professional and social organizations, including *Christ Church Law Club*, *Oxford University Law Society*, and *Oxford University Union Society* (the best known of Oxford's debating societies.) A Christ College rowing team calling itself *The Gentlemen's Eight*, when not racing on the river Isis, dressed in peculiar fashion. (A photograph of *The Gentlemen Eight* appears later in this volume.)

Oxford's social scene never ended, or so it seemed. Parties, dances, receptions, teas—the choices nearly overwhelmed an American Rhodes Scholar at Oxford. Many of the invitations are handwritten in beautiful script and typically displayed colorful coats-of-arms. Smith still has several of the attractive and beguiling invitations. One is from the Dean of Christ Church to come to "the Deanery" (the quarters of the College's dean and his wife). Another is from "The Master and Wardens of the Worshipful Company of Grocers."

THE MASTER AND WARDENS OF
THE WORSHIPFUL COMPANY OF GROCERS
request the honour of the company of
Mr. W. R. Smith
at a Reception to
Rhodes Scholars, Dominion Undergraduates and Students
on Friday, June 2nd, 1950
AT
GROCERS' HALL, PRINCESS STREET, E.C.2
at 3:30 p.m.
H.R.H. PRINCESS MARGARET HAS KINDLY
CONSENTED TO BE PRESENT

Athletics: Oxford Beats Cambridge

At Oxford, students enjoy opportunities to participate in various sports. The 1948–1949 Oxford student guide states: "All the principal sports (among them such sedentary occupations as chess and bridge) are offered at all [Oxford] colleges." The most authoritative historian of American Rhodes Scholars, Frank Aydellote, has written: "The two things which are likely to mean the most to the American Rhodes scholars are talk and sports." That was true during Smith's three years.

Unlike American universities and colleges that have full-time staff coaches, at Oxford athletics are in the hands of undergraduates, for the most part on a residential college basis. The students organize the teams and clubs, provide their own coaches, and arrange their own schedules.

At Oxford, athletic programs exist on two tiers: the college level and the university level. Students from each college have their own teams for inter-school and intramural sports. In contrast, university-wide sports are conducted through "clubs," comprised of players from various colleges who together represent the university against other clubs outside Oxford. The clubs typically engage in what Oxbridgians consider the major sports: rowing, rugby, and cricket. In these three sports, the centuries-old rivalries between Oxford and that *other* university from East Anglia (Cambridge) are highlights of the year.

At Oxford, Smith participated in lacrosse, basketball, rugby, cricket, and rowing. Two—lacrosse and basketball—were Smith's fortes, both of which he played at the university (club) level for three consecutive seasons

Lacrosse (invented in Canada from an native Indian game), has been a major sport in British Commonwealth countries for well over a century, especially so in England. Smith began playing lacrosse after McGurk explained the game to him and invited him to a club practice. According to McGurk, Smith was very interested in trying it, adding, "being a natural athlete, he quickly became a starter on the university lacrosse team," for which he ultimately was awarded three "half-blues," the American equivalent of letters in varsity sports. Blues, as distinguished from half-blues, are awarded for participation on the university's major teams—rowing, rugby, and cricket. Half-blues are awarded for other university or club-level sports. To earn a blue or half-blue, one has to play against Cambridge, Oxford's arch-rival.

Of all athletic pursuits at Oxford, Smith found lacrosse to be the most rewarding. In addition to hurling the rubber ball from the crosses, lacrosse involves bumping, blocking, and thumping (Smith's description of the contact nature of the game). Smith and McGurk played defensive positions, McGurk in the "point position" while Smith played the "third man," a position that required him "to thump" the opposing team's players. Thumping was sort of like blocking and tackling in football. "I was not very good at catching and throwing the ball," Smith says, "but I was rather good at bumping and thumping," adding, tongue-in-cheek, "I became a famous thumper."

Smith played his first game on the University lacrosse team in 1949 against Kent under a "fog-shrouded greyness." The match was for the Southern Counties Championship. Describing the match, Oxford's student magazine, *The Isis*, said: "The murky weather hampered the scoring. The handful of hardy spectators who braved the weather and managed to find the field in the fog were treated to the spectacle of alternatively disappearing and reappearing players as the battle swirled from one end of the pitch to the other." The match ended in a draw, five to five.

Moreover, *The Isis* account praised "the new boy from America," saying "of the individual players, newcomer Reece Smith of Christ Church deserves a bouquet for his determination and nimble-foot agility on defense." Turning to the team as a whole, however, the article cautioned that "the [team's] aggressiveness necessary to beat Cambridge has still not developed." That year, it never did, for in the Fall of 1949, Cambridge beat Oxford in lacrosse for the thirteenth straight time. An article in *The Isis* lamented that the Oxford team "lacked handling abilities."

A year later, on November 23, 1950, a far different headline appeared in *The Isis*: "Oxford Beats Cambridge 6–5; First Time in Fourteen Years," though Smith describes the win against Cambridge as "the first since the signing of the *Magna Carta.*" The upset occurred during Smith's second season as a starting member of the lacrosse team. The evening of the triumph, both teams attended the traditional Oxford/Cambridge Lacrosse Clubs Banquet. (A picture taken at the time reveals a jubilant Smith at a table with Oxford and Cambridge lacrosse players.) In the fall of 1951, the two universities again played each other in lacrosse and, with Smith and McGurk, Oxford again beat Cambridge (7–3).

English County National Championship Cup

Smith played in every one of the University's lacrosse matches over three seasons. Besides defeating Cambridge twice, the team's most notable achievement was winning the "English County Cup" in Manchester, England. In this annual competition, teams from all participating counties compete for the opportunity to participate in the national championship match. The Oxford University team represented the county of Oxfordshire. At the end of the lacrosse season, the two county teams having the best won-lost-draw record play each other for the national county championship. In March 1951, the Oxford University team beat a team from Surrey 5 to 4 to win the County National Championship Cup.

Getting to the championship match held in Manchester, however, was anything but easy for Smith. Hours before daybreak on the day of the match, carrying helmet, stick, pads, and lacrosse gloves, he climbed over a Christ Church wall and trudged nearly two miles to the town's railway depot. There, he and his teammates boarded a train to London, where they had an English meal of greasy fish and chips. Afterwards, they boarded another train to Manchester.

Once there, they rode a double-decker bus to half a mile from the lacrosse pitch. Running late and with gear in hand, Smith and his teammates raced to the field arriving only minutes prior to the scheduled match. The effort was well worth it, as Oxford won the national championship! After the win, followed by drinks and comradery with the Surrey opponents, Smith returned to Oxford late that night, again climbing over the wall.

In contrast to lacrosse, Smith's participation on Oxford's basketball team, though enjoyable, involved neither championship games nor matches against Cambridge. But he does remember one evening in particular. He and the Oxford University basketball team traveled to London where they had been invited to play on the same program with the famed Harlem Globetrotters. The forum was jammed with people waiting to see the Globetrotters perform. It was thrilling for the Oxford players to know that hundreds of spectators were also watching them.

Head of the River

Then there was the really big sport at Oxford—rowing. It seemed that everyone at Oxford rowed. Though not a member of the university's team, Smith rowed on one of four Christ Church boats. Each team had its own shell (boat). His crew was called the "Gentlemen's Eight." Heading it was Peter Gladstone, a former Oxford Blue (and grandson of the former British Prime Minister) who had retired from serious rowing but came back to participate on the college level. Gladstone was the Gentlemen's Eight "stroke oar" and, as such, set the tempo for the strokes in conjunction with the shouts of the "coxswain," who sat in the front of the shell looking back towards the rowers.

Each Spring, Oxford colleges compete in what is called "Eights Week," an annual event featuring college rowing crews competing against each other on the Isis (what the Thames is called in the vicinity of Oxford). Each team's goal is to become "head of the river." When Smith was at Oxford, between sixty and eighty shells competed for the title. The Isis is rather narrow and thus prevents the shells from racing abreast. Rather, they follow one another in small groups. Every shell and its crew are ranked and seeded in a prescribed order for lining up prior to beginning of the race. The crew having the highest rating takes the front position in the queue, followed in order from high to lower rated crews. Within each group, the competing shells race against each other, each shell attempting to catch up with the shell ahead and bump it in the rear. Once bumped, a shell must exit that race, and drop back one position for the next race. For the survivors, each crew can work its way up to the head of the line by exchanging starting positions after each race, the ultimate winner being called the "Head of the River."

Though strenuous and tiring, Smith enjoyed competitive rowing on the Isis; still, he admits he was not disappointed when his shell was bumped. That meant his crew had to leave the river and *that* meant some warm English beer after "putting the shell to bed."

Service to the Rhodes Trust

Reminiscing about Oxford, Smith remembers it as a wonderful and amazing experience, one transforming for him personally. The experience reinforced lessons he had learned from his grandmother (Mother Mary) and from his high school football coach (Denton Cook)—to be the best one can be in every endeavor and to avail oneself of every opportunity to grow and learn. Oxford lived up to Smith's expectations. Yes, he was bright, athletic and a hard worker prior to coming up to Oxford (as his earlier successes in high school, college, the Navy and law school had confirmed). But after his three years at Oxford, Smith was a more mature, worldly, scholarly and, most importantly, a socially conscious and involved human being. For Smith, his time at Oxford had been a pivotal experience in his life.

After he left Oxford in 1952, he continued his ties with the Rhodes Scholarship program. In 1956, the Rhodes Trust appointed Smith to be a member of the Florida American Rhodes Scholarship Selection Committee. Thereafter, he worked with the American Secretary of the Rhodes Trust for thirty years. For two decades, Smith headed the Florida committee. His responsibilities included suggesting members to serve on Florida Selection Committees to the American Secretary of the Rhodes Trust. Smith scheduled candidate interviews and communicated all decisions regarding the Florida Selection Committee's business to the American Secretary. Besides his work for the Florida Selection Committee, Smith also served as a member of the Rhodes Trust's Southeastern District (final) Selection Committee.

For several years, Smith has been the secretary of the 1949 class of American Rhodes who refer to themselves as "the 49ers." Each year he asks them to send him information regarding their activities during the preceding year, and then writes a summary of their responses. They are then published in an issue of the *American Oxonian,* a bi-annual publication distributed to all former American Rhodes scholars and other Oxonians.

In 1999, Smith sent letters to each of the "49er," inviting them to gather with the alumni of the classes of 1948 and 1950 at a fifty-year reunion in New York

City. About thirty of his classmates attended. Four years later in 2003, Smith attended a reunion of Rhodes scholars in Washington, D.C. At the meeting, then President Bill Clinton, one of America's better known Rhodes scholars, spoke. Smith recalls it was a memorable occasion, and he was delighted to see many old friends and acquaintances from his Oxford days. (A photograph of First Lady Clinton greeting Smith at the White House appears later.)

* * *

CHAPTER SEVEN

LAW PRACTICE AT CARLTON FIELDS

Post-Oxford: Law Teacher

During his final year at Oxford (1951–52), Smith contemplated what he would do next. Several classmates planned to remain on the continent and he considered that possibility. By 1952, America's leadership in rebuilding Europe under the Marshall Plan was still on-going. Thousands of Americans, including lawyers, were in Europe. Smith contacted a lawyer who worked in the Paris office of the New York law firm of Coudert Brothers. He advised Smith against coming to France to practice law because he was not familiar with the French civil law system and because attorneys not admitted to the French Bar "were at a distinct disadvantage." Smith contacted another American lawyer who was on leave from a Philadelphia firm and working in London with a U.S. government agency; he told Smith there were no openings in the London office, but said he would recommend to his partners back in Philadelphia that they hire him. Though considering the idea, Smith chose not to pursue it, knowing nobody at the firm.

Instead, he began thinking about returning to Tampa, perhaps with the law firm of Fowler White, which had made him an offer three years earlier. Then, out of the blue, as his final year at Oxford was drawing to a close, he unexpectedly received a letter from Dean Henry Fenn of the University of Florida College of Law. Fenn offered Smith a position on the law faculty, explaining that the school needed a one-year replacement for Professor Gene Scoles who would be on academic leave in the fall. Scoles taught conflicts of law, and Fenn knew Smith had studied international conflicts of law at Oxford. Fenn also was aware of Smith's outstanding academic record while studying law at Florida.

Finding the prospect of teaching law exciting, Smith accepted Dean Fenn's offer even though he realized his appointment likely would be only for one year. Nonetheless, teaching law was something Smith knew he would enjoy and find stimulating. Moreover, it would provide him additional time to decide where, and with whom, he would practice law. So, he decided to take the job at UF in Gainesville.

During his year on the law faculty, Smith taught contracts, legal research and writing, and conflicts of law. He found he liked teaching law and working with students. Of course, he had no way of knowing that, within two years, he would be teaching law again, this time on a part-time basis, at Stetson University College of Law.

Coming to Carlton Fields

During his year on the Florida faculty, another unexpected opportunity arose—to join a law firm other than Fowler White. Michel Emmanuel, a Tampa lawyer, contacted Smith in the Spring of 1954 and asked him to consider joining the law firm of Mabry, Reaves, Carlton, Anderson, Fields & Ward. Smith had met Emmanuel a few years earlier when both were law students at Florida. Emmanuel told Smith that his Tampa law firm wished to hire a lawyer to work in trial and appellate practice. Smith drove to Tampa to interview with the firm's partners. The interview went well and he was hired.

Smith has been with Carlton Fields since that day in October 1954 when he first joined the firm. At that time, the firm consisted of twelve lawyers, not all practicing law full-time. Fifty-five years later, as of January 1, 2009, the firm had 300 attorneys and a support staff of 350, located in seven offices: Tampa, Atlanta, Miami, Orlando, Tallahassee, St. Petersburg, and West Palm Beach. For a number of years, the firm also maintained offices in Pensacola and Jacksonville.

From the time Smith joined the firm through the present, he has played a key role in its development. He soon became a partner and for three decades headed the firm, initially as managing partner and after the firm became a professional corporation, as vice president, then followed in succession as president, and chairman of the board. Today he serves as chairman *emeritus*.

Carlton Fields's attorneys have been and remain among the most highly-rated lawyers in the country on the bases of peer review assessments. Martindale-Hubbell, the publisher of the leading nation-wide attorney directory, annually rates the country's lawyers on two measures—legal ability and ethical standards. As explained by Martindale-Hubbell, its Legal Ability Ratings consider "the standard of professional ability in the area where the lawyer practices, the lawyer's expertise, and other professional qualifications." The rating A signifies "very high to preeminent." The second component—the General Ethical Standards Rating—signifies "adherence to professional standards of conduct and ethics, reliability, diligence and other criteria relevant to the discharge of professional responsibilities." Lawyers who meet this standard are rated V, meaning very high. In a recent year, eighty-eight percent of Carlton Fields's eligible lawyers were awarded the highest AV(r) rating.

The first year Smith was eligible, he received the top AV(r) rating. An official of Martindale Hubbell once told Smith that he had one of the highest ratings by his peers the official had ever seen. Smith dismisses the compliment as "all puff." Nonetheless, for nearly fifty years, Reece Smith has held the highest AV(r) rating.

In 2008, another publication that ranks attorneys—*The Chambers Guide to American Leading Business Lawyers*—listed forty Carlton Fields attorneys among the top lawyers in Florida. The Chambers Guide also recognized the firm for "excellence" in twelve specialities of business practice, ranking it first in Florida in three areas: construction practice (for the sixth straight year), insurance law, and white collar crime and government investigation practice.

Smith is one of many lawyers at Carlton Fields who have gained recognition in the profession of law. He was the first member of the firm elected a Fellow of the American College of Trial Lawyers, a national honorary organization that elects outstanding trial lawyers. In 1992, five other partners were members of the College: Broaddus Livingston, Davidson Dunlap, Sylvia Walbolt, Alan Sundberg, and Tom Clark. Smith suggests that the firm's reputation for trial and appellate excellence is demonstrated by the fact that Carlton Fields "had more members in the American College of Trial Lawyers that year than any other Florida firm."

Founders and Early Partners— Giddings Eldon Mabry

The firm's reputation for excellence began when it consisted of only three lawyers: Giddings Mabry, Governor Doyle Carlton, and Judge OK [his first name] Reaves. Each man possessed a strong moral and religious ethic; all were practicing Baptists and adhered to high moral and ethical standards. According to Sylvia Walbolt, a former chair of Carlton Fields, all of the founding partners firmly believed that a lawyer must "do what was right, even it that meant losing money or a client. They were the conscience of the firm from the beginning."

Carlton Fields traces its roots to Giddings Eldon Mabry. Born in Tupelo, Mississippi, in 1877, he opened his Tampa law firm in 1901 at age twenty-four. Mabry earned his law degree at Cumberland Law School (then located in Lebanon, Tennessee.) Attending law school at that time was not the normal path to becoming a lawyer in America. Rather, those who aspired to be attorneys either read the law on their own or served as apprentices to lawyers (or both).

The second lawyer to join Giddings Mabry's firm was his father, Milton Harvey Mabry, who earned a law degree in 1872 from Lebanon School of Law (later renamed Cumberland). After graduation, Milton Mabry practiced six years in Mississippi. In 1878, Mabry, when his son Giddings was two years old, moved to Florida and opened a law office in Leesburg. A few years after coming to Florida, Mabry was elected to the state's House of Representatives. A year later, he was elected Florida's Lieutenant Governor and served four years. Subsequently, Milton Mabry was appointed to the Florida Supreme Court, becoming its chief justice. He served on the state's highest court until 1903, when he retired from the bench.

He then moved to Tampa to join his son in law practice, and the firm's name was changed to Mabry & Mabry, but not for long. The elder Mabry soon discovered that law practice was no longer personally fulfilling. After practicing with his son for a relatively short time, Justice Mabry returned to Tallahassee to become clerk of the Florida Supreme Court. Milton Mabry had another son with ties to Tampa—Dale Mabry. Dale rose to be a captain in the United States Army Air Corps and became famous for his pioneer work in lighter-than-air aircraft (then called airships). Colonel William "Billy" Mitchell described Dale Mabry as one of the "really experienced" airship captains. Tragically, in 1922, Dale Mabry died at the controls of the dirigible *Roma* when, due to a malfunction, it crashed and burned at Langley Field, Virginia. (A major thoroughfare in Tampa now bears his name.)

During the period Dale Mabry was flying airships, Giddings Mabry practiced law in Tampa. Giddings quickly became known as a hardworking and competent lawyer. At one point, he placed an advertisement in the Martindale Hubbell directory that read:

> Careful, personal attention given to every item of business, large or small. I hold no Claims. I either collect them within a reasonable time or return them. No inquiries necessary on claims sent to me. I report frequently and regularly with each claim. All commercial reports are thorough, reliable, and up-to-date and are made promptly.

Giddings Mabry was a highly regarded citizen as well as a prominent lawyer. He was active in his Baptist church and served on the Board of Trustees of Stetson University. He served as the Tampa City Attorney from 1910 to 1913, and then as County Attorney for Hillsborough County from 1917 through 1923. Smith followed in Mabry's footsteps, also becoming Tampa's City Attorney while serving as a full-time member of the firm.

Smith describes Mabry as "a thoughtful and generous man who cared about those who worked with him." Newer members of the firm were quite pleased when Mabry insisted on distributing the firm's profits in a manner to enable the younger members to become equity partners. Although Mabry often gave advice to his partners and associates, that advice was not *always* on the mark. One day shortly after Smith joined the firm, he asked Mabry about investing in stock of a company named Walt Disney. Mabry warned: "Don't do it. It's too speculative. Mickey Mouse will never catch on."

Poor investment advice notwithstanding, Smith says that Mabry was "a fine citizen and an able lawyer," adding "he had a quiet, but effective influence upon the firm's partners, many of whom were more publicly prominent than Giddings chose to be." In summing up his significance to the firm, Smith says: "Mabry was a solid rock upon which the firm could build." In 1968, Giddings Mabry died in Tampa at the age of ninety.

Governor Doyle Carlton

In 1912, Giddings Mabry joined Doyle Elam Carlton in a partnership they called Mabry and Carlton. Except for a few short intervals, including when Carlton was Florida's governor, their partnership flourished for over sixty years.

The Mabrys and the Carltons were both prominent Florida families. Though the Mabrys moved into the state in the late 1880s, Carlton's ancestors went back at least to the mid-1830s in Florida, years before it gained statehood in 1845. *Florida's early families such as the Mabrys and Carltons are referred to as "Florida Crackers." Today, some people use it in a disparaging manner, but that is not its origin. According to Florida historian Michael Gannon, when cattle raising was widespread across central and southwest Florida in the latter part of the nineteenth century, cowmen "worked the herds with eighteen-foot-long braided buckskin whips that, when cracked, sounded like rifle shots across the palmetto prairies. According to one theory it was the whip-cracking that gave rise to 'Crackers' as a sobriquet for native Floridians."*

Another common usage of the term is referencing a second, third or longer generation Floridian. Many of Florida's early leaders were from out of state. "Not until 1929 and the election of Doyle E. Carlton," writes Gannon, "would Florida have a native son from a native institution [Stetson University] as governor."

The two-story wood home in Wauchula where Doyle Carlton was born on July 6, 1887, today stands in "Cracker Village" at the Florida State Fairgrounds in Tampa. Carlton was one of nine children of Albert and Martha McEwen Carlton. He received his undergraduate education at the Stetson University in DeLand, Florida, earning a bachelors of arts degree while concurrently graduating from Stetson's School of Business. After Stetson, Carlton went to the University of Chicago Law School, but transferred a year later to Columbia

University Law School in New York. The move permitted him to take the Florida bar examination earlier than had he remained in Chicago. Earning his LL.B. in 1912 from Columbia, Carlton came to Tampa to join Giddings Mabry in practicing law.

With Carlton on board, Mabry was able to focus his practice more on probate and real estate matters. In contrast, Carlton essentially tried cases, and was noted for his oratorical proficiency. Smith comments that clients thought "Doyle used compelling and persuasive argumentative skills in the courtroom, often making fiery arguments and having an adeptness of connecting with juries. His arguments were lucid and straightforward, and absent of sophistry."

In 1917, Carlton used his public speaking talents when he ran for the Florida Senate. He won and served, as Smith puts it,"two remarkable years." Smith adds, "Doyle is properly credited with leading the fight in Tallahassee for women's suffrage and for the state providing free text books for elementary school children." Following the Senate term, Carlton returned to the law firm. Like Mabry before and Smith later, he became Tampa's city attorney, thus combining his private practice of law with public responsibilities of being Tampa's head lawyer.

Then, in 1928, Carlton ran for Florida's governorship. His opponent was Fons Hathaway, a Florida state official who allegedly had incurred expensive car repair bills for his personal automobile that he had submitted to the state comptroller for payment. The problem — as Carlton pointed out during his campaign — was that the car mysteriously disappeared. Waiving Hathaway's bills in front of campaign audiences, Carlton asked rhetorically: "Where is this fine car"? The exhortation resonated with voters, and Carlton easily carried the election. He subsequently served four years as Florida's governor.

From the outset of his term, Governor Carlton confronted deteriorating economic conditions as the Great Depression spread and deepened. Many Floridians nonetheless considered Carlton an effective governor, but not everyone agreed given the economic despair shared by so many. That despair is revealed in a poem of the era, *Leven Cent Cotton*, one stanza of which follows:

> *Leven-cent cotton, forty-cent meat,*
> *How in the world can a poor man eat?*
> *Pray for the sunshine, cause it will rain,*
> *Things gettin' worse, drivin' us insane.*
> *No use talkin', any man's beat*
> *With leven-cent cotton and forty-cent meat.*

Months prior to Carlton taking office in January 1929, Florida had suffered a singular human and economic catastrophe. In 1928 the deadliest hurricane in Florida's history hit the Keys, creating a path of destruction from south

Florida through the Everglades to the shores of Lake Okeechobee. Historian James Clark writes: "The death toll [from the unnamed storm] was estimated at 2,000, the majority of whom were migrant workers." In addition to that disaster, Florida's great land boom of the early- and mid-1920s collapsed in late 1927. Not long afterwards, Florida's farmers suffered economic devastation caused by a wide-spread infestation of Mediterranean fruit-flies that wiped out a large segment of the state's citrus crop.

Thus, Governor Carlton presided over Florida's government while the state experienced the wide-spread economic problems during the Great Depression. Compounding the situation, he had to deal with the Florida Legislature that Clark describes as "an all-time low" in Florida's history. In 1931, the legislators increased their own pay at a time when state's economy was in deep distress and spending for education and other public priorities were severely cut. Governor Carlton caused the legislature to cut his salary by one third, an act that did not go unnoticed by Florida's citizens.

Also in 1931, the legislature established pari-mutual horse racing in Florida. Governor Carlton vetoed the bill. Not deterred, the legislature overrode the veto. Clark writes: "There were rumors that more than $100,000 was paid to legislators to vote for the racing." Carlton said he had refused a $100,000 bribe to sign the pari-mutual betting bill and declared: "If my name is worth that much, I think I'll just keep it." Carlton's honesty was never seriously questioned when he held public office or when he practiced law. In reflecting on his colleague, Smith says: "He always conducted himself with the highest ethical standards and with complete integrity."

In the 1932 state election, Florida voters threw twenty-six of the ninety-five state legislators out of office, a record number, after thirty-one chose not to seek reelection. Carlton had decided not to seek reelection and returned to Tampa to practice law with his partners Mabry and Reaves. To fill Carlton's position during his leave of absence, the firm had hired Morris White, later a principal partner of Fowler White, to be its primary litigator. The firm's name then became Mabry, Reaves, Carlton & White. In 1936, upon the urging of many Floridians, Carlton entered the race for a seat in the U.S. Senate, but lost in what was deemed an upset. Smith says that reputedly Carlton "was too busy" in his law practice to campaign.

Although Carlton never again sought public office, he responded favorably to requests for public service. President Dwight David Eisenhower appointed him to be a member of the first United States Commission on Civil Rights. Years later, President Kennedy appointed Carlton to the National Agricultural Advisory Commission. In Florida, Carlton served as president of the Florida State Chamber of Commerce from 1951–1952, and also played a key role in helping the Ringling Museum in Sarasota become a state institution, today recognized as a distinguished art museum.

In his work for the firm, Carlton brought in major clients. Moreover, he taught new lawyers the nuances of trial advocacy, especially how to try jury cases. But his greatest contribution, according to Smith, was that "Carlton taught the firm how to lead." After Carlton's death in 1972, at the age of 87, the *Tampa Tribune* wrote:

> No Floridian ever made greater contributions to his State, and in such varied areas of vital interest as Doyle E. Carlton, Sr. While governor, he was the first citizen of Florida. He remained first in the hearts of Floridians until his death.

Judge OK Reaves

The firm of Mabry and Carlton got busier as Florida went through its first major land boom of the early and mid-1920s. Mabry and Carlton realized they needed another lawyer and recruited a fellow Baptist, Judge OK Reaves, a highly respected attorney and jurist from Bradenton, Florida. Resigning from the bench in 1921, Judge Reaves joined Mabry and Carlton. The firm's name became Mabry, Reaves, and Carlton because Carlton insisted that his name be last in deference to Judge Reaves's age.

Judge Reaves's first name truly is "OK" As the story goes, after looking at his newly-born infant son, his father declared, "he's OK!" Smith says the proud father was not commenting on the baby's physical condition, but was "complimenting his new son." Born in 1877 in Sarasota County, Reaves attended public schools in Manatee County. After taking courses at a business college in Jacksonville, he decided to become a lawyer and subsequently earned a law degree from Stetson University College of Law. Stetson was the first law school in Florida and OK Reaves was a member of its second graduating class in 1903.

Reaves practiced law in Bradenton from 1903 through1915. During part of that time, he also served as a legislator in the Florida House of Representatives. Governor Trammell in 1914 offered Reaves the post of Florida Attorney General after the then attorney general had decided he was going to resign. But the incumbent changed his mind, so in 1915 Trammell appointed Reaves a circuit judge in Florida's Sixth Judicial Circuit (which then encompassed much of west and south-central Florida, including the cities of Fort Meyers, Sarasota, Bradenton, St. Petersburg, Clearwater, and Dade City.) Reaves held court throughout the area, often "riding the circuit" on a coastal steamer. During his judicial tenure, he was active in the organized bar and was a founding member of the Florida State Bar Association (forerunner to The Florida Bar), serving as president for two years.

After resigning from the bench, Judge Reaves joined Mabry and Carlton in their Tampa law firm. When Reaves announced he intended to resign, a citizens campaign was mounted to persuade him to reconsider. It failed and in a letter to the *Bradenton Herald* the judge explained he was leaving the bench to pursue a new challenge. In the same letter, Reaves spoke out against the "deplorable situation" in sections of Florida where there was little outrage over mob lynchings, declaring: "Let no man assume to be wiser than the law.... [G]oing outside the law is criminal and will only produce more crime. This [judicial] circuit must be altogether free from the mob spirit."

Later, Florida's Governor Hardee offered to appoint Reaves to the Florida Supreme Court, but he declined. By then, he and Carlton had become what Smith describes as "a litigation dream team." Carlton made the opening and closing statements, usually winning over jurors and judges through his persuasive oratorical skills. Judge Reaves, on the other hand, was a legal scholar who exhaustively researched all the relevant points of law before making cogent legal arguments in trial and appellate courts. The combination worked wonders and their reputations as lawyers grew with each courtroom success.

Judge Reaves "was an exemplary role model of a professional lawyer," Smith says, adding: "He was a man of great legal ability and humor whom we all enjoyed and from whom we never ceased to learn." According to Smith, Reaves became one of Florida's expert chancery lawyers, developing a reputation for hard work, top lawyering skill, and bed-rock integrity.

Outside the firm, Reaves was an active citizen, serving as president of both the Florida Baptist Convention and the Florida State Bar Association, a trustee of Stetson University, and a member of the Florida State Board of Law Examiners. Well-liked and respected in the community, Reaves neither was pompous nor took himself too seriously. He also had a dry sense of humor. Smith offers an example: "When Reaves was in his nineties, he told Broaddus Livingston that he was 'worried about the hereafter.' Livingston asked how that could be, pointing out: 'Judge, you have been a devout Christian all your life.' Judge Reaves replied: 'Yes, but I voted for Franklin Roosevelt in 1932.'"

Judge Reaves significantly contributed to the firm in many ways, perhaps most importantly, in mentoring the next generation of the firm's lawyers, especially Smith. Sylvia Walbolt notes: "There is no doubt that OK Reaves was the most important role model for Reece," an assessment with which Smith agrees. In his 1992 unpublished history of the Carlton Fields law firm, Smith wrote: "If Mr. Mabry taught us to care, and Governor Carlton how to lead, it was Judge Reaves who showed us what a great lawyer should be." Smith continued: "He taught us a great lesson in professional development. We asked him: 'How do we get clients, Judge?' His advice: 'Work as hard as you can for those you have and the others will come because of your reputation.'"

When a visitor comes to Smith's office at Carlton Fields, he points to his desk and with pride declares: "That was Judge OK Reaves's desk." When the judge retired, he gave Smith the solid oak, rectangular desk, one Smith still uses and describes as "one of my most prized possessions." Judge OK Reaves was 93 when he died in 1970. Like other early partners of the firm, Reaves continued to work at the office until shortly before his death.

Smith and Others Lead Firm Forward

In 1933, D. Wallace Fields, a native Kentuckian, graduated from Stetson University's law school and in the same year was admitted to practice in both Kentucky and Florida. After practicing several years in DeLand, he was offered a job by the Carlton firm under unusual circumstances. Smith explains:

> When Mr. Mabry met Wally, he said: 'Wally, I'm sick and I'm going to North Carolina this morning and try to get myself in better physical condition. I want to hire you. We'll pay you $75 a month and I want you to take over my work and when I get back I want to see it in as good order as I leave it with you. Just work hard.'

Fields took the job and Mabry immediately left the office. Fields found Mabry had 110 real estate matters pending and some fifty estates in probate pending. Upon return, Mabry found the real estate matters had been completed, the estates were in apple pie order, all fees were collected, and a lot of money had been made for the firm for that day and age. In commenting on Fields's accomplishment, Smith notes: "It was a good way to start."

Fields later became a leading oil and gas lawyer in Florida. In the early 1940s, Fields and Carlton began representing oil companies that were expanding oil and gas exploration in Florida. Fields drafted oil and gas leases in the Panhandle area of the state. Smith notes: "Wally Fields was one of a few Florida lawyers who practiced oil and gas law, at one point representing seventeen oil companies." Fields drafted Florida's first oil and gas code. The man who is *the* "Fields" in today's Carlton Fields law firm, was, Smith says, a soft-spoken, kind and generous gentleman:

Throughout his active years in the firm, Wally was one of our most friendly and popular members. We liked him. So did our clients. Like his mentor, Mr. Mabry, Wally Fields counseled us to be considerate of one another and to share generously the rewards of our work.

Fields retired from Carlton Fields in 1977 and died in 1991.

Additional lawyers came to the firm in the decade after World War II who contributed both to the firm and to the community. Marvin Green, for example, served sixteen years on the Hillsborough County Board of Public Instruction (several as chair). During this period, the U.S. Supreme Court handed down its 1954 decision of *Brown v. School Board of Topeka*. Green was instrumental in persuading the Hillsborough Board to work for orderly integration of the public schools. Around the same time, Mitch Emmanuel, a veteran of World War II, joined the firm. He was the son of Greek immigrants and his hiring broke a cultural barrier at the firm.

Meanwhile, A. Broaddus Livingston (who joined the firm two years after Smith), became a leader of the growing organization, serving in time as both the firm's president and, later, chair. Smith underscores that Livingston's interactions with the firm's other lawyers "exemplified the importance of collegiality," noting: "Broaddus Livingston was one of our most popular members."

Thomas Clark also came to the firm in the mid-1950s. Smith notes that "he always put others first." Clark was "the firm's father confessor who, like me, had a bleeding heart for the underdog." The two worked together to promote social causes including the firm's diversification, promoting the hiring of women, Jews, Blacks and Hispanics. President Carter appointed Clark to the federal Court of Appeals for the Fifth Circuit. He later sat on the newly formed Eleventh Circuit of Appeals.

Growth in Diversity and Size

From the time Giddings Mabry opened his law office in Tampa in 1901 through 1960, the firm experienced intermittent periods of growth and retrenchment. One of the more significant growth spurts occurred during the Florida's boom years in the 1920s. But the Great Depression and then the war led to serious retrenchment. By 1940, the firm had five lawyers. Its growth did not begin until after World War II. By the time Smith joined the firm in 1954, even then only a few lawyers in the firm were actively practicing.

A "second generation" of lawyers came during the 1950s and 1960s. It was in the 1960s when firm began to diversify. Before then there had been no Jewish, women, or minority lawyers at the firm. For that matter, none of Tampa's large firms had members from these groups. Then, in 1961, Carlton Fields hired Edward Cutler, who had relocated from Philadelphia. This was the first time a large established Tampa law firm had hired a Jewish lawyer. And what a lawyer he was.

"Ed Cutler," Smith says, "influenced the firm in several ways. He brought to the practice of law in the Tampa Bay region a level of legal sophistication that had not been seen previously." Sylvia Walbolt comments: "Cutler had an intellectual mastery of wide-ranging areas of law; and he was meticulous." She adds: "Some of us called him Zorro because he marked the work of other lawyers with a red pencil, scribbling over pages like Zorro moving his sword wildly through the air." Smith assesses Cutler as "an exceptionally knowledgeable lawyer, a competent attorney, and a diligent worker." In an unpublished history of the firm, Smith wrote:

> No lawyer I have known in forty years at the bar mastered more fields of law than Ed Cutler—jury and bench trials, probate and real estate matters, labor, tax, securities, secured transactions, bankruptcy—you name it—Ed could hold his own with specialists in almost any area of the law. He loved the law and even enjoyed working on a Saturday afternoon.

In the early 1960s, Carlton Fields broke down another barrier to entry—gender. The attitude for the most part in Florida had been: "Women need not apply." At Smith's urging, the firm hired Sylvia Hardaway ("Walbolt," after marriage), thereby becoming its first woman attorney. After law school, Walbolt joined Carlton Fields where for some years she worked primarily with Smith in trial and appellate practice. Smith says that a partner had commented: "Sylvia thought while Reece talked." He agrees.

> Sylvia's thinking contributed materially to successful results obtained in several important firm cases in the late '60s and early '70s, including sustaining a record personal injury verdict, representation of Florida Power Corporation in a novel antitrust case, and a branch banking case that went to the U.S. Supreme Court.

When Smith took a leave from Carlton Fields to be Interim President of the University of South Florida (discussed later), "Walbolt," he says, "assumed the responsibility for many of my clients and undertook the leading role she plays today in the firm's work. Her career has been remarkable." Smith emphasizes that Walbolt "blazed the trail for women lawyers."

In the 1990s, the firm initiated a domestic partner benefits program, one of the first in Florida. In 1999, Carlton Fields was Florida's first large firm to elect a woman—Sylvia Walbolt—to head the firm as chair.

In recognition of her lawyering skills and professionalism, Sylvia Hardaway Walbolt was the second woman lawyer in the country to be inducted as a Fellow of the American College of Trial Lawyers. Following Smith's example, she has been active in *pro bono* matters and has received several awards for that work. Examples include her receiving The Florida Bar President's "*Pro Bono* Service Award for the Thirteenth Circuit" in 2007, the "Tobias Simon Award" from the Florida Supreme Court for "outstanding service in the area of *pro bono* legal representation" in 2008, and "The Medal of Honor of the Florida Bar Foundation" in 2009. Sylvia Walbolt is also a recipient of the annual "William Reece Smith, Jr. Public Service Award," presented by Stetson University College of Law "to an individual who epitomizes the best in lawyering, public service, and professionalism in the tradition of Reece Smith."

For decades, African-American lawyers found it virtually impossible to find employment with Tampa's large law firms. But the situation began to change and Carlton Fields played a major role in brining it about. In 1971, Carlton Fields hired its first African-American attorney, Eurich Griffin, who subsequently was elected a shareholder of the firm. Then, in the 1980s, the firm elected an African-American woman—Mary Scriven—to shareholder status. Subsequently, she was appointed a United States Magistrate judge and, more recently, was appointed a United States District Judge.

In 2007, Gary Sasso became the firm's first Hispanic chief executive officer and chair. Later he, was honored for his leadership in championing diversity within the firm, receiving the 2008 "Best Practices CEO Diversity Leadership Award" at the Fifteenth Annual Diversity and Inclusion Leadership Gala in Washington, D.C., sponsored by the "Diversity Best Practices" organization. The group describes itself as "the preeminent organization in the nation for national corporate and law firm leaders to share best practices and develop innovation solutions for cultural change." The diversity transformation of Carlton Fields to a large degree has resulted from the persistent urging of Reece Smith. He always pushed the issue and persuaded his colleagues to open the firm's doors to persons who didn't look the same as the firm's then current lawyers. He continues to do so today.

Public Service and *Pro Bono*

Two law professors—Marc Galanter and Thomas Palay—in a study found America's large law firms have rapidly grown by "increased rationalization, specialization, hierarchy, meritocracy, diversity, and market orientation." The authors concluded large law firms are increasingly governed by the bottom line. Smith agrees. In a 1992 firm history, he wrote: "competition has increased under the pressure of consumerism, and the [legal] profession has become more like the business community it has long served." With Smith's example and leadership, however, Carlton Fields became, and remains, one of the leaders in Florida in *pro bono* activities.

Smith notes that members of the firm have "long engaged in representing disadvantaged persons without compensation, *pro bono publico*." In his 1992 history, he explained how the firm's *pro bono* activity evolved:

> Initially we accepted representation in criminal cases upon assignment through state and federal courts, before the days of public defenders, and worked with the Legal Aid Society of Hillsborough County. Commencing in the 1970s, we were one of the first Florida firms to give productive hour credits for *pro bono* representation. Our policy in this regard has been defined and redefined as we grew and economic pressure became greater. But we continued to esteem *pro bono* representation.

Today, the tradition of *pro bono* work at Carlton Fields continues. *The Vault Guide to the Top 100 Law Firms* (2007 edition), ranked Carlton Fields third nationally in *pro bono* undertakings. Smith's public service imprint on Walbolt and others at the firm has been, and continues to be, invaluable in assuring the firm's adherence to its core values. In 1990, the firm honored Smith for his service as President and Chairman of the Board. His service, however, was not over. Smith continues to serve as the firm's beacon and carries its banner.

* * *

CHAPTER EIGHT

CASES BEFORE THE U.S. AND FLORIDA SUPREME COURTS

A Generalist Lawyer

Smith has tried and argued cases before Florida municipal, county, circuit, and district courts of appeal judges as well as before the justices of the Florida Supreme Court. On the federal level, he has argued cases before magistrates, district court judges, courts of appeals tribunals, and the chief justice and associate justices of the U.S. Supreme Court. He has appeared in scores of administrative proceedings before various state and federal regulatory agencies including the Interstate Commerce Commission, the Internal Revenue Service, the Securities and Exchange Commission, and the Federal Communications Commission. Smith also lobbied Congress and the Florida Legislature on behalf of clients and causes, including the American Bar Association.

A review of Smith's notes used in writing briefs and in preparing for oral arguments before both the Florida Supreme Court and the United States Supreme Court reveal his acumen in getting to the heart of a dispute. In his arguments, he focuses on the key legal issues, but also brings in the profundities of social and political aspects of the controversy. His analyses are straightforward, disentangling claims and counterclaims, and pointing out superficialities of purported distinctions. This chapter examines the first case Smith worked on at Carlton Fields, one that ended up in the Florida Supreme Court, and the four cases Smith took to the U.S. Supreme Court.

First Appellate Case before Florida Supreme Court

The year Smith joined Carlton Fields—1953—Judge O.K. Reaves asked him to assist in a case brought by a group of Manatee County citizens against the Manatee County Commissioners and the Manatee County School Board. The Board had passed a resolution calling for the issuance of $1,750,000 in bonds for rehabilitation work in the County's schools. Under Florida law, the bond issuance needed voter approval in a special election. The County School Board set the election and subsequently the bond issuance was approved by a relatively small margin of around 500 votes.

Under Florida law, the results of the special election required certification by a district's circuit court. Mabry, Reaves, Carlton, Fields & Ward represented a citizen of Manatee County who petitioned the circuit court to invalidate the election. Attorneys Reaves and Smith argued the bond election was illegal because Florida statutory law provided that only county commissioners had the power to call for a special election, not a county school board. Further, even if the school board had the legal authority to call a special election, the bond issue election was asserted to be invalid because voters who had not previously registered were allowed to vote. The School Board had published a registration deadline several days before the scheduled election. Many voters, including the petitioners, had missed the deadline and did not go to the election sites, believing they had no right to vote. On the other hand, some who had not registered early but went to the polls anyway were allowed to vote. Finally, Reaves and Smith presented testimony of a witness who had checked registration lists and found 84 names of persons who voted in favor of the bonds, but who were ineligible to vote because they owned no property in Manatee County and thus would not be subject to an increased *ad valorem* tax.

After Reaves and Smith presented their evidence and legal argument, Circuit Judge Lynn Gerald ruled for their client, declaring the bond election was invalid; first, the county commissioners had not called for the special election in the manner required by Florida law and, second, Manatee County's Supervisor of Voter Registration had allowed previously unregistered voters to vote, in contravention of Florida law mandating that voters register prior to election day. The School Board appealed to the Florida Supreme Court.

Between the filing of the appeal and the argument before Florida's highest court, the Supreme Court's 1954 desegregation decision of *Brown v. Board of Education* was rendered. Reaves and Smith argued that additional grounds supported the invalidation of the bond election: the School Board's plan for spending the bonds' proceeds would violate the equal treatment and equal protection requirements of the federal Constitution set forth under *Brown*.

In the eyes of some, the issue was not as clear cut as Reaves and Smith urged. Lawyers for the respondents argued that the Florida Constitution allowed segregated schools, the United States Supreme Court's edict notwithstanding. The Florida Supreme Court seemed to agree. A majority of justices of the Florida Supreme Court concurred in an infamous opinion written by Chief Justice Glenn Terrell that approved the School Board's call for a special election, as well as the late voter-registration procedure. The Court held that *Brown* did not require *immediate* implementation of desegregation or that all students to be afforded substantially equal facilities in every school district.

In disagreeing with the *Brown* decision, Chief Justice Terrell wrote that it was "a great mistake," and added:

> Whether or not the [older] doctrine of "separate but equal" has a place in the field of public education is a question of policy determinable by the legislature. It is not a judicial question ... Likewise, the question of segregation is for the same reason a legislative rather than a judicial question.... The effect of the *Brown* decision will retard rather than accelerate the removal of these inequalities.

Associate Justices B.K. Roberts, T. Frank Hobson, E. Harris Drew, and John H. Murphree concurred in Chief Justice Terrell's opinion, while Justice Elywin Thomas did not concur with its reasoning but concurred in the court's decision. The lone dissenter was Justice John Mathews, whose opinion generally agreed with the arguments of Reaves and Smith. Moreover, Justice Matthews sharply disagreed with the majority on the impact of the *Brown* decision, writing in his dissent: "If [the bond] proceeds are used to build segregated schools, the Federal Constitution will be violated."

Admission and Cases before the U.S. Supreme Court

On August 30, 1960, Smith and twenty-six other Tampa-area lawyers were admitted to the Bar of the United States Supreme Court. The ceremony took place in connection with the 83rd Annual Meeting of the American Bar Association. At the admission ceremony, William Reece Smith, Jr., raised his hand, repeated the oath, and was sworn in by the Honorable Earl Warren, Chief Justice of the United States. When Smith took his oath, he did not anticipate that someday he would argue a case before the Supreme Court, let alone four cases.

Reapportionment: *Swann v. Adams*

Arguably his most important case was *Swann v. Adams*, which ended up three times before the Court: *Swann v. Adams*, 378 U.S. 553 (1964), *Swann v. Adams*, 383 U.S. 210 (1966), and *Swann v. Adams*, 385 U.S. 440 (1967).

The reapportionment case that Smith undertook led to the *Swann v. Adams* trilogy. Historical perspective is required to understand its importance. Beginning in the late 1940s, and intensifying in the 1950s, Americans increasingly demanded that their votes have equal importance when electing members to state legislatures and to the U.S. Congress. Often huge disparities in population existed in legislative districts within given states, either by intentional gerrymandering of boundaries for political benefit, or by inadvertently ignoring population shifts from rural to city areas. Gerrymandering sometimes was based on race. In Florida, however, the problem primarily related to population shifts over time, as rural areas had substantially lower growth rates than did the urban regions, allowing rural interests to enjoy increasingly disproportional political power. For much of Florida's history, the majority of state legislators had come from rural districts but, as the populations of Florida's cities rose rapidly, voter disparities increased between urban and rural areas.

The United States Supreme Court began to encounter the same or similar claims in cases brought in other states, leading to the Court's decision in *Baker v. Carr*, 369 U.S. 186 (1962). Certain renowned Constitution law scholars (including Harvard Law School's Lawrence Tribe) consider the *Carr* decision to be among the Court's most significant. Even Chief Justice Earl Warren suggested that *Baker v. Carr* may have been the most important decision the Court decided during his tenure.

Thereafter, in *Reynolds v. Sims*, 377 U.S. 533 (1964), the Court, in a decision by Chief Justice Earl Warren, held the Equal Protection Clause of the Fourteenth Amendment requires apportionment of both houses of a state legislature on the basis of a population equivalency among legislative districts. For example, each district should have relatively the same number of voters. For several decades that had not been the case in Florida. In fact, at the time Smith filed *Swan v. Adams*, Florida had one of the greatest disparities in population among its election districts.

Florida Historian Peter Klingman observes: "Despite frequent calls for the Florida legislature to reapportion the state to reflect the growth and shifts in population, the state's legislators pressured by the rural interests—especially in northern Florida where they had the largest numbers—resisted the change." Rural-based legislators became popularly known as the "Pork Chop Gang" (a pejorative phrase coined by a *Tampa Tribune* editor and columnist, James

Clendinen). The "gang's" leader was Millard F. Caldwell, the twenty-ninth Governor of Florida who served from 1945–49. Closely tied to the rural and agricultural interests, Governor Caldwell steadfastly resisted redistricting during his term. Caldwell was also a staunch segregationist and segregation sentiment was strongest in rural sections.

During the ensuing decade, demands for reapportionment grew, but the "porkchoppers" gave no ground, even when the Florida Legislature met in special sessions to consider making changes. Increasingly, however, demands for change became better organized and more vociferous. In the mid-1950s, Professor Manning J. Dauer, head of the political science department at the University of Florida, became a strong voice for Florida reapportionment. His proposed plan in time was adopted by the courts (explained below), and, as a result, he has been called "the father of the Florida reapportionment law."

In 1960, Florida's voters elected Farris Bryant as the state's thirty-fourth governor. Governor Bryant, like his predecessors, was a conservative Democrat and was generally satisfied with the *status quo* apportionment of districts in the state. Nonetheless, the Governor knew Florida politicians from urban areas were pushing for reapportionment and he scheduled a special session for January 1963 to address the issue.

In late 1962, however, the Supreme Court's one-man, one-vote decision of *Baker v. Carr* was handed down, effectively overturning the Court's earlier precedent of *Colegrove v. Green*, 328 U.S. 549 (1946). *Baker v. Carr* held that a state's legislative apportionment had to comply with the requirements of the federal Constitution's Fifteenth Amendment (guaranteeing the right of citizens to vote) as well as the Fourteenth Amendment's equal protection requirement. In short, *Baker v. Carr* opened the door for those challenging mal-apportionment to file suit in the federal courts, which now had both the power and obligation to review state reapportionment legislation. In time, *Baker v. Carr* would have monumental importance for Florida.

Facing increasing calls for reapportionment, and given the prospect of judicial review of their action (or inaction), one might expect that Florida's legislators would speedily enact a plan that would pass judicial scrutiny. Instead, Florida politicians were not listening and had no intention to change the *status quo ante*. Litigation ensued.

Smith represented five mayors of Florida cities, who were seeking a reapportionment of the Florida Legislature to assure each urban voter's ballot would have substantially equivalent value when weighed against votes from rural areas. Julian Lane, Tampa's mayor, recommended that Smith be the mayors' attorney and they retained him. Smith had not yet become the chief attorney for the City of Tampa, but he was well known and recognized throughout

Florida for his integrity and lawyering skills. An editorial in the *Tampa Tribune* supported his selection as the mayors' lead attorney, commenting that "William Reece Smith, Jr.,has been hired to protect the rights of Hillsborough County voters."

On January 28, 1963, one day before the Florida Legislature was to convene for its third special session within a five-month window, Smith, representing the Mayors' Conference on Fair Legislative Apportionment, filed suit in federal court against the Legislature. Styled *Burdick v. Horne,* the suit sought to mandate legislation that would assure "substantially equitable representation" among Florida's election districts, in accordance with *Baker v. Carr.* The lead plaintiff was Sylvan Burdick, mayor *pro tem* of West Palm Beach. Respondents included Florida House Speaker Mallory Horne, Senate President Wilson Carraway, State Treasurer J. Edwin Larson, and State Comptroller Ray Green.

The petitioners sought a declaratory judgement before Judge Harold Carswell, the U.S. District Court Judge for the Northern District of Florida, declaring sections of the Florida Constitution unconstitutional, under the right-to-vote and equal-protection-of-the-laws mandates of the federal Constitution. They also asked the court to require the Florida Legislature to act in accordance with the Supreme Court's *Baker v. Carr* ruling. Smith submitted a proposed plan for reapportionment intended to meet the "substantially-equitable" election district standard. He suggested the court might enforce its mandate by ordering the state not to pay legislators for the session until they enacted a reapportionment plan.

Prior to the filing of *Burdick,* a Miami lawyer named Peter Sobel, representing himself, filed a similar case called *Sobel v. Adams* in the U.S. District Court for the Southern District of Florida. The *Sobel* suit, like *Burdick,* asked the court to mandate the Florida Legislature to enact a new reapportionment plan in line with the requirements of *Baker v. Carr.* The Miami district court had not yet ruled in the *Sobel* action. Consequently, Smith requested Judge Carswell to "accelerate" the case on his calendar and "enter forthwith" its declaratory judgment.

While the *Sobel* and *Burdick* cases were pending, in special session the Florida Legislature on February 1, 1963, enacted a new apportionment scheme for Florida. But the changes were so minor they would have little impact, and huge disparities in populations among election districts remained. Max Swann, a Florida State Senator and resident of Dade County, sued to invalidate the new reapportionment law. The first of the named defendants, Adams, was the Secretary of State for Florida. Because the suit raised a question of federal constitutional law, a three-judge federal district court was convened to decide the case. The district court panel upheld Florida's reapportionment legislation. Subsequently, the *Swann* and *Burdick* cases were consolidated under the name *Swann v. Adams,* and the lower court decisions were appealed to the Supreme Court.

In Smith's jurisdictional brief to the Court, he stressed that the disparities among voting districts remaining after the 1963 reapportionment violated the constitutional requirements established in *Baker v. Carr*. Smith highlighted the still-existing gross statistical disparities regarding the significance of a single vote. Dade County, with a population of roughly one million people, had two elected state senators, while Columbia County, with a population of 25,000 had one senator. Comparing the ratio of the population of Columbia County to that of Dade, a vote in Columbia would have roughly twenty-five times the weight of a vote in Dade.

In his brief, Smith explained that, over the years "a crazy quilt pattern of senatorial districts emerged in peninsular Florida featuring no relationship to either population or economic factors." He added that substantial and serious apportionment inequities had existed in Florida for years, and even though the state's governors had repeatedly called the Legislature into special sessions to consider reapportionment, and though the legislature had changed its apportionment scheme in 1963, the state still had not achieved a fair and substantially equitable distribution of its senatorial election districts. Those districts remained in violation of the requirements of *Baker v. Carr*.

On June 22, 1964, the Supreme Court, in a *per curium* opinion, reversed the lower court ruling and remanded the case for reconsideration in light of the Court's week-earlier decision in *Reynolds v. Sims*, 377 U.S. 553 (June 15, 1964). In *Reynolds*, the Court held that a state must make an honest and good faith effort to construct district lines "as nearly of equal population as practicable." Smith's appeal prevailed; he had achieved an important victory. Or so it seemed.

The battle, it turned out, was not over. In response to the U.S. Supreme Court's *Swann v. Adams* decision, the Florida Legislature enacted a revamped reapportionment plan in 1965. In a baffling manner, the plan was upheld by a three-judge federal district court panel. Though conceding the Legislature's newest enactment would be *prospectively* unconstitutional, the tribunal nevertheless held that it could be implemented in the Florida's *next* state-wide election, postponing reapportionment at least for another four years.

Talk about delay. Not surprisingly, opponents of the district court's ruling appealed to the Supreme Court yet again. In another *per curium* opinion— the third—in *Swann v. Adams*, the Court reversed the Miami three-judge district court panel, holding the panel had erred by delaying "effectuation of a valid apportionment in Florida until at least 1969." The Court held the lower court must require a valid reapportionment be adopted in Florida before any new elections.

Would the Florida Legislature now, finally, adopt a plan that would pass scrutiny by the U.S. Supreme Court? The Legislature did meet and passed a new plan, one that the federal district court in Miami upheld, declaring Florida's mal-apportionment problem had been remedied. Not so, countered Smith, still representing the Mayor's Conference on Fair Apportionment. For a third time, the case was appealed to the U.S. Supreme Court.

Rather than issuing a third *per curium* reversal, the Court issued an opinion authored by Justice Byron White in *Swann v. Adams*, 385 U.S. 440 (1967). Rejecting the Florida Legislature's 1966 attempt to reapportion the state's voting districts, the Court held the plan failed to comply with the constitutional requirements for reapportionment. Justice White wrote that Florida's newest effort was flawed because it continued to sanction "unacceptable disparities" among the state's voting districts. Reversing the district court's decision, the Court once more remanded the case and again ordered the district court to determine if "acceptable reasons for the variations among the populations of the various districts in respect to both the senate and house of representatives," existed, adding that if the Legislature was unable to do so, the district court must impose an acceptable plan.

On remand, the district court was persuaded that a plan submitted by a "friend of the court" in an *amicus curiae* brief by Professor Manning Dauer of the University of Florida was workable and constitutional. The plan limited the maximum variance among the state's voting districts to a fraction slightly over ten percent. After approval of the district court, the Florida Legislature enacted the Dauer plan. Though the state's adoption of the plan did not resolve all legal issues, and although challenges in courts did not cease, a fair and more equitable apportionment had been devised and was being implemented.

The *Swann v. Adams* trilogy not only changed the inequitable voting system in Florida, it confirmed a basic principle of separation of powers in America. The federal courts' powers of judicial review of legislative action (or inaction),were first articulated by the U.S. Supreme Court in one of its most historic decisions—*Marbury v. Madison*, 5 U.S. (1 Cranch) 137 (1803). When a politically powerful public political body including Congress or a state legislature refuses to follow the mandates of the federal Constitution as interpreted by the U.S. Supreme Court, those who have been denied their fundamental Constitutional rights may seek judicial review.

Federalism: *First National Bank of Plant City v. Dickinson*

Smith and his colleague Sylvia Walbolt worked together on an important banking case that ended up before the Supreme Court: *First National Bank of*

Plant City v. Dickinson, 396 U.S. 122 (1969). Smith argued the summary judgment motion and Walbolt wrote the briefs.

Under Florida law at that time, state banks were not allowed to provide customers off-site services such as automated deposit drop-offs, as that was deemed to be a branch bank. A federal regulation arguably allowed national banks operating in Florida to do so. The genesis of the dispute between national and state banking interests began when the Plant City National Bank instituted new services for its customers, including providing an armored car that picked up deposits and delivered cash at the customers' homes and places of business, and also establishing off-site "secure receptacles" in which customers could leave deposits.

The petitioner, First National Bank of Plant City, sought to protect its purported right to offer branch banking services, even though Florida law prohibited this. The case was filed in the U.S. District Court for the Northern District of Florida, and then went to the U.S. Court of Appeals for the Fifth Circuit. Intervening on the side of the First National Bank to protect the federal government's interests was William Camp, U.S. Comptroller of the Currency. Camp and the U.S. Treasury were represented by Deputy U.S. Solicitor General Springer. William Ruckelshaus, U.S. Deputy Attorney General, and Erwin Griswold, U.S. Solicitor General, signed the briefs for the Treasury.

Smith and Walbolt represented the respondent, Fred Dickinson, Jr., the *ex officio* Florida Commissioner of Banking, who regulated state chartered banks. They also represented three intervening state banks—Hillsboro Bank of Plant City, First Ruskin Bank, and Peoples Bank of Lakeland. The challenge facing them was large. At the time, the Solicitor General had won something like 95 percent of his cases before the Supreme Court.

The principal issue before the Supreme Court was whether state or federal law controlled the regulation of branch banking in Florida; as such, it raised a question of federalism. The outcome of the litigation was important to Florida banking interests because, should the Supreme Court decide that *national* banks could offer branch banking services in Florida, while *state-chartered* banks controlled by state law could not, the national banks would have a strong competitive advantage over the state-chartered banks.

In an earlier decision, *First National Bank of Logan v. Walker Bank & Trust Co.*, 385 U.S. 252 (1969), the Supreme Court held that under the McFadden Act a national bank could establish a branch only under the same conditions that state law would authorize a state bank to do so. The Walbolt-Smith brief dove into the legislative history of the National Banking Act of 1864 and the McFadden Act of 1927, noting that the latter "granted national banks the right to have only intra-city branches where state banks were allowed to have them under state law." They quoted the law's sponsor, Congressman McFadden:

As a result of the passage of this act, the National Bank Act has been so amended that national banks are able to meet the needs of modern industry and commerce and *competitive equality* has been established among all member banks of the Federal Reserve System. [Emphasis in original.]

The doctrine of "competitive equality" between state and national banks, as mandated under the McFadden Act, was not a new concept, having been in effect for over a half-century. Citing the Court's earlier decision in *Logan v. Walker* (where the Court had declared that "the clear cut" purpose of the McFadden Act should not be frustrated), Smith and Walbolt's brief noted that policy was a continuation of the "competitive equality" established in the 1864 National Banking Act. This was a pivotal point.

Smith argued the case before eight of the nine justices of the U.S. Supreme Court on behalf of Florida and the three state-chartered banks. The ninth seat on the Court was vacant because the Senate had not voted on the President's pending nominee, Judge Harold Carswell, the district court judge who had tried the case.

When the Supreme Court's *Plant City v. Dickinson* decision was subsequently announced, it relied heavily on the legislative history argument presented in their brief. Writing for the majority of the Court, Chief Justice Burger explained that the purpose of Section 36 of the McFadden Act "is to maintain competitive equality" between state and national banks. The Court held that the bank's pick up, drop-off delivery services using armored cars, and its off-site locations for deposits practices *did* constitute branch-banking activities. As such, they were prohibited under the McFadden Act's competitive-equality mandate.

In 2007, the U.S. Supreme Court again addressed the relationship between national and state banks in *Watters v. Wachovia Bank*, 550 U.S. 1 (2007), (though not on the issue of branch banking). This time, the Court's majority sided with the U.S. Comptroller of the Currency and held for the national banks over state banks. The majority opinion was written by Justice Ruth Bader Ginsburg, who addressed the *Plant City v. Dickinson* decision in a footnote. She wrote that the *Plant City* decision applied to the facts of that case, but not to the present one. In a dissenting opinion, Justice John Paul Stevens underscored that the "competitive equality" principle that had been affirmed in *Plant City* should apply in *Watters*. Justice Stevens quoted a passage from *Plant City* that set out the history of the competitive-equality doctrine, a history that Smith and Walbolt had incorporated in their brief decades earlier.

Bill of Rights: *Shadwick v. City of Tampa*

A motorist named Shadwick was arrested and charged with impaired driving in violation of a Tampa ordinance. After he failed to appear for a scheduled hearing, the arresting officer went before a clerk of the Tampa Municipal Court and, in a sworn affidavit, alleged that the motorist had violated the city ordinance on impaired driving. The clerk issued an arrest warrant. Subsequently, the no-show driver was picked up and taken to jail. His lawyer moved to quash the arrest warrant because it had been issued by a non-judicial officer, thereby violating the requirements of the federal Constitution's Fourth Amendment. The defendant contended that only a "judicial officer" had the legal power to issue an arrest warrant.

The judge of Tampa's Municipal Court did not agree and denied the motion to quash. The decision was appealed and eventually reached the Florida Supreme Court, which held the that the clerk and the deputy clerks of the municipal court of the City of Tampa "are neutral and detached magistrates for the purpose of issuing arrest warrants and are within the requirements of the United States Constitution." *Shadwick v. Tampa*, 250 So.2d 5 (FL, 1971).

Throughout these proceedings, Smith was City Attorney for Tampa, and he won the case both in the Tampa Municipal Court and Florida Supreme Court. But the litigation was not over. After losing in Florida highest court, Shadwick appealed to the United States Supreme Court, which had jurisdiction because it involved an interpretation of the federal Constitution by the Florida's Supreme Court. The Court took the case because it raised an issue that had been decided differently by various U.S. Courts of Appeals.

Smith and Gerald Bee, Jr. (an assistant city attorney appointed by Smith) represented Tampa before the Supreme Court. In their brief, they traced the history of the Court's interpretations of the Fourth Amendment, focusing in particular on the conflicting decisions of the Courts of Appeals on the specific issue of *who*, under the Fourth Amendment, has the power to issue arrest warrants. Justice Lewis Powell delivered the opinion of a unanimous Supreme Court, affirming the Florida Supreme Court's *Shadwick* decision and thereby agreeing with Smith and the City of Tampa. Justice Powell traced the interpretive history of the phrase "judicial officer," noting that the Court's prior decisions did not require a judicial officer to be a lawyer and that the term "judicial officer" often has been used interchangeably with "magistrate." Reviewing earlier precedents, Justice Powell concluded:

> The substance of the Constitution's warrant requirements does not turn on labeling of the issuing party. The warrant traditionally has

represented an independent assurance that a search and arrest will not proceed without probable cause to believe that a crime has been committed. *Shadwick v. Tampa*, 407 U.S. 345, 350 (1972).

The U.S. Supreme Court articulated a test to be used in determining who qualifies under the Fourth Amendment to issue warrants:

> [A]n issuing magistrate must meet two tests. He must be neutral and detached, and must be capable of determining whether probable cause exists for the requested arrest or search.... [I]nferences of probable cause [must] be drawn by a neutral and detached magistrate instead of being judged by the officer engaged in the often competitive enterprise of ferreting out crime.

The Court rejected any *per se* invalidation of a state or local warrant system on the ground that the issuing magistrate is not a lawyer or a judge. Smith's arguments prevailed, Tampa's ordinance survived, and the City's practice of allowing the Municipal Court's judicial clerks to issue writs was upheld under the federal Constitution.

Interstate Commerce and Antitrust: *FL East Coast Railroad v. United States*

In December 1963, the U.S. Interstate Commerce Commission (ICC) approved a merger between the Atlanta Coastline Railway Company and the Seaboard Air Line Railroad Company in *Seaboard Air Line Railroad Co.,* 20 ICC 122 (1963). Other railroads, together with the Department of Justice, opposed the merger. Even though the ICC acknowledged the merger would lower or eliminate transportation competition in parts of Florida (including the Hillsborough County and Tampa Bay region), it nonetheless found the "the reduction in competition would have no appreciably injurious effect upon shippers and communities."

One of the opponents to the merger—the Florida East Coast Railroad—sued the ICC to enjoin the proposed merger, alleging it would violate the laws of the United States and, in particular, Section 7 of the Clayton Antitrust Act. The suit was filed in the U.S. District Court for the Middle District of Florida. Attorneys for Florida East Coast Railroad argued that the merger of the two railroads would result in a lessening of competition among the railroads serving Florida and the southeast, causing substantial harm to Florida's businesses and citizens as well as to other common carriers operating in the state. Several federal laws applied to the proposed railroad merger. Particularly relevant was Section 5(11) of the Interstate Commerce Act setting out a "limited application" of federal antitrust laws to common carriers regulated by the ICC; the Transportation Act's declaration of fostering competition among carriers; and the Clayton Act's prohibition of mergers found to be against the public interest because they would significantly reduce competition.

Following argument, a three-judge district court panel threw out the ICC order, holding that, by not considering the relevant products and geographical areas that the merger would affect, the agency failed to properly determine whether the merger violated Section 7 of the Clayton Act. The Seaboard and Atlantic Coast railroads appealed to the U.S. Supreme Court. In *Seaboard Air Line Railroad Co. v. United States,* 383 U.S. 154 (1965), the Court, in a *per curium* opinion, reversed and remanded the case back to the U.S. District Court for the Middle District of Florida. The Court cited *McLean Trucking Co v. United States,* 321 U.S. 67 (1944), where it had articulated the test for balancing the interests of free competition protected by the antitrust laws against the benefits of limited competition applicable to regulated carriers under the Interstate Commerce Act. Finding the lower court had improperly applied that test, the Court vacated the order and remanded the case "for a full review of the [ICC's] administrative order and findings pursuant to the standards enunciated by this Court."

At this point, Smith filed a suit on behalf of the City of Tampa seeking to block the merger. Smith was knowledgeable about ICC regulations and was admitted to practice before the Commission. In opposing the merger of Florida's two largest railroads, Smith argued that the merger would not be in the public interest because it would eliminate rail competition in the Tampa Bay area. At the earlier ICC hearings, the Commission found Tampa was "the only major population center" that would be without any competing network of rail companies. Nonetheless, the ICC concluded the merger's benefits were more significant than the impact of less competition. Subsequently, two other opponents intervened—the Railroad Executives Association and the Southern Railroad Association.

Smith and the interveners asked the District Court to enjoin the merger, arguing that under the Supreme Court's balancing test, the negative impacts on competition outweighed the benefits of the merger. On remand, the District Court applied the *McLean Trucking* balancing test, and concluded the benefits of the merger would outweigh any negative impacts of lessened competition. The court found the merger would increase efficiency and produce economic benefits in reducing the costs of rail services. The court accordingly upheld the merger, noting the ICC had primary jurisdiction in regulating common carriers.

After the court's ruling, opponents of the merger, including Tampa, petitioned the U.S. Supreme Court to vacate the district court's judgment. In a *per curium* opinion in *Florida East Coast Railroad Co. v. United States*, 386 U.S. 544 (1967), the Supreme Court affirmed, without comment, the lower court's opinion approving the merger of the Florida railroads. Though the judicial challenge did not succeed, Tampa's City Council commended Smith for his efforts in the litigation, commenting that he had gone "above and beyond the call of duty."

* * *

CHAPTER NINE

TAMPA CITY ATTORNEY

In the fall of 1963, Tampa Mayor Nuccio invited Smith to meet him "at the Silver Ring at 4:30." Reece replied he had a conflict that afternoon and could not meet at that time. Nuccio exclaimed: "*Not* in the afternoon—at 4:30 a.m.!" The mayor liked to meet constituents, city officials, and job seekers in this setting over strong Cuban coffee. It was there where Nuccio offered Smith the city attorney job. He may have done so in part on the recommendation of Smith's law partner, Doyle Carlton, and also because he knew Smith was a young, energetic, respected, and established lawyer. At that time, Smith was president of the Hillsborough Bar Association and knew most of the lawyers in the community as well as public officials throughout the county region.

After talking with his partners at Carlton Fields, Smith accepted the position. He and Nuccio understood that it was a part-time job (as it had been previously) and that Smith would continue to work at the firm as long as there were no conflicts of interest. He became Tampa's new city attorney.

Nuccio also asked another respected business person, William Earle Patterson, an executive at Tampa's First National Bank, to join his administration. The *Tampa Times* and the *Tampa Tribune* ran stories about the Smith and Patterson appointments. Bob Turner of the *Times* wrote: "The first big shakeup of the new city administration under Mayor Nick Nuccio came today as he named a new city attorney and comptroller and announced wholesale replacements of other key personnel." Two days later, the *Tribune* editorialized: "[I]f future appointments match the general caliber of those announced, Nuccio will be signifying to citizens that the detailed operation of Tampa's government ... will be in good hands," adding that they brought youth and a record of energetic achievement to city hall. Later, in Tampa's Latin publication *La Gazeta*, Roland Manteiga editorialized:

> The best thing Mayor Nuccio has going for him in the betterment of relations between his office and the City Council is a young man named Reece Smith. The City Attorney waves a magic wand when he talks and renders his opinions to the City Council. He has complete com-

mand of their respect due to his brilliant and knowledgeable manner in explaining the legal rights and wrongs of actions they plan to undertake. They [City Council members] think he's 'the most.'

Meanwhile, Herschel Cribb in a story in the *Tampa Tribune* wrote:

> [Reece] Smith is a conspicuously lucid speaker amid the sometimes muddle of council meetings. No councilman yet has been able to ask him a question he couldn't answer on a legal point once he had looked into it (and usually before). Too, he has functioned as a sort of informal moderator in some of the more tempestuous council sessions which turned on legal points. Notably fair, Smith has proved a sure and articulate guide for councilmen in matters of municipal law.

The laudatory press comments on Smith's performance often were in sharp contrast with those written about the City Council. In one *Tampa Tribune* article, the writer criticized the caliber of leadership of the members of the City Council, going so far as to wonder if they could "make it in" private enterprise, but went to say: "Thanks to the wise council [sic] of the Rhodes Scholar who is serving as City Attorney—without his direction all would be chaos." Though the Council was often at odds with the mayor, Smith says it was understandable, in part because the Council members represented various constituencies and consequently often voiced different priorities for the city.

Though coming from divergent backgrounds, Smith and Nuccio worked well together. In the Latin tradition, Nuccio invariably addressed his city attorney as "Mr. Reece." They respected and listened to each other. What differences they had typically were resolved after frank and open discussions. Newspaper accounts describing Smith's work as Tampa's City Attorney portray him "as a voice of reason in the midst of conflicts among city leaders" and "a leader who remained calm in times of anxiety and knee jerk proposals." Bob Turner, a *Tampa Times* commentator, in 1967 wrote: "Speculation by some influential watchers of City Hall [is that] Reece Smith would make Tampa a fine mayor."

Shepherd v. Manatee County Port Authority

During the time Smith was City Attorney, he became involved in a case, the outcome of which could have a substantial negative impact on Tampa and its Port Authority. The City of Tampa, however, was not a party to the litigation.

The Manatee County Commissions put forth a plan to fund and develop a port capable of accommodating ocean-going cargo vessels, along with facilities for loading and off-loading goods (especially phosphate fertilizer), the port to be located in lower Tampa Bay close to a shipping lane into the Bay from the Gulf of Mexico. Favoring the port were commercial and business interests in Manatee County.

On the other hand, Hillsborough and Tampa commercial and business interests generally opposed the Manatee County proposal, largely because the Manatee port would be only twenty miles south of Tampa's port, and would be expected to take away business. Smith represented a Manatee County taxpayer, Hazel B. Shepherd, who opposed the Manatee County port project.

In furtherance of the new port plan, the Manatee Commissioners adopted a resolution in June 1964, designating itself the "Manatee County Port Authority." Shortly afterwards, the new Authority issued a resolution calling for the issuance of $750,000 in revenue bonds to finance acquisition of property and the initial construction of a port near Piney Point on lower Tampa Bay's southeastern shore. The bonds would be secured by a pledge of income generated by the port facilities and also by a pledge of race track revenues payable to the County. That presented legal problems for many.

The Manatee Port Authority petitioned the Circuit Court to validate the issuance as required under Florida law. The State of Florida moved to dismiss the validation petition, claiming that the Manatee Port Authority had no authority to issue the bonds "because it had no separate existence as a legal entity." The Circuit Court disagreed and validated the bond issuance. The State appealed the decision, but the Florida Supreme Court affirmed the lower court's decision in *State of Florida v. Manatee County Port Authority*, 169 So.2d 169 (Jan. 20, 1965).

Efforts to stop the Manatee port, however, were not over. About a year later, the Manatee County Port Authority passed another resolution, this one to issue revenue bonds in the amount of $18.5 million to construct the new port and related structures on 570 acres of land. Included would be phosphate loading facilities to be leased exclusively to the Atlantic Coast Line and Seaboard Airline (in reality a railroad) for forty years. Sixty percent of the bond proceeds would be used for the construction of the loading facilities and related railroad tracks accessing those facilities.

As before, the Manatee Port Authority filed a petition in the Circuit Court to validate its new bond issuance and, once again, the Circuit Court validated the issuance. Again the State appealed, but this time other parties joined: Hazel Shepherd, represented by Smith, and the Tampa Port Authority, represented by Tampa lawyers Thomas MacDonald, Jr., John Van Voris, and Richard Hampton. In his brief, Smith argued (as did other appellants) that the Manatee Port Authority had no legal right to use public bond revenues to assist private businesses. In addition, Smith emphasized that the Manatee port project would cause Tampa's port to be "second rate."

The Florida Supreme Court concluded that neither the advantage to one community nor the disadvantage to another was a basis to judge the merits of the project. On the key legal issue, however, the Court held in a split-decision that the use of the bond's proceeds was illegal, as it would "enhance and assist private enterprise" in violation of Article IX of the Florida Constitution. The opinion applied to all three appellants and is reported in *Shepherd v. Manatee County Port Authority*, 193 So.2d 165 (Dec. 14, 1966, *reh. den*, Jan. 23, 1967); *State of Florida v. Manatee County Port Authority*, 193 So.2d (Dec. 14, 1966, *reh. den*, Jan. 23, 1967; and the companion case of *Tampa Port Authority v. Manatee County Port Authority*, 193 So.2d 165 (Dec. 14, 1966, *reh. den*, Jan. 23, 1967). Smith and his client prevailed, to the benefit of the City of Tampa.

Multiple Roles and Issues

Due to the wide-range of legal issues that any city attorney must deal with, persistent legal research is a necessity. Municipal law matters relate to occupational licenses, civil service jobs, construction law, public bonds, utility regulation, court personnel and management, employment law, governmental powers, taxation, defending lawsuits, appearing before numerous administrative agencies and boards, working with the police and fire officials, and on and on. Smith handled a wide range of matters when he was Tampa's City Attorney.

One involved Mayor Nuccio's nominee for Chief of Police, J.P. Mullins. The Thirteenth Judicial Circuit's State Attorney Paul Johnson, was investigating if Mullins was eligible for the job because his homesteaded residence was in Pasco County, though he was renting a room for $25 per month at the time in Tampa. Tampa's City Charter required that city officials "reside" within the city. Was the rental of the room sufficient to comply with the "to reside" requirement of the charter? Legally the problem was more complex than it appeared. Several members of the City Council believed Mullins was violating the City Charter, including Dick Greco, a young and often outspoken critic of Mayor Nuccio.

Not surprising, the local press jumped on the issue. The *Tampa Times* argued in an editorial that the chief of police was living outside the city. A later editorial, under the heading "*Intent of the Law Was Abused*," commented that though no grounds were found for prosecuting Mullins, it seemed "particularly egregious for a member of the police department to flagrantly violate the laws regulating employees of the city." The competing *Tampa Tribune* also raised possible criminal ramifications because Mullins had continued to vote in Tampa after he declared in 1967 that his principal residence was in Pasco County.

Since the mayor and city council did not see eye to eye, they asked Smith to research the problem and issue a legal opinion on Mullins's eligibility to serve as chief of police. Smith did so. He noted that the issue turned on the interpretation of the words "residency" and "domicile" as used in the city charter. The aim of the charter's provisions, he wrote, "seems to require city officials to live where they work and be readily available to perform their duties." He continued:

> The questions of residency and domicile, are essentially matters of fact about which reasonable persons may disagree. It is important to understand that the conclusions I state are by no means certain. Close questions are involved which might well be resolved differently in a court of law or by a different person.

Smith concluded the police chief originally was domiciled in Pasco County but that the issue became moot after he announced he was giving up his Pasco County residence and returning to live full time in Tampa. As a result of Smith's opinion, the City Council confirmed Nuccio's appointment of Mullins as chief of police. The *Tampa Times* noted afterwards that "Smith's opinion had been praised by councilmen for its thoroughness and clarity [because it] answered to their satisfaction questions raised about … the dual residence hassle."

As City Attorney, Smith often became involved in civil service matters. In one case, he warned county commissioners against adopting a proposal to create a county-wide civil service board that would have jurisdiction over certain classes of City employees. Smith explained: "It should be the prerogative of city government to determine what persons or positions should be classified as department heads." The *Tampa Tribune* quoted Smith as saying that the appointment of civil service board members is the responsibility of the mayor and *not* the city council.

In another realm—municipal finance—Smith worked on several issues that affected the city's credit rating. He lobbied the state legislature to change an existing law, one that prohibited Tampa from charging costs for indigent prisoner health care against the City's general fund. State law at that time required the City to pay the costs from the City's debt-repayment fund. This caused the City's municipal bond rating to be lower, which in turn raised the City's cost of borrowing. Smith argued that the City's indigent health care costs required it to take over $100,000 from its debt repayment fund; if the legislature changed the law, it would save the City needed funds.

The range of issues Smith responded to as City Attorney also included whether the City Council could investigate the fire department (yes); whether the hours that trains passed through the City could be restricted (no); whether a third city judgeship should be created (a decision for the Council); whether the City could impose and enforce a system of occupational licenses (yes); and whether the City Council could ban door-to-door evening solicitations (no).

Occasionally, Smith had to respond to a proposal that was patently impermissible. For example, in response to citizen complaints about long delays due to railroad trains passing slowly through town, Council members wanted to compel the railroads to elevate the tracks and build road underpasses, all at the railroads' expense. Smith advised the Council that it would be preferable if the city negotiated with the railroads rather than to use "legal muscle," opining that the railroads would vigorously resist and that there was little likelihood the city would prevail in the courts.

New Mayor; Good Government Award

Nick Nuccio's mayorship came to an end after he was defeated for a second term by City Councilman Dick Greco, Jr. Greco was only 34 when he was elected mayor in 1967. Having served on the City Council while Smith was City Attorney under Mayor Nuccio, Greco came to admire and respect Smith and asked him to stay on as Tampa's City Attorney during Greco's new administration. This was the first time a sitting city attorney had survived a change in administration. Smith and Greco worked well together for five years, four during Greco's first term, and the fifth during Greco's second term as mayor. Smith resigned as City Attorney when he returned to full-time law practice in his firm, having been elected President-Elect of The Florida Bar.

Smith's contributions to Tampa as city attorney were officially recognized by the City Council in 1972, when it awarded him a "Certificate of Commendation." Following Smith's stepping down as City Attorney, the Tampa Junior Chamber of Commerce bestowed on him its "Good Government Award" for "initiative and contributions beyond ordinary responsibilities to improve [Tampa] Government...." The *Tampa Tribune* reported that Smith was selected for the Good Government Award "because of his unselfish approach to his position." The Junior Chamber of Commerce told the *Tribune*: "No man ever gave more unswervingly of himself in an effort to assist those with whom he came in contact. [He] brought to public service a new character of professional craftsmanship."

Merger of Municipal and Circuit Courts

After Smith returned to his full-time law practice, Tampa's mayor hired him and his law firm to represent the City in a complicated matter that arose due to a constitutional amendment approved by the state's voters in March 1972. The amendment made major revisions in Article Five of the Florida Constitution dealing with the state's judiciary. The revised article established a new trial court system by eliminating all municipal courts and transferring their work to the county courts. Smith worked hard for voter approval of the new amendment, one that declared the state's judicial power "shall be invested in a supreme court, district courts of appeal, circuit courts, and county courts."

Prior to the 1972 revisions, the Legislature had authorized several judicial categories, including civil courts of record, criminal courts of record, juvenile courts, county courts, municipal courts, and justice-of-the-peace courts. It was confusing and inefficient. Moreover, several sitting magistrates and judges on the legislatively-created courts were not required to have law degrees.

The reorganization was to commence on January 1, 1973, and to be completed no later than January 1, 1977. Though no longer Tampa's City Attorney, Smith was named Special Corporate Counsel by Greco to assess the legal ramifications of the court reorganization mandate and oversee its implementation. Smith was concerned because the State had not sufficiently dealt with the process and ramifications of transferring municipal courts into county courts. One issue concerned the pensions and benefits of court employees and judges. Another involved where the additional circuit and county courts would be housed.

The merger was especially problematic for Tampa and Hillsborough County because the number of circuit judges would increase from ten to twenty-one, and county judges from five to eight, while all municipal judges would be abolished. New facilities had to be built or rented. How would this be funded? The State would pay salaries for the additional circuit judges, but significant other costs remained that the City of Tampa and Hillsborough County would have to cover. Essentially, the financing problem was for the County Commissioners and City Council to resolve.

In addition to finances, various legal problems involving the city had to be dealt with and Smith was given the primary responsibility for doing so. Regarding the reorganization of the county/municipal court system, he worked with Judge Neil McMullen (supervising circuit judge) and Fred Bagett (executive assistant to the Florida Supreme Court). Time was a major consideration. In a letter to Burton Loebl, the North Miami Beach City Attorney, Smith wrote: "There are added advantages to effecting a merger as promptly as possible."

Meanwhile, Tampa Municipal Judge Robert Johnson was concerned about the municipal court probation officers whose jobs would be eliminated under the new Article V. State Representative Elvin Martinez suggested that the County contract with the City for the services of Tampa's probation officers. Smith approved the idea.

Other challenges included what to do about separate city and county jails, locations for court records as well as bookings for people arrested, and job classifications. Smith worked with city and country law enforcement personnel to establish a central booking system for the county sheriff's office and the city's police department. They worked out job issues and several other issues as well.

After considerable effort, Smith drew up the final plan for the merger that Hillsborough County Sheriff Malcolm Beard, Tampa City Mayor Dick Greco, Tampa Police Chief J.G. Littleton, City Council Chairman R.L. Cheney, and County Commissioner Chairman Maurice Bach each approved. An editorial in the *Orlando Sentinel* applauded the agreement, stating:

> The [merger] plan provides a practical example of the possibilities for efficiency and economy through eliminating duplication in local government. With Reece Smith at the helm, it may well become a pilot program for similar cooperation between the city and the county which can bring about other savings and reductions of red tape.

As a result of Smith's work, Tampa became the first municipality in Florida to merge its municipal courts into the county and circuit court system.

Downtown Land Use

A few years later, Tampa's Mayor Sandra Freeman appointed Smith to the "Mayor's Committee on Downtown Land Use," which was considering changes for amending the land use code to accommodate various land use objectives of Tampa, in particular regarding property bordering the Hillsborough River. Smith and members of the committee traveled to other cities—including San Diego, Salt Lake City, and Portland—to learn how each had divided up their waterfronts to specific mixed uses. He returned from this exploratory journey more convinced than ever that public waterfront property within a city is a *very* precious asset, one that should be open and green and accessible to, and used by residents and visitors alike. Smith opposed allowing commercial development adjacent to the river as it flowed through downtown Tampa for at least one block inward, thus allowing Tampa to put in public parks with landscaping and walking paths. To stroll along the Hillsborough River from Tampa Heights to the Bay—well, to Smith, nothing could be finer (except playing football for South Carolina).

As it turned out, Smith's efforts were to no avail. A majority of the members of the Mayor's Committee on Downtown Land Use sided with the Chamber of Commerce and Tampa's commercial and banking interests that insisted the river-front property be zoned for commercial use, arguing doing so would create new businesses and jobs while solidifying the city's financial base.

Smith's Contributions Are Recognized

The City of Tampa has recognized Smith for his contributions to the community's welfare on many occasions and in various ways. One was naming official "Reece Smith" days in his honor. Tampa, however, was not the only city to do so. In July 1977, the mayors of both Tampa and Temple Terrace officially proclaimed July 12th "William Reece Smith, Jr. Day" in recognition of his achievements when interim President of the University of South Florida and for the positive affects that resulted, not only for the University, but also for the City.

Two years later, Tampa's Mayor William F. Poe formally recognized Smith for his service to the city years earlier when he was city attorney, designating September 27, 1979, "Reece Smith Day. "

> Whereas from 1963 through 1972, William Reece Smith, Jr. effectively and efficiently served as City Attorney and Head of the Legal Department of the City of Tampa; and in 1975 was the Vice-Chairman of the Commission to Revise the Charter of the City of Tampa, I, William F. Poe, Mayor of the City of Tampa declare 27 September 1979 Reece Smith Day.

But that was not all. In 1981, Smith's home town—Plant City, Florida—added to the commendations when the City's Commissions proclaimed January 12th "William Reece Smith Day" in honor of *both* Smith and his father—William Reece Smith, Sr.—for their achievements and for their contributions to Plant City in particular.

* * *

CHAPTER TEN

Pursuing the Public Interest

Not long after Smith arrived in Tampa to practice law, he spoke to the Plant City Women's Club—a group his grandmother Mary was a leading member of for over two decades. He told the assembled women that civic clubs represent "the concerned effort of individuals who are banded together without compulsion of political governments or personal gain." Years later, Smith returned to Plant City and gave another speech to a group of civic organizations. He spoke on "leadership," more specifically on "what it means and how it is confused with other concepts such as power or prominence." Smith underscored that leadership involves—stepping up to improve the social circumstances under which people live, and to do so without seeking prominence or praise. In his own words.

> Leadership is a positive quality that excludes seeking power for self-serving or evil goals, or seeking prominence as an end in itself. Though prominence may come as the result of leadership, many pass through life in near anonymity while providing inspiration and guidance to others. We think of leaders as persons who rise to the great occasion and leave their likeness standing in bronze or stone. Yet, in many respects, the greatest leadership is that which is displayed by concerned and loving parents in rearing their children; by dedicated teachers who introduce the young to learning and life; by workers who, through counsel and example help lighten daily tasks and alleviate anxieties; by people of all ages and walks of life who seek to improve the social circumstances in which we live.

Smith continued: "Leadership brings to mind the capacity to accept responsibility and the ability to provide guidance for those within our sphere of influence." But there is more—"the development of philosophical and emotional maturity." Smith explained:

No person can lead—indeed no person can really succeed in life—until he is first in tune with himself ... He must be inwardly able—not merely desirous or willing—but actually able to live with himself ... Those of early promise are not always the ones who ultimately lead.

In assessing Smith's leadership speech, Florida historian Peter Klingman commented that not only did the speech reflect Smith's philosophy, it revealed "the essence of the man."

Bettering Race Relations: 1967 Riots

Smith grew up in a segregated community with segregated public schools. For most Floridians (as throughout much of the country), housing and school segregation was taken for granted. Nonetheless, as Smith matured, the "accepted" state of affairs troubled him. When he was Tampa City Attorney, he confronted the issue directly.

On June 11, 1968, Martin Chambers—an African-American youth and a suspect in robbing a camera store—was spotted by Tampa police in east Tampa. Chambers reportedly was shot by the police in the back as he ran from them. Anger swept the African-American community and riots broke out. Mayor Nuccio asked Smith to go with the police to the riots. In the midst of the mayhem, Smith, using a bull horn, read the "riot act" statute and called for the rioters to disperse. They did not.

Rather, rioters began burning and looting homes and businesses in an area just north and east of the city's downtown. Smith found himself in the midst of a whirling social and political controversy, with the responsibility of counseling the mayor and chief of police on the appropriateness of possible responses under the law. They turned to Smith as City Attorney for advice, telling him that it seemed the police had two options. They could remain outside the area of the city where the majority of the burning and looting was taking place, and concentrate their efforts on preventing the riots from spreading into other areas including the primarily white-owned businesses in nearby downtown. Or, the police could march into the middle of the rampage and attempt to stop the burning and looting. But, by doing so, they risked not only their own safety, but also the safety of the area's inhabitants because the rioters' anger was so intense that it seemed likely a massive police presence could lead to further shootings, personal injuries, and perhaps even deaths.

Smith along with a young lawyer from Carlton Fields, Dan Walbolt (whom Smith had appointed as an assistant city attorney), hurriedly researched the issue and concluded that ordering the police to retreat and concentrate their efforts on protecting a more defensible area on the edge of the riot would be lawful. They relied on a line of cases holding that, so long as the decision to order police to retreat was done in good faith and with the belief that the decision would prevent further injuries and damages, the City could do so.

During that time, high racial tensions and resulting riots were occurring in cities across the country, including Los Angeles, Detroit, and several Florida cities. Because of the actions of the mayor, police chief, and other civic and community leaders, the damage in Tampa was limited in comparison with many other cities.

One reason was because Smith had persuaded city officials to promptly issue a parade permit to groups that wanted to demonstrate their unhappiness over recent events that they claimed had precipitated the riots. The parade was to take place at a later time after tempers cooled. The parade was held and both those in the parade and onlookers remained peaceful. The marchers, however, made it clear that they were frustrated over a lack of meaningful dialogue between city officials, police, and the Black community.

1987 College Hill Disorder

The 1967 Tampa riot and its aftermath was not the last time Smith was asked to step in to address race relations problems in the midst of a crisis. In 1987, an African-American man died after a Tampa police officer allegedly used a carotid neck-hold on him. Around the same time, an official report cleared police of alleged racism in the 1986 arrest of the nationally-known Tampa native and professional baseball player, Dwight Gooden. These events precipitated racial riots in the College Hill neighborhood of Tampa. During the mayhem, a Korean grocery store was sacked and burned, an event reported nationwide.

By the next evening, after tempers had cooled, Smith accompanied police officers to a meeting in College Hill with predominantly young African-American men. Tensions between the two groups were high. Many voiced a deep hostility toward police and city officials, while city representatives blamed the demonstrators who had broken the law. Smith encouraged both groups to turn their frustrations into a productive discussion of the underlying concerns of the African-American community. Though neither the city nor the protest leaders were satisfied when the meeting ended, the tensions had eased. They agreed further talks were necessary, as underlying problems and mistrust remained. More needed to be done and Smith knew it.

The gutting of the Korean grocery store was the immediate issue that needed a response. Smith and leaders of the Tampa Chamber of Commerce assisted the Korean store owner in obtaining an insurance settlement. They also spearheaded a successful effort to raise citizen contributions to pay for the restocking of the store. But the larger issues remained.

Having no doubt that police/community relations in Tampa had to improve and that a deep mutual distrust existed, Smith put together, under the auspices of the Chamber of Commerce, a bi-racial committee, and obtained a federal grant for a study of Tampa's Police Department by the District of Columbia Police Foundation. The resulting report was used for training Tampa police officers in bettering race relations. The Rev. Leon Lowry, a recognized and respected leader of Tampa's African-American community, described the Committee's action and consequent police training to improve race relations as "unprecedented." The Chamber's Bi-Racial Committee became a permanent body and continues to work to improve race relations in the City.

"Florida Classic" Dispute

Smith's involvement in race issues still was not over. In 1914, long before Smith was born, Mary Bethune opened the Daytona (Florida) Normal and Industrial Institute for Negro Girls. Bethune, an African-American, became one of the most respected educators in Florida's history. The Institute merged in 1923 with the Cookman Institute of Jacksonville and was renamed Bethune-Cookman College (BCC). In the latter part of the 1970s, Smith was named a trustee of BCC, which remains a predominantly African-American institution of higher learning.

Soon thereafter, he became involved in a dispute involving "The Florida Classic," the annual football game between BCC and Florida A&M University (another largely African-American institution). The long-standing football classic between the schools was on the verge of being cancelled, primarily due to a disagreement over the allocation of the game proceeds. BCC President Oswald Bronson asked Smith to represent BCC in negotiations with Florida A&M, negotiations that had been urged by Governor Bob Graham and the African-American members of the state legislature. Winter Haven lawyer Robin Gibson (chair of the then Florida Board of Regents) represented Florida A&M and Smith represented BCC. The dispute was mediated by Charles Reed, then Governor Graham's Chief of Staff. Following several meetings, the parties agreed to divide the game's proceeds equally and to recommence the game in Tampa during the upcoming Thanksgiving holiday.

Smith and Otis Andrews, assistant to Tampa Mayor Sandra Freedman, were asked to serve as co-chairs of the Florida Classic. Andrews and Smith worked together to assure the football game would be held annually in Tampa, ultimately to the satisfaction of both universities. For years thereafter, Smith continued to co-chair the Classic.

His involvement in the Classic and his service as a trustee of BCC caused him to become well known and respected by African-American leaders throughout Florida as they gained confidence in his objectivity and sincere efforts to improve race relations. During the 1990s, Smith was called on twice to help resolve race-related controversies. The first involved claims of a coalition of Tampa Bay African-American organizations that its constituents had been excluded from planning events related to Super Bowl XXV. Warren Dawson, an African-American who earlier had been an assistant Tampa city attorney, spoke for the coalition, threatening a boycott of Super Bowl events. He held a press conference with national media representatives to publicize the coalition's grievances, which included claims of social and economic discrimination. The Tampa Chamber of Commerce asked Smith and other community leaders to meet with Dawson and other members of the coalition to address the problems.

As a result of these meetings, Tampa officials and the Chamber of Commerce became more active in developing and promoting opportunities for African-American businesses. It pushed businesses to employ more black men, especially youths. Smith headed the drive to promote a Careers Tampa program designed to place a minimum of 200 African-Americans having high school educations in jobs. Looking back, Smith says that "the controversy before Super Bowl XXV turned into a community success story," adding "the [African-American] coalition felt constructive progress was made."

Another controversy developed in 1993 when African-Americans became unhappy over a proposed berthing in Tampa's port of a pirate ship named *The Whydah,* which earlier had transported slaves. The plan was to convert the vessel into a museum. The African American community reacted swiftly. Reverend Art Jones, an African-American community leader, voiced concerns that went beyond the presence of the ship to include the issue of the lack of economic opportunity for minorities. Tampa's Chamber of Commerce again got involved, and Smith worked behind-the-scene in negotiations. All the parties agreed that the museum idea was absurd and, instead, developed an agenda and implementing plan for economic development and job opportunities to benefit the city's minorities.

In the 1990s, Smith became involved with an issue of long-unpaid attorneys fees in a civil rights case that was tried in the 1950s. Not long after the 1954 landmark decision of *Brown v. Board of Education,* the NAACP sued the Hillsborough County School Board to implement the Supreme Court's *Brown* desegregation mandate. Thurgood Marshall (later an associate justice of the U.S. Supreme Court) filed the Tampa case for the NAACP pursuant to Section 1983 of the U.S. Code. Following hearings and briefs, a federal court in Tampa ordered the Hillsborough School Board to implement a desegregation plan to be approved by the court. At that time the NAACP lawyers did not make a claim for attorneys fees, but they did years later in the early 1990s when Warren Dawson, local counsel for the NAACP, filed a suit in a federal district court for payment of the fees for the NAACP attorneys.

Tampa federal Judge Elizabeth Kovachevich denied the request, in part because of the long delay of the NAACP in filing the claim. Dawson came to Smith and asked if he would join him in representing the NAACP in petitioning the court for reconsideration. Smith agreed and filed additional pleadings. In time, Judge Kovachevich reversed her earlier decision and allowed some $300,000 in attorneys fees for the NAACP lawyers.

Did Smith's involvement make the difference? Probably not, he says, "because it was a team effort." (Incidentally, the judge awarded attorney fees to Dawson but not for Smith. He appealed to the U.S. Court of Appeals for the Eleventh Circuit where a three-judge panel remanded the case for mediation. Eventually, Smith received some compensation for his professional services.

Because of Smith's persistent efforts to improve race relations in both Tampa and Hillsborough County, along with his efforts to protect the rights of citizens regardless of race, he was named the first recipient (outside the Bing family) of the "E.L. Bing Award," named after a highly respected administrator in the Hillsborough County School System who was an African American.

Defending the First Amendment

Not only has Smith worked to improve race relations, assure minorities access to jobs and education, and to encourage the basic value that all human beings deserve to be treated with dignity, fairly, and uniformly under the law, he has also worked in other areas to protect basic constitutional rights. One example, already mentioned, was his insistence that women not be discriminated against in job access or advancement. Smith practiced what he preached in his own firm.

In another area, Smith protected the guarantees of the First Amendment. In 1997, he was appointed to replace Dean Erwin Griswold of Harvard Law School as one of three co-chairs of the Emergency Committee to Defend the First Amendment. The other two co-chairs were Norman Stokes, a professor

of law at New York University, and Michael McConnell, a professor of law at
the University of Utah Law School.

Several members of Congress had proposed amending the Constitution to
permit the United States or any State to outlaw the desecration of the American flag. The Committee to Defend the First Amendment was composed of
prominent lawyers and law professors, many of whom were political conservatives. In common, they nonetheless understood that, as disgraceful as such
acts were, the First Amendment to the Constitution protected free speech and
peaceful protest and that right should not be altered.

This was not the first time Smith supported the First Amendment when unpatriotic speech and expression were challenged. When he was president-elect
of the American Bar Association in 1979, a tenured faculty member at the University of South Florida in Tampa publically advocated "the overthrow" of the
U.S. government during the height of the Vietnam war tensions. An editorial
in *The Tampa Tribune* demanded that the faculty member be fired, asserting
that his advocacy was beyond the realm of academic freedom.

Smith certainly did not defend the substance of what the faculty member said,
in fact, he could not have disagreed more. But Smith did understand that,
under the Constitution, the professor had a right to voice unpatriotic advocacy in a public institution. It was not a matter of academic freedom, but a
basic tenet of constitutional law. The United States Supreme Court had held
that advocacy to overthrow the government was protected free expression, absent a clear and present danger. The professor was not fired. Smith did not
waiver and the matter soon passed out of the collective consciousness of the
community. The constitution right the issue the incident raised, however, was
one to be protected.

Smith liked to quote "a wise judge"—Chief Judge Pound of the New York
Court of Appeals—who once had said "the rights of the best of men are secure
only so long as those of the worst are protected." Smith in turn has been quoted
countless times for a sentence he has used repeatedly: "We must remember that
a right lost to one of us is lost to all." The context was a speech he gave to the
American Civil Liberties Union when president of the ABA. Smith said:

> When we are angered and threatened by the acts and words of others,
> we must remember that a right lost to one of us is lost to all. The ACLU
> remembers, and it acts. Its task is sometimes distasteful and often un-
> popular. [But] the cause it serves so well is an imperative of freedom.

At heart, Reece Smith is a moderate leaning toward the conservative. But he
never has wavered in his commitment to the rule of law, the Constitution, and
its Bill of Rights.

Community Service

Throughout his career, Smith has been active in promoting the economic development of Tampa and the greater Tampa Bay region. In the late 1980s, he became a member of the Committee of 100, the economic development arm of the Chamber of Commerce. In 1991, he became chair of the Committee. Smith also was a member of an informal group of twenty of Tampa's business and professional leaders concerned about the City's well being and economic development. They met intermittently to candidly discuss the city's shortcomings, problems and challenges, and invited speakers to talk about these matters. The group became known as the "Damn Committee." Smith explains: "It was first called that by wives whose husbands said they would not be home until late."

The Damn Committee was not the first group of Tampa citizens to meet periodically to discuss City affairs. In the 1950s, Smith was part of a group of young professionals called the "Thinking Thirties." To be a member, you not only had to be in your thirties, you also had to be concerned about improving conditions in the City. "We did not accomplish a whole lot," Smith says, "but we did rectify an irritant." Across the street from Tampa's old City Hall stood a giant rotating beer can atop a brick foundation. The Thinking Thirties thought the display was inappropriate for downtown community development. "Our objective," he explains, "was to remove what we considered a rotating eyesore and we succeeded."

Smith also supported Tampa General Hospital when it faced serious financial problems in the early 1980s. Tampa General was (and remains) a community hospital that served (and continues to do so) as the teaching hospital for the USF Medical School, and also provided medical care for indigent patients. Due to the hospital's weakening financial condition, payments becoming due on previously issued revenue bonds, which had been sold to finance a recent addition to the hospital, were about to default. If that happened, the favorable credit ratings of both Hillsborough County and the City of Tampa would suffer and the hospital's financial problems would intensify. Terrell Sessums, then Chair of the Chamber of Commerce, appointed Smith to head a task force to study and make recommendations regarding the hospital's financial condition. He prepared a report that recommended, among other things, temporary enactment of a higher local sales tax, and then successfully lobbied the state legislature for enabling legislation. This resolved the hospital's financial problems, at least for the time being.

In 1988, three Tampa women—Colleen Bevis, Marion Rogers, and Ann Murphy—were involved in the welfare of children. They asked Smith to chair a committee to obtain voter approval in a referendum for a tax-supported Children's Board. He agreed, though he knew getting the referendum passed would be challenging, given that a tax increase would be necessitated. But they succeeded as voters approved the referendum, albeit by a small number.

Smith has been involved in several philanthropic groups in the Tampa Bay area. While teaching part-time at Stetson University College of Law in the mid-1950s, he had a student named Harvey S. Firestone III, of the famed Firestone Tire and Rubber Company family of Ohio. Harvey III suffered from cerebral palsy that Smith observed first hand. Being well aware of the difficulties encountered by victims of cerebral palsy, Smith for years supported the Tampa Chapter of United Cerebral Palsy, later serving on its board of directors, and ultimately becoming its president. As head of the chapter, he oversaw the development of new and expanded recreational, camping, and nursery programs that afforded victims of the cerebral palsy opportunities to experience the normal activities and happiness of childhood. Smith's philanthropical work also has extended to the Greater Tampa Visiting Nurses Association. In addition, Smith's *bono* service has included serving on the local boards of directors of the Tampa chapters of the American Red Cross and the American Cancer Society.

President of Tampa Philharmonic Orchestra

In 1958, when Smith was only thirty-three years old, he became president of the Tampa Philharmonic Orchestra Association (TPOA) "because," he says, "no one else would take the job." His self-effacing comment notwithstanding, Smith's willingness to spearhead the fine arts speaks to his conviction that the privileges of being a professional has a responsibility to promote those interests, including cultural, that benefit the community's citizens.

Being president of the TPOA was not just a title, far from it; it quickly became a challenge to build a better orchestra. He realized that there were too many (all somewhat amateurish) orchestras competing and trying to survive in the Tampa Bay region. Musicians in St. Petersburg, Sarasota, Clearwater, Orlando, as well as Tampa, had respectively assembled into small, radically underfunded associations in an effort to bring the world of classical music to the region. The talent was spread too thin and the revenues near non-existent.

Smith felt that these various musical groups should join into one, not only to have a higher quality orchestra, but also to have one that might attract the financial resources for survival. He helped persuade the Tampa and St. Petersburg orchestra groups to merge. That was not easy, given the mistrust between the leaders of those cities. In fact, Smith had to arrange the meeting, which would make or break the deal, to be held on a boat in the middle of Tampa Bay, half way between the two city centers.

The meeting on the bay was held, talks ensued, and a merger was forged. The name was changed to the Tampa Bay Philharmonic Orchestra. Subsequently, groups from Sarasota and Clearwater joined, and the name changed to Florida's West Coast Orchestra. Today, it is called the Florida Orchestra and has achieved wide acclaim among concert goers, lovers of music, and professional musicians. Smith never imagined that, as a young man and new lawyer in the Tampa Bay area, he would have a role in developing a world class orchestra in his community.

Service to Florida

In 1975, Florida Governor Reuben Askew announced that he was creating a Florida State Human Rights Advocacy Committee to advocate on behalf of peoples' welfare rights before the state's Health and Rehabilitative Services Department (HRS). Askew described the committee "as a third party mechanism for protecting the constitutional and human rights of any client." In January 1976, the governor appointed Smith to be the first chair of the eight-member committee. He served as the chair for several years. Smith's service was duly noted when he received a National Humanitarian Award in 1977. He also received an award from B'nai B'rith for his work as chair of the Human Rights committee and for other work on behalf of the state's public universities.

In 1979, while Smith was president-elect of the ABA, Florida Governor Bob Graham appointed him to an executive commission designed to deal with problems of public higher education in the state. Officially called the Florida Post-Secondary Education Planning Commission (but more commonly referred to as the Florida Commission on Higher Education), it was charged with reviewing and assessing the State University System with the goal of bringing "excellence to post-secondary education system in the public institutions of Florida." Smith's selection to head the Commission was lauded in an editorial in the *St. Petersburg Times*: "The choice of Tampa lawyer, William Reece Smith, Jr., to lead a statewide assessment of Florid's higher education system is solid insurance that the study will be worthwhile—not just another thick, dust-covered report."

Smith and other members of the Commission on Higher Education put together an ambitious set of recommendations. Their report called for across-the-board salary raises for university faculties to take Florida up to or above the national median, supplements for merit and distinction, reduced faculty-stu-

dent ratios, more release time for faculty research and more administrative assistance to faculties. The Commission recommended a billion-dollar endowment to enhance the quality of the state university system. Smith went to the
Florida Legislature to urge it to support "appropriate sums which the Board of
Regents and state universities would be able to allocate as seen fit." The recommendations were supported by editorials in the *St. Petersburg Times* and in
other newspapers as well. The *Times* editorial read in part: "Under Chairman
William Reece Smith of Tampa, the panel of distinguished Floridians has drawn
recommendations that will have great impact if they inspire a long-term commitment to quality."

During the time Smith chaired the Commission, he pushed for higher salaries
for state university faculties that would be competitive with those at compa-
rable institutions of higher learning around the country. The Commission also
studied a proposal to combine Florida State (FSU) and Florida A&M (FAMU)
universities into a single institution. Though many in-state government organizations supported the merger, it was strongly resisted by citizen groups.
After studying the matter, Smith and the other commission members concluded that FSU and FAMU each had a distinctive mission and that it would
not be in the best interest of public higher education for them to merge.

* * *

CHAPTER ELEVEN

IMPROVING THE JUDICIARY

Polling Lawyers on Jurists' Competence

Many of those who signed the American Declaration of Independence in 1776 and who drafted the United States Constitution were lawyers. For the most part they had received their legal training at one of the Inns of Courts in London. When they came to the American Colonies, they brought with them the English common law. No one doubted they were learned lawyers. But the English norm of training lawyers for entry into the profession was not the same in America where, for several decades, neither law schools nor inns of court existed. Moreover, by the mid-nineteenth century, America's ethos had become more populist, believing any adult could become a lawyer, doctor, or minister with minimal formal education—they could learn what they needed to know on their own as they went.

The most famous (or notorious) example of this ethos outcropped in Indiana where, from 1851and for seventy years thereafter, any person of legal age could practice law if he (women then were not considered eligible) was a registered voter and was vouched for by an existing member of the bar as having "a good moral character." After the War Between the States, however, more and more law schools opened their doors, and states began to raise the standards for entry into the profession. Nonetheless, even after the required educational bar was raised, the problem of the character of lawyers remained, and a mere assertion that one had a good moral character often did not mean it was so. Raising the ethical standards of lawyers and jurists was, and remains, a challenge.

For decades, Smith has worked on raising standards of professional competency and on highlighting ethical issues in the practice of law. As president of the Hillsborough County Bar Association in the early 1960s, Smith chaired a committee that proposed to poll all county bar members regarding the qualifications of candidates seeking judicial office. He persuaded his colleagues that the quality of judges would improve if members of the bar assessed the qualifications of existing judges for re-election, as well as those who aspired to become judges and who had announced their candidacies.

After the polling proposal was publicized, many lawyers and members of the press voiced serious reservations. Alton Pittman, a local Tampa attorney, challenged the bar's proposal, describing it as a "not so subtle means of garnering political support for particular candidates." In response, Smith noted that such polls had become more commonplace because the ABA and local bar associations were "looking for ways to insure that the public is served in judicial offices by lawyers of the highest integrity and ability." He also pointed out that the American Judicature Society had published studies documenting the benefits of lawyer polling as to judicial qualifications.

After studying and debating the issue for two years, the Hillsborough Bar Association adopted the measure by a unanimous vote in an open meeting. Smith wrote a letter to the media:

> Of course, the voting public is free to accept or reject the judgment of those participating. But the good faith of the lawyers of our community in seeking to discharge a recognized duty should not be doubted.

Judicial Qualifications Commission

In 1966, the newly-revised Florida Constitution created the Judicial Qualifications Commission (JQC). Florida's judges were not all pleased. Jack Turner, an elected state judge sitting on the Eleventh Circuit Court in Miami, had special reasons for his displeasure. Prior to being elected to the Eleventh Circuit, Judge Turner had served as judge of the Criminal Court of Record for Dade County. In April 1973, he was indicted on charges that he committed a narcotics felony. Subsequently, he was tried before a jury and acquitted.

Despite the vindication, the JQC investigated Judge Turner for misconduct, causing him to file a petition for prohibition in the Florida Supreme Court, asking the Court to order that the JQC cease any further action against him. The case, *The State of Florida ex rel Jack M. Turner v. Judicial Qualifications Commission*, involved several provisions in Article V of the Florida Constitution, one of which prohibited investigations into *prior term* alleged offenses. Turner relied on the provision in challenging the right of the JQC to investigate or to take action against him. Richard Earle, Jr., then Chair of the JQC, appointed lawyers Reece Smith, Thomas McDonald, John Germany, and Sam Daniels to serve as the Commission's counsel, and named Smith chief counsel.

Smith and the other JQC attorneys developed their legal arguments to present to the Florida Supreme Court. First, the Court lacked jurisdiction because Turner's suit had not been presented to the Supreme Court on direct appeal from the lower court as the law required; second, the JQC had no power to discipline judges but only to recommend discipline to the Court; third, if the Court upheld Turner's motion to prohibit the JQC from further investigation of his activities, this would damage the scheme of checks and balances between the judicial and the executive branches under the Florida Constitution; and fourth, Turner was a member of the state's judiciary in both his prior and present offices, thereby permitting JQC to proceed under the specific Article V because in both instances he held "judicial office."

Complicating the *Turner* case was the possibility that two of the sitting justices on the Florida Supreme Court were being investigated themselves by the JQC. Smith asked Earle if there was any truth to the allegations, strongly believing that if any of the sitting members of the Court were under investigation, they should recuse themselves. Earle replied that, whether rumors of judicial misconduct were true or not, "as Chair of JQC, I cannot reveal to you the names, if any, of Justices of the Supreme Court who are under investigation by the Commission." Smith ultimately did not request any justices to recuse themselves.

In December 1973, attorney Sam Daniels filed the brief for the JQC with the Florida Supreme Court and, along with Smith, went to Tallahassee for oral arguments. Afterwards, Smith wrote Earle: "Realizing the problems we face, Sam [Daniels] and I are reasonably optimistic, probably because we are convinced we are right [but] the outcome remains to be seen." In due course, however, the Florida Supreme Court granted Judge Turner's petition of prohibition, proscribing the JQC from further investigation regarding Turner's tenure when he was a Dade County Criminal Court judge. Historian Klingman notes that following the Florida Supreme Court's decision, "a storm of protest both within the legal profession and the media arose."

What began as a dispute between Turner and the JQC in the Florida Supreme Court became much larger when a controversy erupted between the JQC and the Florida Legislature. The JQC wanted to preserve the confidentiality of its investigations, while members of the Legislature demanded that the records be made public. The House Judiciary Committee issued a subpoena to JQC Chairman Earle, demanding he appear and testify about on-going investigations. Earle replied that he would go to jail before turning JQC confidential records over to the Legislature. Though the Legislature did not hold Earle in contempt, the controversy continued. In the meantime, Earle asked Smith to petition the Florida Supreme Court to reconsider its decision in *Turner*. Smith did so, though he had little hope the Court would reverse its earlier decision.

But battles often are waged on two fronts. Upon the advice of Smith and others, the JQC adopted a proposal for changes to Article V of the Florida Constitution that would give the JQC power to promulgate its own rules, including the power to oust or reprimand a judge for misconduct "whenever committed." Moreover, the changes gave the JQC power to investigate complaints about judicial wrongdoing even after the judge left office. In an effort to address legislative and media concerns about the confidentiality of JQC proceedings, a compromise was proposed: the JQC would make its findings in any investigation of alleged judicial misconduct public, provided in its judgment it would be in the public interest to do so. In other words, it would make its own rules on disclosure.

The stage was set for resolving the long-standing controversy. The proposal would give the JQC greater investigative and rule-making powers, while requiring that its findings of fact in completed investigations be publically accessible. Subsequently, the Court, the JQC (represented by Smith) and the Governor agreed on language for the proposed Article V amendments and placed them on the November 1974 ballot. They were approved by the voters and, Klingman notes, "the JQC wound up a very much-strengthened institution." JQC Chair Earle emphasized that the stronger and more effective JQC in Florida "was due in large measure to the work of Reece Smith."

Merit Selection of Judges

Should judges be elected or appointed? That question has been debated since the First Continental Congress convened in Philadelphia over two-hundred years ago. When Smith became president of The Florida Bar, all circuit and appellate judges in the state were elected. After learning how other states selected judges and listening to debates on whether judges should be elected or appointed, Smith came down solidly in favor of the *initial* appointment of judges on the basis of merit selection. The divisive debate continued in Florida from the late 1960s through the 1970s.

In 1940, Missouri became the first state to adopt merit selection. The "Missouri Plan" called for establishment of a non-partisan nominating board consisting of the Missouri Supreme Court's chief justice (chair), three lawyers elected by the state bar association, and three laymen appointed by the state's governor. By 1964, Alaska, Nebraska, Iowa, and New Mexico had adopted Missouri-type plans applying to both trial and appellate court judicial aspirants. Five states (Florida being one) had adopted a non-elective procedure for the lower courts. In Florida, however, that practice was limited to candidates seeking judgeships on the Metropolitan Court of Dade County.

Smith was aware of the merit selection procedures in other states when he became president of The Florida Bar, and still believed that merit selection's advantages far outweighed its disadvantages. While president-elect of The Florida Bar, he had worked with Governor Askew and others in implementing Article V of the state's constitution. One provision authorized a Judicial Nominations Commission (JNC) to assist in filling interim judicial vacancies, which Smith believed would "give Florida the most modern court system in the United States." Pursuant to the revised Article V, Askew established the JNC framework in 1971. The following year, Askew appointed Smith the Commission's first chair.

The JNC's powers only affected *interim* vacancies, however, and had no impact on the election or re-election of Florida judges. To Smith, this was a significant limitation. In an article in *The Florida Bar Journal* in December 1972, Smith noted that certain candidates for judicial office had not been forthright with the public in the 1972 fall election. Examples included one election campaign where a judge implied that he sat on a higher court, but did not, while in another case a judicial aspirant said he was a judge, when he was not.

Moreover, several candidates running for judicial office had friends pay for publicity on their behalf. This practice particularly troubled Smith since it raised concerns about how such indirect financial aid might affect the jurists' independence and neutrality. He acknowledged that such improprieties might have occurred more through "thoughtlessness and ignorance than by malicious intent." Smith did not couch his words, however, as to the inappropriateness of shady campaign practices. Louis Salome, political reporter for the *Miami News*, wrote: "Smith believed most of the practices were really not unlawful, but that they were highly unprofessional and do discredit both to the candidate and to the office he seeks." Salome quoted Smith: "The conduct of a number of [judicial] candidates was disgraceful." Salome added an editorial comment: "Smith pulled no punches."

As a leader of the state bar, Smith frequently spoke out in support of an expanded JNC screening program. He believed that if the quality of Florida's judiciary was to improve and if the public was to acquire a greater respect for both the legal process and the legal profession, judges must be chosen on the basis of ability, not political cronyism. Revised Article V of the Florida Constitution provided for the first time that judicial elections in Florida be conducted in a non-partisan manner, seemingly removing judges from politicking, though they would continue to be elected. For many, including Smith, the new constitutional change raised hopes that judicial selection would improve.

With increased interest in judicial merit selection from the media, Smith increased pressure for such a system to be adopted in Florida. In an interview reported in the *Tampa Tribune* in February 1973, Smith endorsed a Missouri-type plan, arguing that initial appointments should come from the JNC. He realized that Florida likely would not immediately implement merit selection of judges at *all* levels, though he preferred that it do so, but he was supportive that a merit based system exempting circuit and county judges be adopted at a minimum. At least all the appellate judges in the state would be appointed on a merit basis.

Aware that the work of the JNC would be greatly expanded if merit retention were adopted in Florida, Smith invited JNC members to an "institute" at Florida State University to discuss the issue. He was also aware that opposition to his goal of a merit-based selection plan was mounting. An editorial in the *St. Augustine Record* stated: "If there exists a living example of the failure of the appointive judicial system, then the one employed by the Federal government stands immediately in the forefront as a glaring reason judges should remain under the choice of the electorate." In addition to certain critics in the press, many sitting judges strongly opposed merit selection. At the same time, voices also were heard from the other side and letters or editorials favoring merit selection appeared in the print media across the state.

It took time and effort, but through his powers of persuasion and charm, Smith ultimately won over other leaders of The Florida Bar to support merit selection of judges. Nonetheless, and in spite of his success in getting the Bar's leaders to publicly support merit selection, he knew that judges and lawyers in the state remained sharply divided.

In May 1973, Smith testified before the Florida Legislature in support of a bill authorizing merit selection of judges. His testimony received a mixed reception, with several legislators publically voicing concerns about removing the election of judges from the voters. Judges too largely were concerned about how it might affect their retention.

On May 16, 1973, the Florida House ultimately killed a proposed constitutional amendment that would have opened the way for the merit selection of judges. Smith lamented the House vote but vowed to continue the fight. His efforts and the efforts of others ultimately succeeded.

In 1976, proponents of merit selection won a significant victory when Florida voters approved an amendment to Article V that required merit appointment of Florida appellate court judges as well as justices of the Florida Supreme Court. Though pleased with the new system, Smith was disappointed that merit selection did not extend to the state's trial judges because they often faced no real opposition in the elective system and, consequently, escaped any meaningful peer review. Indeed. Smith was certain that judicial elections where candidates ran unopposed often encouraged less qualified aspirants to seek judicial positions.

Today, Smith acknowledges that the job of convincing the general populous of the advantages of merit selection of trial judges in Florida has not been entirely successful. In the 2000 general election, Florida voters rejected a proposal approved by The Florida Bar that would make merit selection a process applicable to all circuit (trial) court judges, though it can be adopted on a circuit by circuit basis.

Raising Judges' Ethical Standards

In the early 1960s, a Miami judge who was seeking re-election kept a list of names of attorneys whom he had successfully solicited for endorsements. When Smith was on a judicial ethics panel and was asked if he thought this practice was ethical, he replied: "Absolutely not!" His outspokenness on judicial improprieties has continued ever since. When president of The Florida Bar in the early 1970s, Smith was aware not only that certain aspirants who ran for judicial positions in Florida engaged in highly questionable and inappropriate activities, he also knew that many sitting judges compromised their independence through maintaining special interests and by having a weak work ethic, thereby bringing discredit to the judiciary. As bar president Smith pushed for new ethical standards that would replace earlier guidelines, which had been in effect since 1924, with only minor changes adopted by the Florida Supreme Court in 1971. Smith wanted Florida to adopt the higher ethical standards for judges that had been drafted by the ABA.

Under Smith's direction, a committee of The Florida Bar recommended new ethical rules for judges based on the ABA Code of Judicial Conduct. After approval by the Bar's Board of Governors, Smith took the recommended rules to the Florida Supreme Court asking the Court to adopt them. Smith suggested that the Court approve the new judicial conduct rules for Florida, pointing out that ABA has spent a great deal of time and effort in formulating them, and that they had been well thought out. The ABA rules required judges to make full financial disclosure of outside income (excepting investments) to prevent any real or appearance of a conflict of interest, and prohibited the involvement of judges in any outside business enterprise or in holding any part-time job while serving on the bench. Finally, the rules limited judges' involvement in political activities.

An editorial in the *Tampa Tribune* echoed Smith's point, declaring that it is "vital that a judge above all keep his private life above reproach." The editorial strongly supported the Florida Supreme Court's adoption of the ethical rules for Florida judges. In time, the Supreme Court implemented the new rules.

Chair, ABA Committee on the Federal Judiciary

In 1946, the ABA considered creating a judicial screening body to evaluate the credentials of persons being considered for federal judicial appointments. It was not until the administration of President Dwight Eisenhower, however, that the ABA's involvement in the process began. Perhaps most responsible was Bernard "Bernie" Segal, a prominent corporate and civil rights lawyer from Philadelphia who persuaded U.S. Attorney General Herbert Brownell to submit names of all prospective federal judicial nominees to the ABA for screening. The ABA "Standing Committee on the Federal Judiciary" was created, which Segal subsequently chaired for six years. For over two decades, the Department of Justice sent a candidate's name for a federal judgeship to that ABA Committee in confidence. The Committee reviewed the candidate's credentials, experience, and reputation and issued its recommendation on the candidate's qualifications for the position.

In 1973, ABA President James Fellers asked Smith to chair the ABA judiciary committee and he did so from 1974 through mid-1975. During that time, Smith received a phone call from President Reagan regarding a state court judge named Sandra Day O'Connor. President Reagan told Smith that he was about to announce the nomination of Judge O'Connor to be an associate justice of the U.S. Supreme Court. President Reagan considered his call a courtesy to Smith and to the ABA. But it was more than that. The White House was circumventing the tradition of submitting the name to the ABA committee for evaluation and input prior to public announcement. In Smith's view, Reagan's action undermined the ABA's role as an independent fact finder and evaluator of judicial qualifications. Smith recalls: "The President politely told me that the ABA's views on Judge O'Connor were still welcome and might be expressed in the Senate Judiciary Committee. I chose not to argue the point, realizing that the change was a *fait accompli*."

During Smith's tenure as chair of the ABA Judiciary Committee, a controversy arose over President Richard Nixon's nomination of Connecticut Governor Thomas J. Meskill to the U.S. Second Circuit Court of Appeals, a nomination made only hours before Nixon resigned from office under threat of impeachment. One historical account described what happened:

> Meskill's appointment met with fierce opposition. The American Bar Association deemed him unqualified ... Faculty members at Yale and University of Connecticut law schools joined to issue a scathing letter indicating Meskill was 'insensitive to the rights of the poor and the disadvantaged, and indifferent to civil and political liberties.'

Under Smith's chairmanship, the ABA Standing Committee on the Federal Judiciary found Meskill "unqualified" for the appellate post. But that was not the end of it. The nomination still was sent to the Senate where, Smith says, "a bitter battle ensued." By a close vote, the Senate confirmed Meskill's nomination. During the debates, ABA president-elect Ed Walsh told Smith to get involved by "using hard-ball tactics." Smith resisted, believing the Senate debate was an internal political battle. Walsh apparently disagreed and declined to reappoint Smith to another term as chair of the committee. In looking back years later, Smith notes that "Meskill proved to be a good judge."

* * *

CHAPTER TWELVE

LEADERSHIP ROLES IN VARIOUS BAR GROUPS

Chair, Tampa and Hillsborough County Bars

When Smith entered law practice in 1954, he joined the Tampa and Hillsborough County Bar Association (the name "Tampa" was later dropped). From the outset, he participated in the bar's activities while encouraging other lawyers to do likewise. In 1959, he was appointed a member of its board of directors; during his term he worked to raise the ethical standards of lawyers and to develop procedures to obtain and retain qualified judges. In January 1963, he was elected its president.

While serving in that capacity, Smith also was active in The Florida Bar, the ABA, and the ABA Junior Bar Conference. Throughout his bar-related activities, he continued to practice law at Carlton Fields, while also serving nine years as Tampa City Attorney. He was incredibly busy on many levels.

Early Work for The Florida Bar

Smith became a member of The Florida Bar after graduating in 1949 from the University of Florida law school and being admitted to practice law under what was called "the diploma privilege." In due course, he served on The Florida Bar's Professional Ethics and Judicial Administration committees. In 1954, he was named a director of The Florida Bar's Junior Bar Section, where he sought to increase participation in bar activities among lawyers who were thirty-five years old or under. A year later, Smith became chair of the Bar's Committee on the Uniform Commercial Code, a position he held for two years. Subsequently, he chaired the Bar's Committee on Legal Forms and Work Sheets, overseeing the compilation and publication of materials relating to procedures and forms tailored for Florida law.

But of all his early experiences in The Florida Bar, Smith says the most significant was his work on its Committee on Professional Ethics. In 1960, he became chair of the committee, and for four years, oversaw the handling of complaints that lawyers allegedly had violated the Canons of Professional Ethics. Throughout his tenure as chair, Smith advocated for stricter enforcement of the canons. He traveled around the state speaking to local bar association groups on professional ethics whenever the opportunity arose. A story in the *Newsletter* of the Orange County Bar Association noted that Smith was "an outstanding speaker who is imminently qualified to discuss legal ethics."

After Smith became president of The Florida Bar, he continued speaking about professional ethics. But his speech topics grew as America faced growing social unrest during this period. The upheavals of the 1960s and first few years of the 1970s were in everyone's consciousness. Heading the list was the national discord over the war in Vietnam, creating a debate that in some cases degenerated into riots, the most violent of which was the National Guard killings of students at Kent State University in Ohio. Then, within a year of the Kent State tragedy, there was the infamous break-in at the Democratic Party national headquarters in the Watergate Hotel in Washington, D.C. Eventually it was learned that it had been orchestrated by confidants of President Richard Nixon, many of whom were lawyers sworn to uphold the rules of professional ethics and to act in accordance with the rule of law.

It was during those troubling times that Smith headed the state bar in Florida. In the Spring of 1973, he was invited by the senior class of the University of South Florida to give the commencement address before 4,000 graduates. Smith was awarded an honorary doctor of laws degree from the University of South Florida at this commencement.

In his remarks, Smith pointed to the illegal and unethical conduct of the lawyers who had taken part in the cover up of the unlawful Watergate break-in. Criticizing their breach of their public and professional responsibilities, Smith declared: "Lawlessness by constituted authority is the newest danger facing America," adding, "No claim of self-justification for unlawful acts can ever change the unlawfulness of the acts." Smith knew that many in the audience were opposed to the Vietnam war and distrusted governmental authority, some questioning the very principle of the rule of law. He said:

> I hope that you are no less concerned about the problems of our nation and the shortcomings of society. These still cry out for commitment. Thus, I would urge you to remain concerned about society's difficulties. Be radical if you wish, there is still plenty to be radical

about, but not through lawless disruption, but rather by using legal and political processes created under the rule of law.

President, Florida Bar Foundation

In 1970, the year before Smith became president-elect of The Florida Bar, he became president of a related organization—the Florida Bar Foundation (FBF). The FBF was and remains the charitable arm of the Bar. The majority of its grants supports legal assistance for the poor in the state.

Prior to serving as the FBF president, Smith learned from William Gossett that he had been selected a Fellow of the American Bar Foundation (AFB). The AFB, like the FBF, serves as the ABA's charitable arm. Gossett (a former ABA President) wrote Smith he had been selected because of "[your] public and private career has demonstrated outstanding dedication to the welfare of the community, to the traditions of the profession and the maintenance and advancement of the major objectives of the American Bar Foundation." As an ABF Fellow, Smith learned about the public service funding provided by such foundations and headed that effort in Florida while serving as the FBF president.

During the year Smith headed the FBF, he also was running for the presidency of The Florida Bar. His opponent was a well-known Miami attorney, Ed Atkins. When the votes were tallied, Atkins carried Dade County two to one, but it was a different story in the rest of the state. Smith explains: "My margin of victory got larger as we moved away from Dade, reaching fourteen to one in West Florida." He had campaigned hard for the position, traveling throughout the state for many months. The story of Smith's presidency of The Florida Bar follows this chapter.

Positions in the JBC and ABA

While an ABA member, Smith was appointed to several ABA committees including those dealing with membership, credentials, constitution and by-laws, and administration. He chaired a special task force on "Lawyer Utilization," and was appointed to the council of the ABA's General Practice Section. To his surprise, he also was assigned to the ABA's "World Peace Through Law Committee," his first step into the international law arena, which years later culminated in his becoming president of the International Bar Association.

Smith had joined the ABA when he was twenty-eight and was eligible for membership in the ABA Junior Bar Conference (JBC). He soon joined the JBC after attending an ABA meeting in Philadelphia, an event he recalls vividly. The ABA "assigned me to a hot and noisy hotel room on the second floor above the hotel kitchen's exhaust fan." He did not have a good night's sleep. With a smile, today Smith says: "That was when I decided to become more active in the ABA in order to get a better room in the future."

At the Philadelphia meeting Smith met several of the leaders of the JBC, a group having some 25,000 members at the time. The JBC—today called the ABA Young Lawyers Division—was one of eighteen sections within the ABA. In time, Smith was elected to the JBC Executive Council, representing the six southeastern states within the (then) Fifth Federal Circuit—Florida, Georgia, Alabama, Mississippi, Louisiana, and Texas.

In 1960, Smith was elected chair of the JBC and automatically became an *ex officio* member of the ABA House of Delegates. While JBC Chair, he testified before a subcommittee of the House Judiciary Committee in support of legislation that would require the government to compensate lawyers representing indigent defendants in federal courts. Though it did not pass, the plan was adopted years later when Congress established the Federal Defender Program.

During his chairmanship, Smith also testified before the Senate Finance Committee in support of a bill to establish voluntary pension plans for the self-employed, which included the majority of the JBC members. He told Congress that young lawyers and other self-employed professionals were discriminated against under the tax laws then in effect, in contrast to those working for corporations. He said: "A corporate pension plan is one of the most compelling arguments inducing lawyers to enter corporate service.... [The] private practice of law is a bulwark of freedom. [It] should be strengthened and encouraged, not discouraged and weakened because tax incentives are not available." Despite Smith's lobbying, Congress did not adopt the plan at that time, though it did so years later.

As head of the JBC, Smith oversaw institutes designed to assist new lawyers make the transition from law school to practice. He traveled to ABA conventions and legal education conferences around the country, speaking at many of the events. Once he participated in a conference on the economics of law practice along with Lewis F. Powell (then chair of the ABA Committee on the Economics of Law Practice, and later an associate justice of the U.S. Supreme Court). Smith also traveled with the renowned New York City lawyer, Whitney North Seymour, who was the ABA president at that time and they became good friends. Both spoke at bar meetings, Seymour as the ABA president, and Smith as the JBC chair.

On one occasion, Smith traveled to Ecuador to speak at a meeting of South American lawyers about the JBC's activities. He recalls how he began to speak in Spanish. After a few moments he stopped and in Spanish asked his audi-ence to raise their hands if they understood him. "About half did so," Smith says. "Then I changed to English and using my southern drawl asked if they un-derstood me now." "No hands went up," he says, "so in broken Spanish, I con-tinued speaking."

In 1963, while chair of the JBC, Smith was named Assistant Secretary of the ABA, the first of several offices he held within the organization. As assis-tant secretary, he sat in the meetings of the ABA Board of Governors. After four years, he was elevated to the position of ABA secretary at its 1967 national convention in Houston.

Other Leadership Positions

Smith participated in several national law-related organizations including the *American Bar Endowment* (ABE). The ABE was established by the ABA as a not-for-profit corporation to receive gifts and bequests and to set up an income-producing fund that would "distribute grants to promote justice through education and scientific research in the field of law." Smith held var-ious positions in the ABE, and ultimately was named to its Board of Direc-tors. In 1976, he became the Endowment's president, a position he held for two years. Smith's efforts on behalf of the ABE continued for fourteen years following his presidency.

In the early 1960s, Smith was named a Fellow of the *American Bar Foundation* (ABF). The ABF has become the preeminent provider of empirical research fundamental to legal institutions and processes, by supporting independent research utilizing social science analysis. He served on the ABF oversight com-mittee on research.

In the 1970s, Smith was selected to be a member of the executive commit-tee of the *National Conference of Bar Presidents* (NCBP), an organization that he was first associated with while president of The Florida Bar. The NCBP was formed in 1950 "to provide information and training to state and local bar as-sociation leaders." In 1978, he became president of the NCBP, one year before he became incoming president-elect of the ABA.

Smith enjoys telling a story about an a NCBP meeting at which he sat next to a man named Gates. The man said that his son had quit Harvard and had worked at home in the garage on some project." And what a project it turned out to be. The son of Gates was none other then Bill Gates, Jr., founder and CEO of Microsoft.

In 1966, Smith was elected a member of the *American Law Institute* (ALI), an elite group of prominent judges, lawyers, and academicians who are charged with carrying out the Institute's mission. The Institute was incorporated "to promote the clarification and simplification of the law and its better adaption to social needs, to secure the better administration of justice, and to encourage and carry on scholarly and scientific legal work." One of the principal projects the ALI has undertaken since its founding is the development of "Restatements of the Law," which are scholarly and exhaustive studies laying out the doctrinal principles and policies of the common law areas such as agency, contracts, and conflicts of law. Today Smith serves as a member of the ALI Executive Council and continues to attend and participate in the Council's meetings. Smith also has worked with the *American Judicature Society* (AJS), which has the mission of improving both state and federal courts and upgrading the quality of judges. He joined the AJS in 1960, and was selected a director on its Board in 1976.

* * *

CHAPTER THIRTEEN

President of The Florida Bar

Florida's Legal Profession

In 1972, Smith was sworn in as president of The Florida Bar. James Urban, an Orlando lawyer who chaired the meeting, mounted the podium at the Walt Disney World Convention Center in Orlando to welcome Smith and the other 4,200 attendees, telling the crowd that it was the largest bar gathering in Florida's history.

After being sworn in, President Smith spoke to the throng, first underscoring that The Florida Bar's 13,500 attorneys made it the country's fifth largest state bar organization. He listed many of its significant accomplishments, including establishing Florida's Judicial Nominating Commission. Smith said: "Now we have the opportunity of assuring that only qualified persons are appointed to judicial office." He also praised the dedicated work by the legislature and organized bar in revising Article V of the Florida Constitution, noting that Florida "now enjoys a new prominence as a leader in judicial reform."

Smith then turned to his agenda as president. First was increasing "the delivery of legal services to the poor," an issue that remained a top priority throughout his presidency. He told his audience: "Though we live in a nation dedicated to equal justice for all, a recent Florida study indicates we are yet unable to say that poor and disadvantaged persons are receiving adequate legal services." He acknowledged that even though federally supported legal service programs "have advanced the cause of justice, [they] can only be part of any response." He mentioned possible steps that might be taken: a judicare system for Florida (similar to medical group insurance); a greater use of paralegals in routine legal matters; and more involvement by Florida lawyers in providing *pro bono* legal aid services.

Changing his focus to attorneys' fees, Smith told the attendees that "the Florida legislature had recently warned lawyers to eliminate excesses if they exist, especially regarding condemnation, probate, and contingency fees." He raised concerns about the validity and wisdom of the Bar's recent adoption of a recommended statewide minimum fee schedule: first, the minimum fees might be higher than the marketplace would set them and, second, minimum fees might cause the Bar problems under state and federal antitrust laws (he was prophetic).

Then, responding to a concern voiced by what seemed to him an increasing number of Florida lawyers—whether the state's law schools were producing more lawyers than seemed warranted, given a comparative scarcity in jobs for attorneys—Smith acknowledged that there was one law student for every three and one-half lawyers in the country. He projected that in 1974, "two years from now," Florida law schools were expecting to graduate 3,000 lawyers. "Even so," he said "we should not deny legal education to qualified students who seek it." He then commented: "We must [also] be aware that more lawyers from disadvantaged minority groups are needed," adding, "it is our responsibility to assure adequate opportunity for access to the profession regardless of race, and access to legal services regardless of economic circumstances."

Smith ended his remarks by lamenting that the funds available for the administration of justice in the nation and in Florida "are grossly inadequate," adding "today we spend less money for the entire federal court system than is needed to build a single supersonic bomber," and noting that "the same is true for the Florida court system." Unfortunately, Smith observed, "we act as if justice is a cheap commodity. And, to paraphrase Goethe, "we must not only labor, but pay for that which we possess." He asked the lawyers attending The Florida Bar convention "to work together in furthering the concerns of a great profession and take part in directing its course. We may be able to do little as individuals to influence the course of events," Smith concluded, but "working collectively through The Florida Bar, the opportunity is offered to direct our ultimate destiny."

Historian Klingman described the presentation as "a remarkable survey of ideas, not only of current issues and conditions, but also those that [Florida's lawyers] would face in the future." In Klingman's view, "it was vintage Smith."

News Media/Bar Conferences

Prior to Smith's becoming president of The Florida Bar, members of the state's news media criticized the Bar's lack of transparency, arguing that much of its work was done in secret, especially attorney discipline. In addition, representatives of the media were concerned about other issues involving the media/bar relationship in Florida. Smith recognized that a mutual mistrust between the press and the bar seemed to be increasing. He knew this had to change, a point he had made in his inaugural speech.

Within a month after becoming president, Smith organized the Bar's first ever "News Media-Bar Conference." Held in August in the state's capital, Smith brought together over forty media representatives who met with leaders and members of The Florida Bar. The extensive program included concurrent sessions, often utilizing panels consisting of media and bar representatives.

Topics included the media's scepticism regarding proposals to change the state's resign-to-run law; the media's unhappiness with judges prohibiting press and TV journalists from bringing cameras into courtrooms; and the media's complaint that it was being denied the right of free speech by having limited access to certain "closed" criminal proceedings. Other topics dealt with the Bar's concerns that media coverage displayed a lack of understanding of "legal technicalities," as well as implementation of the new revised Article V of the Florida Constitution dealing with the judiciary and the state's justice system. Still other discussions focused on issues that concerned the media and the Bar—attorneys' ethics, fees, and discipline, while one panel—consisting of criminal lawyers and media personnel chaired by James Clendinen, editor of the *Tampa Tribune*—dealt with the constitutional rights of defendants in criminal prosecutions.

Smith considered the bar-media conference (he sometimes called it a "pow-wow") an important opportunity for a candid and open discussion of the media's and the Bar's concerns about their relationship and the issues that produced conflict. He sought the views of media personnel and bar leaders and asked all to be outspoken about their concerns. Smith believed that each side had to understand their respective points of view in order for the media and bar "to work together."

One issue Smith felt strongly about was the state's resign-to-run law, which required a state officeholder to resign when announcing candidacy for an elective position. Smith was concerned because the law applied to any sitting judge who desired to run for higher judicial office. Believing the resign-to-run law should not apply to judges, he told members of the press, as well as the public, that the statute was "improvident and ought to be repealed." Smith noted that judges sitting on lower courts were afraid to run for higher court positions for fear of losing their current posts. To resign from one's position, run for a higher judicial post, and then lose had a serious practical and humanitarian impact on the former judges. "Beyond the potential hardship on their livelihood," he said, "it was equally troublesome that they could lose their state retirement benefits." Smith's efforts to have the law repealed did not succeed and it remains today in Section 99.02 of the Florida Statutes.

A perpetual media concern was the extent the Bar imposed confidentiality in attorney disciplinary matters. It came up again at Smith's second Media-Bar Conference in Miami Beach in 1972. A story in the *Miami Beach Times* quoted Smith as saying: "Disciplinary actions against lawyers are not secret." Smith acknowledged that "a large majority of claims against lawyers turned out to be unfounded"after being investigated. The task of sorting out spurious claims from serious charges of ethical violations, however, was a difficult one. Confidentiality in the preliminary steps of investigations prevented innocent lawyers from having resentful and spurious attacks on their reputations made public. The issues changed, however, when preliminary findings of serious ethical violations.

A few days after the Miami news-media conference ended, the *Miami Review and Daily Record* in an editorial declared:

> William Reece Smith, Jr., president of The Florida Bar, performed a fine public service in conducting the recent seminar in Miami for media representatives.... Mr. Smith pointed out that the bar is making good progress in updating and streamlining its disciplinary procedures.

The editorial writer continued: "We salute the Florida Bar in its efforts to bridge the gap between the legal profession and the media." Meanwhile, Mike Henderson wrote in an article the *Pensacola News-Journal* that "Reece Smith reflects a changing attitude toward the press, a willingness to talk with the press and the public."

Creation of Florida Legal Services, Inc.

During his inaugural address, Smith pointed out the deficiencies with the delivery of legal services in Florida, especially referring to those who were unable to afford to hire attorneys. Legal service programs were operating, but they were able to assist only a relative small portion of the poor. Forty of Florida's sixty-seven counties had no legal aid programs of any kind.

To help rectify that situation, Smith, along with many others, worked on creating, funding, and implementing Florida Legal Services, Inc. During his presidency of the Bar, Smith urged its Board of Governors to set up a "coordinating office of legal service programs," the preliminary step in establishing a nonprofit corporation. Smith declared that "a person's income should not limit his access to legal assistance."

Smith appointed a committee to draft articles of incorporation and by-laws for a proposed "Florida Legal Services Corporation." The proposed articles in part read:

This corporation is organized exclusively for the purpose of furthering justice for those living in poverty; of helping to provide legal services for persons who would not otherwise have the means to obtain a
lawyer's assistance; of conducting research pertaining to the legal problems of the poor; [and] of educating the poor of their legal rights and
responsibilities....

In January 1973, The Florida Bar filed a charter for the Florida Legal Services Corporation with the Florida Secretary of State. In reporting the news, the
St. Petersburg Times noted that the Florida Department of Community Affairs
"has asked Gov. Reuben Askew to recommend a one million dollar legislative
appropriation that would support contracts with Florida Legal Services, Inc."
  A dispute arose, however, over the composition of the governing board of the
new corporation. The original draft of the articles incorporation called for a
nineteen-member board composed of five lawyers appointed by the Bar's president (Smith); five lawyers appointed by the chair of The Florida Bar's Legal
Aid and Indigent Committee, which represented poor people; and nine appointed by the Governor, at least six of whom should be poor or selected from
organizations representative of the poor. In addition, the draft articles specified that the poor shall not be "less than one-third" of the boards membership.
Opposition to the proposal came from several Florida lawyers who did not like
the membership composition or the requirement regarding the number of positions allocated to the poor and those who represent them. There was concern
that a majority of the board should be members of The Florida Bar.
  In response, Smith redrafted the articles of incorporation, reducing the
board's number from nineteen to fifteen; requiring that at all times the majority of the board's composition be members of The Florida Bar; reserving
to the Bar president the power to appoint the majority (eight) with the advice
and consent of the Bar's Board of Governors; and reducing the Governor's appointments to seven (five of whom to be poor or selected by organizations
representing the poor). The proposal was approved, and a charter for Florida
Legal Services, Inc. (FLS) was filed in the Secretary of State's office in January
1973. A news release stated: "Florida Legal Services has become the first statewide
organization aimed at giving the poor legal help in civil matters."
  In February 1973, Smith wrote Governor Askew asking him to support a
budget request of approximately $1.8 million from the Florida Department of
Community Affairs. "The funds," Smith wrote, "are to support a program for
state involvement in civil legal services," explaining that "FLS would serve as a
principal vehicle for implementing the program." The grant, however, did not
materialize. Askew responded to Smith, writing that he was unwilling, "albeit

reluctantly," to authorize funding of FLS under the circumstances, adding that he would "be happy to help in any appropriate way in the fund raising from private sources."

With the Governor's vocal (if not financial) support, consensus among bar leaders was that the FLS project must go forward somehow. A study by Professor Harold Levinson of the University of Florida surveyed every program of legal assistance then in existence in Florida. The report revealed that legal aid services for the poor in the state were meager. In forty-six Florida counties "there were no organized legal service programs," while in several counties "publicly and privately supported [legal aid] programs were struggling, ... and were ineffective in providing meaningful [legal] services." Following the report's release, Smith told the media that it "vividly demonstrates the unmet needs of indigent persons in Florida for civil legal aid in the State." He emphasized the need for action was now "all the more obvious." The FLS Corporation had to move forward.

Smith appointed Robin Williams, an attorney at Legal Services of Greater Miami, to be the first executive director of the FLS. Smith believes that Williams's acceptance of the position "was an act of dedication and faith" because the corporation had "no significant financial assets at that time." Shortly after the FLS directors were appointed, Smith invited Williams and the directors to an organizational meeting in Tallahassee. At the meeting, the directors defined the corporation's goals, agreeing that the primary objective was for it to serve as a statewide support agency for delivering legal services to the poor by a providing financial support of "civil legal aid offices in every county in the state where none existed."

In an effort to obtain funding for FLS, Smith sought a $300,000 grant from the Florida Department of Community Affairs to support a statewide legal services center, compensate its staff, and allow pilot programs to be established. An appropriation bill to fund the grant, however, was defeated in the Florida House. When it seemed that the FLS project was, in Smith's words, "on the brink of failure," he and others intensified efforts to raise money privately. They succeeded. The McIntosh Foundation of Palm Beach provided the seed money needed for FLS's initial work. Without it, Smith believes, the organization might never have opened an office. Smith credits Howell Ferguson, the lawyer who worked for legal services in Palm Beach County, for convincing the Foundation to make the grant.

Additional financial assistance eventually came from Department of Community Affairs, which channeled funds from the federal LSC agency. At the same time, Smith worked with the Florida Bar Foundation (which he had headed two years earlier) for a matching grant. Although many helped in getting the necessary funds to support FLS, Smith singles out Thomas Norman, Jr., who was with Florida's Human Affairs Department, for his dedicated work.

The project was on track. Smith announced that "modest offices" for LSC had been obtained in Tallahassee and that a staff of lawyers and assistants had been hired. He called on all Florida lawyers to accept "their special obligations to assure access to legal assistance and, thereby, to justice." Smith cautioned that the "Bar's continued support will be required."

Once the organization work was completed, Governor Askew appointed Smith to be the first President of FLS. The Corporation continues today to assist in the funding of legal service programs throughout the state. A 2008 report describes FLS as "the voice for Florida's poor, disadvantaged, and vulnerable." That year the FLS supported thirty legal aid field offices in the state and seventeen in-house full-time attorneys, and utilized in excess of 250 private lawyers. Additionally, FLS managed several programs including: "Migrant Farm Worker Justice," "Medicaid Reform Fairness," "Statewide Affordable Housing," "Employment Law Advocacy," and "Children's Legal Services."

In handwritten notes that Smith made while FLS President, he commented on the continuing struggle during the agency's first three years in obtaining funding. At one point, he wrote: "future—still in doubt, clouds of despair." But in time and after much effort the clouds lifted. The new affluence brought new responsibilities. Smith's notes include a list of FLS accomplishments, including opening new legal aid offices in the state, developing paralegal training programs, starting an elderly legal-assistance program, enlisting support from the state's law schools, developing model documents for a legal aid handbook, and coordinating legal aid programs throughout Florida.

Smith lists people who were instrumental in the success of FLS, including: Michael Abbott, Reubin Askew, Marshall Cassedy, LeRoy Collins, Howard Dixon, Paul Doyle, Howell Ferguson, Bob Graham, Robert Guttman, Earl Hadlow, Harold Levinson, Neil McMullen, Hugh MacMillan, William Manikas, Steve Mickel, Richard Miller, Thomas Norman, Pat Pattillo, John Smith, Daniel Thompson, and Bob Williams. Smith's notes conclude: "Am terribly proud of accomplishments by these dedicated people. Their achievement; no one else's."

Florida: First State to Adopt an IOLTA Program

By the time his presidency of The Florida Bar ended, members of the Bar, including Smith, had become aware of a new method to assist in the funding of legal services to the poor. Smith and others found the concept innovative and believed it would work in Florida. Nonetheless, it took several years to get the system adopted and implemented. The program is called "Interest on Lawyers' Trust Accounts" with the acronym IOLTA (in Florida the acronym IOTA is often used).

The story of the development of Florida's IOLTA program—the first such plan implemented in the United States—is fascinating. Smith early on heard about a unique method for funding legal assistance programs in British Columbia. There, the organized bar had instituted a system whereby interest on attorneys' short-term bank accounts was funneled to an agency that used the funds to make grants to organizations providing legal aid to the poor.

Wanting to learn more about how the Canadian system worked before his term ended, Smith appointed a committee chaired by his partner at Carlton Fields—Ed Cutler—to learn more about the British Columbia program. In due course, Cutler's committee reported back to Smith. As a result, Smith became a strong supporter of the funding idea. Meanwhile, knowledge of the program spread within the organized Bar, attracting the attention of prominent lawyers and jurists.

One of these was Randolph Berg of the Florida Justice Institute, a respected public-interest lawyer who, after learning about the Canadian program, became a strong advocate for its adoption in Florida. Another was Florida Supreme Court Justice Arthur England of Miami. Justice England along with attorney Russell Carlisle of Fort Lauderdale had gone to Vancouver, British Columbia, to visit a friend. While there they learned about its innovative system for funding legal aid services. They returned to Florida enthusiastic about Florida adopting a similar scheme. But before that could happen, the system had to be explained to Florida judges and lawyers and, eventually, to the state's legislators and the general public. It would not be an easy sell, but because the Canadian system was based on a practice already widely used in Florida—lawyers' trust accounts—the implementation of the system would be relatively painless and would not require any new tax support from the general public.

Attorneys routinely hold clients' funds in special accounts known as client trust accounts. Most of the time these are individual trust accounts where the client is both grantor and named beneficiary, and the lawyer is the trustee and depositor.

But in the case of small sums of money a different practice was used in Florida as well as in several other states. When the amounts were small and only to be held for a short time, they were commingled in a single interest-free trust account. Unlike the individual client trust accounts, these small-sum accounts were paid no interest, due to the administrative costs of doing so. (An example of a small sum to be held in a commingled trust is a client's advancement to cover the cost of filing fees.) If all the nominal short-term lawyers' trust accounts could be consolidated into a single account, however, the total would be large and the pool large enough to generate interest. Then, the interest could be channeled through the Florida Bar Foundation and eventually distributed to organizations supporting legal services to the poor.

Justice England, Donald Middlebrook, and Russell Carlisle, with Smith's support, went before the Board of Governors of The Florida Bar seeking approval for a statewide IOLTA program. The Board appointed in turn a committee to study the idea. Under Article V of the Florida Constitution, the state's highest court has rule-making powers over the state's judges and lawyers. The Bar committee suggested that under this constitutional grant of authority, the Florida Supreme Court create and implement an IOLTA program in the state. In furtherance of this end, the Board of Governors petitioned the Court for such a rule. Attorney Russell Carlisle argued in support of the petition. In due course, the Florida Supreme Court approved the petition in an opinion written by Justice England. The matter, however, was not a slam dunk.

Several years of court challenges followed, many filed in Florida's state courts, but all in time were resolved in favor of the IOLTA program. These cases included: *In re Interest on Trust Accounts*, 356 So.2d 799 (Fla. 1978), and *In re Matter of Interest on Trust Accounts*, 372 So.2d 67 (Fla. 1979).

One of the later challenges, however, was nearly a deal breaker. The case was *Cone v. Florida Bar*, 626 F. Supp. 132 (M.D. Fla. 1985), *aff'd*, 819 F.2d (11 Cir.), *cert. denied*, 108 S. Ct. 268 (1987). Filed in a federal district court in Florida, the named individual plaintiffs represented a class of individuals who allegedly had lost interest on their money in their lawyer's pooled IOLTA accounts. Rather, the interest from the pooled accounts was directed to the Florida Bar Foundation pursuant to the rules of the Florida Supreme Court.

A comment published in the *Florida State University Law Review* summarizes the facts: Evelyn Glaeser claimed that the $2.25 interest generated on her $13.75 principal held in trust by the law firm of Holland & Knight and used in Florida's IOTA was taken without just compensation. The suit challenged the program, claiming it violated the due process clause of the Fifth and Fourteenth Amendments, and constituted conversion of property and breach of fiduciary duty. Glaeser's class action was filed in the U.S. District Court for the Middle District of Florida. The district court denied her claim. She then appealed to the Eleventh U.S. Circuit Court of Appeals, which affirmed the district court's ruling. *Cone v. Florida Bar*, 819 F.2d (1986). In 1987, the Supreme Court denied her petition for a writ of *certiorari*, thereby leaving stand the Eleventh Circuit's ruling that Florida's IOLTA plan was not prohibited by either the Constitution's Fifth or Fourteen Amendments.

The *Cone* decision opened the door for states throughout the country to adopt IOLTA programs similar to Florida's. By 1987, six years after the Florida's implementation of the country's first IOLTA program, forty-two other states and the District of Columbia had adopted IOLTA-type programs. Twenty years later by 2007, *every* state and several territories had an IOLTA program to help fund legal-aid services programs. Though the details of the plans differ, their combined impact has to a significant degree countered the drastic curtailment of federal funding for legal services that went into effect during the Reagan administration.

The decade-long efforts to create, and then defend, the IOLTA program in Florida succeeded, causing Smith to repeat his favorite dictum: "Meeting the legal needs of the poor is not a race for the short winded." Smith was very pleased that Florida was the first state in the nation to implement such a program. "Arthur England and Russell Carlisle," Smith says, "without doubt are the ones most responsible."

Minimum Fee Schedules

When Smith gave his state-of-the-profession speech at The Florida Bar 1972 convention, he told the assembled lawyers that the high cost of legal services seemed to result in part due to local bar association sanctioned minimum-fee-schedules. He suggested that lawyers who strictly adhered to these minimum fee schedules were negatively impacting the availability of legal services to low and middle-income people. Smith appointed a committee to investigate the matter. After studying the issue, the committee recommended that minimum fee schedules should be disapproved. With report in hand, Smith convinced the Bar's Board of Governors to announce that the Bar would not support local bar organizations that maintained or established minimum fee schedules for their members. The press praised the action.

In an article published in *The Florida Bar Journal*, Smith wrote that lawyers' fees in Florida tended to be high, making legal services unaffordable to poor persons and less affordable to middle-income persons. He also mentioned his concerns about possible antitrust ramifications of adopting minimum fees, even though the schedules were not mandatory. Subsequently, in a letter to Bar members, written when he was the Bar's president, Smith noted that the tacit support of local bars' minimum fee schedules "no longer has the approval of The Florida Bar." Under the headline "Bar Junks Suggested Fee Schedule," the *St. Petersburg Times* praised the pulling of the approval plug. Smith hoped the state's lawyers would be encouraged to be more modest in their fees when

Reece Smith, 16 months old, Plant City, Florida, 1927

Smith's parents: Wm. Reece Smith Sr. and Gladys Moody Smith

Smith's maternal grandmother:
Mary Noel Estes Moody ("Mother Mary")

Three generations:
Wm. Reece Smith Jr.,
Wm. Reece Smith III,
Wm. Reece Smith Sr.

Smith's father and mother
with their grandson,
Wm. Reece Smith III

Three generations:
Wm. Reece Smith III,
Wm. Reece Smith IV,
and Wm. Reece Smith Jr.

NROTC Commander T.D. "Buck" Isom, Vice-Commander Smith

Smith, quarterback, University of South Carolina, 1944, played in first "Gater Bow" in Jacksonville, Florida.

Wm. Reece Smith Sr. and USNR Ensign Wm. Reece Smith Jr., 1945

American Rhodes Scholars aboard the ship *Isle de France, Life Magazine,* 1949, (Smith, bottom row, 2nd from right)

Smith and Oxford friends, December 1949, in Rome at the Coliseum

Gentleman's Eight rowing krewe, Christ College, Oxford, 1950 (Smith — the cowboy — 2nd from left)

Oxford's champion lacrosse team, 1951, Smith, upper row (2nd from left)

Meadow Building, Smith's residence hall, Christ Church, Oxford

Giddings Mabry.
Founded in 1901 the
firm that in time became
Carlton Fields.

Governor Doyle Carlton
joined Mabry in 1912.

Judge OK Reaves joined
Mabry and Carlton in 1921.

Smith, president, Carlton Fields,
on balcony of Tampa office

Carlton Fields
named partners;
Fields, Ward,
Emmanuel, Smith
and Cutler, circa
1960s

Carlton Fields
lawyers Cutler,
Walbolt and Smith
at *Pro Bono
Publico* meeting,
New York City

USF presidents Carl Riggs, John Allen, John Brown, Smith and Cecil Mackey

USF President Smith
playing donkey basket-
ball with USF students,
1977

Smith canoeing with USF
students (not shown),
Hillsborough River, 1978

Maori girl greets American
Bar Association President
Smith in Auckland,
New Zealand, 1980

Chief Justice of the United States Warren Burger with
ABA President Smith, Houston, 1981

Wm Reece Smith

With warm best wishes

G.g Bush

Smith introducing Vice-President George H.W. Bush at ABA meeting,
New Orleans, 1981

Smith and overseers of the ABA Pilot *Pro Bono* Projects, Chicago, 1982

Smith attending the Opening of the Courts, London, England

Otis Andrews and Smith, co-chairs, Florida Football Classic, 1983

International Bar President Smith and Kenyan Law Society officials in Nairobi, 1990

First Lady Hillary Clinton greets Smith, East Room of White House,
20th anniversary of the Legal Services Corporation, 1994

Smith; Elaine Jones, Director, Legal Defense Fund; and Washington, D.C.
attorney John Pickering, New York City, 2000

Lord Henry Wolfe, Chief Justice of England, and Smith, London, 2000

Former Attorney General Janet Reno and Smith at Inns of Court dinner, 2006

Sylvia Walbolt toasting Smith at his 80th birthday party, in offices of Carlton Fields, 2005

Benefactor Joy Culverhouse, Smith, and Stetson Law Dean Darby Dickerson, at dedication of Wm. Reece Smith Jr., Courtroom, Tampa, 2004

Smith, 83, teaching professional responsibility at Stetson University College of Law, 2008

William Reece Smith, Jr. Portrait, Board Room, Carlton Fields, Tampa

rendering legal services to the economically deprived members of society who could not pay "the going rate."

Cuban Lawyers

On another front, Smith resolved an issue concerning lawyers who had fled the Castro regime in Cuba. They had lawfully immigrated to Florida and wanted to be allowed to continue to practice law. Each had earned an accredited law degree and was licensed in Cuba to practice. But under Florida Bar rules, they would have to go back to law school and start over, in effect requiring them to earn a second law degree before being allowed to sit for The Florida Bar examination. To many, including Smith, this seemed an excessive burden, given they had already undergone a complete law school training curriculum in their home country. Smith knew, of course, that before *anyone* can be admitted to The Florida Bar, the aspirant *must* first take and pass The Florida Bar examination. The issue raised by the Cuban lawyer immigrants was whether, before they sat for The Florida Bar examination, they had to complete *a full three-year* law school curriculum in America.

Smith and the Bar's Board of Governors concluded that lawyers who were exiled from Cuba should be granted credit for their legal education success in Cuba. Smith went before the Florida Supreme Court, asking it to appoint a committee to study the best method of identifying former Cuban lawyers who had valid credentials and allowing them to take a short course of legal education in Florida prior to being permitted to sit for the examination. The Florida Supreme Court accepted Smith's proposal and the program was implemented. Some years later, in appreciation of Smith's efforts, the exiled Cuban lawyers who had become members of The Florida Bar gave him a plaque at a special dinner and lauded his advocacy on their behalf.

Funding for Implementing New State Judiciary System

During Smith's presidency of the Bar, he lobbied the state Legislature for increased funding for the state's judicial infrastructure, especially to pay for implementation of the revised Article V (judicial article) of Florida's Constitution. Smith noted that the counties shouldered most of the financial burden, and expressed concern that the state "has yet to provide significant financial assistance," which was required because Florida's "counties cannot long absorb the fiscal shock." The reason Article V was revised was to improve the state judicial system and, Smith noted "that costs money."

As Bar president, Smith crisscrossed the state meeting with state officials, lawyers, the media, and civic organizations affording him opportunity to get his message out regarding judicial ethics, merit selection of judges, problems with minimum fees, discipline of lawyers, and obtaining greater legal assistance to low and middle income people. Another matter Smith addressed during his presidency involved persuading the Florida Supreme Court to adopt most of the ABA's Standards for Criminal Justice.

Accomplishments

In an interview with reporter Philip Morgan of the *Tampa Tribune*, Smith summarized his time as president of The Florida Bar. Among the Bar's accomplishments was "it becoming more attuned to the public interest." He listed the successes as also including raising the Bar's interest in judicial reform; drafting a set of proposed new rules dealing with judicial ethics; advancing the merit selection of judges; fostering a better understanding between the media and the bar regarding their respective responsibilities and concerns; and establishment of Florida Legal Services. Meanwhile, The *Tampa Times* quoted Smith: "Not one of us is going to re-shape the world in the period of one year, but some of the [Bar's] goals were attained." Smith told the *Times* he was especially pleased by the Bar's founding of Florida's first statewide legal service agency for the poor, and having it funded by private foundations.

Smith had indeed put his stamp again on expanding legal services for the poor. And, he was far from over. After thirteen months as interim president of a major university, he would be back at it again, this time as president of the ABA.

* * *

CHAPTER FOURTEEN

INTERIM PRESIDENT, UNIVERSITY OF SOUTH FLORIDA

Unexpected Opportunity

During the early 1970s when Smith was practicing law at Carlton Fields and, concurrently, was active in state and national bar associations, he found time to be concerned about the problems of public higher education. His interest in part was the result of his belief in the necessity and value of quality education, a belief nourished during his time at Oxford, and subsequently enhanced while chairing the Florida Joint Legislative-Executive Committee on Post-Secondary Education. Smith oversaw the preparation of a report evaluating Florida's university system that resulted in a series of recommendations to improve academic quality. In doing so, he worked with the leaders of the Florida Legislature, state universities, Governor Reubin Askew, and members of his administration. One such person Smith worked closely with was Chester Ferguson, chair of the Florida Board of Regents that oversaw all of the state's public universities.

Ferguson wielded great influence in Florida, and Smith felt honored when, on a number of occasions, he invited Smith to consider a university presidency. "Yes, he called more than once," Smith recalls, adding: "Chester sought to interest me in being a state university president—Florida State University, in particular, was mentioned." Another was the University of South Florida. Today, Smith wryly comments: "I resisted, thinking Chester was simply seeking to get me out of my firm, a rival of MacFarlane, Ferguson." More seriously, Smith adds: "I was intrigued by the idea."

In the summer of 1976 while attending an ABA meeting, Smith received a phone call from Marshall Criser, then chair of the State Board of Regents. Criser told Smith that Cecil Mackey, President at the University of South Florida, had resigned to become president of Texas Tech University. (An article in the

USF student newspaper, *The Oracle,* reported that President Mackey cited dwindling funds for education in Florida as a major reason for his departure.) Criser asked Smith if he would serve for "a few months" as acting president. Smith was well qualified, Criser thought, having served as co-chair of the Task Force on Missions and Goals of USF, and also having served as chair of the Council of Advisors to President Mackey.

Smith, surprising even himself, agreed. He later explained that his presidency was to be for a limited time, and that his trial calendar was relatively light at the time. Chester Ferguson had nominated Smith to be USF's interim president. When discussing the possibility with Criser, Smith learned that due to a Board of Regents' policy, an "acting" university president was ineligible for later appointment as the "regular" president. But given that Smith had the backing of Criser, Ferguson, and others to remain at USF following his interim service, the Board appointed Smith "interim president" rather than "acting president," thereby making Smith eligible at the end of his temporary term to become the University's regular (permanent) president.

University of South Florida

When Smith became Interim President, USF was a relatively new institution of higher education in Florida. The University had been founded in 1956 and had admitted its first class in 1960. Smith was appointed its Interim President in 1976 and served for a little over one year. USF by then had developed into a significant institution of higher learning. During Smith's leadership at USF, the University's growth and development continued and has done so ever since. (By the Spring of 2009, USF had a combined enrollment of approximately 50,000 students, placing it among the dozen largest universities in the country. With its main campus in Tampa and others in St. Petersburg, Sarasota, and Lakeland, the University offered over 200 degree programs at the undergraduate, graduate, and doctoral levels, and consisted of several schools including a college of medicine.)

Appointment and Reaction

After Smith's interim presidency of USF was announced in August 1976, the media reacted quickly and, for the most part, positively. Tampa's Hispanic newspaper, *La Gaceta,* seemed especially pleased: "The Florida Board of Regents could have searched the entire world and not come up with a more outstanding choice [of Smith] to act as interim president of the University of South

Florida." The paper added that Smith "can best be described as a learned man [who] will face this latest challenge with high integrity, intelligence and vigor." The *Tampa Times* quoted Board of Regents member Chester Ferguson: "USF's greatest deficiency is its relationship to the city, and the biggest pitfall is a lack of rapport and support by the people, which Smith's leadership as an academic outsider may bridge." The *Tampa Tribune* quoted Smith: "I will be working with the legislature and citizens in developing programs.... The first obligation of an interim president is to be sure the University sustains the momentum it has."

After Smith's appointment, he received a bundle of congratulatory letters. Clewis Howell, head of a Tampa bank and Smith's friend, wrote: "I have heard nothing but good things about your appointment. It seems to be one of those few occasions where everyone is happy about the decision." Another friend, Daniel Murphy, president of the First National Bank, wrote: "CONGRATU-LATIONS! The Board of Regents made an excellent choice and I am quite sure they would be pleased if you took the job on a permanent basis."

Not everybody was so enthusiastic. In an article in the *Florida Report*, authors Mike Fowler and Fitz McArden complained that the "Board of Regents is obviously a body stacked by attorneys." In suggesting that its members should be elected, they pointed to the Board's appointment of Smith, calling him "a man with no administrative background." It soon became clear, however, this concern was unfounded, as Smith confronted all issues that came his way fairly, competently, and with a commitment to the welfare of the students and faculty and to the advancement of the University.

Student and Faculty Morale

After assuming the USF presidency on September 1, 1976, Smith soon realized that the morale among faculty and students was quite low. He recalls: "My being a lawyer did not help" in the eyes of many. The first thing he did in response to the morale problem was institute an "open door policy." In his first address to the faculty, as reported in *The Oracle*, Smith said: "It is my view that students and faculty are the heart of this institution. While I'm here, I intend to be as accessible as I possibly can be." *The Oracle* emphasized that Smith pledged to maintain the open-door policy for both students and faculty and made his availability a priority.

Smith followed through on his pledge, but he may have gotten more than he had anticipated. His notes reveal that for several weeks after taking office he was "very busy with discontented individuals." Not only did he meet with students and faculty one-on-one in his office, he also met with them in open meetings. On one occasion, he went to Alpha Hall to answer questions and respond to students' concerns. In doing so, Smith carefully listened to their various comments and complaints, a fact that did not go unnoticed by students and faculty. One student government official, Steve Nichols, was quoted in *The Oracle* as saying: "Reece Smith has been great for this university. Smith listens to what students are saying, instead of making a token attempt at listening," adding, "we can be very frank with him." In response to student dissatisfaction with existing dormitory visiting hours, Smith approved expanding the hours.

Besides listening to students, Smith joined in their activities when circumstances permitted. This was especially the case when students were promoting a good cause. Once, he took part in a campus-wide Swing-a-Thon designed to raise money for campus research.

But certainly the most uplifting experience of this sort was Smith's playing in a basketball game between USF faculty members and students. The game raised money for muscular dystrophy. The catch was that the players had to ride on donkeys. This distinctive athletic contest came to be descriptively called "Donkey Basketball."

Another fund raising event involved students auctioning off various donations of items and "experiences" offered by faculty. Smith offered to paddle students down the Hillsborough River in a canoe. His offering raised more money than any other. He smiles when he recalls the adventure.

In still another noteworthy undertaking, Smith rode a bicycle with faculty and students from the Fowler Avenue campus to the County Courthouse. They appeared before the County Commission to urge the creation of bicycle paths leading to the campus. Smith spoke and presented a signed petition urging the Commission to appropriate the necessary funds to construct the paths. The Commissioners agreed to construct a bicycle path along 30th street. Student, faculty, and media reacted favorably to Smith's efforts. *The Oracle* reported that Hillsborough County had hired a bicycle specialist after "President Smith enthusiastically endorsed the bike path to the Commissioners."

Faculty members also were pleased with Smith's accessibility, willingness to listen, and openness. *La Gaceta* reported that "the faculty are pleased as punch with the performance to date of Tampa attorney William Reece Smith, Jr., who is serving as vice president [sic] of the University of South Florida. They like his style and accomplishments." The faculty was also delighted when Smith opened the first faculty club on the Tampa campus.

Town-Gown Relations

Despite the fact that USF had been in operation for sixteen years when Smith became interim president, there was, in his words, "little contact between the University and the [outside] community." For one thing, the "town" knew little about the University and, for another, students were not cheerleaders for the University.

Part of the problem, Smith wrote in 1976, was that "half of the students are residential and the other half just take courses and live off campus." Moreover, he wrote, "USF [at that time] lacks rallying points, such as a football team," wryly noting that "academics do not provide the type of rallying point that football provides." On the other hand, Smith told the *Tampa Tribune* that though he had played football in college and liked sports, "I would rather see the University gain a reputation for academic excellence than for athletics."

In a newspaper interview shortly after assuming the presidency, Smith said that he had high respect for USF, which he regarded as "an important asset to the communities of the west coast of Florida." He continued:

> I think the relationship between USF and Tampa is a healthy one, but I do think it is desirable to strengthen it and to increase the interest and involvement of the community on one hand, but no less the University in the community on the other. What we need is a sense of pride, a sense of belonging. [I believe] that in time, the community will develop pride in USF for the academic stature of the school.

In order to promote USF's growth in reputation and size, Smith took several steps. One was to publicize the University's cultural activities throughout Florida's west coast, especially in the Tampa Bay region. He pushed the idea that the University's academicians could contribute to the betterment of the community, such as historians working on the history of the region, economists studying state and regional resources, business faculty working with small businesses, doctors performing research in the medical school, and marine biologists working on oceanic problems such as red tide that each year killed thousands of fish along the West Coast of Florida.

With the administrative assistance of Nancy Ford—a Tampa community leader and local bank executive whom Smith "borrowed"—Smith spoke before downtown civic organizations twice monthly in an effort to strengthen the campus-community tie. "I became a cheerleader of sorts for USF," he says, "as well as a champion of its interests." It worked. With Ford's help, he formed a "Town and Gown" organization, one that still provides support to USF. Other projects Smith championed included the building of the Sun Dome on campus (discussed below).

USF's Ph.D. Programs

Smith was aware that all Florida public universities, not only USF, were in a financial crisis when he became Interim President. The mid and late-1970s were times of accelerating inflation. Higher public education in Florida was falling behind due to insufficient funding to maintain the status quo, let alone to improve. In an article in *The Oracle*, reporter Ellen Hampton wrote that Smith was concerned about "the mass exodus of qualified educators from the state" due to a lack of funds. Smith registered as a lobbyist to convince the Florida legislature to increase funding for higher education. At the time, Smith told the media "Florida must make a hard decision ... you can't educate more people with less money."

Among the activities that commanded much of Smith's attention during his presidency was persuading the political powers in Florida to allocate funds that USF needed not only to enhance, but just to maintain its programs of higher education. The greatest threat came from the Board of Regents, which wanted to remove many of the USF doctoral programs and move them to the University of Florida (UF). Many within the Legislature and on the Board of Regents wanted to make UF the state's so-called "flagship" university, which was alright with Smith, but not at the expense of the other two major thriving state universities—Florida State University (FSU) and USF.

Realizing the seriousness of both the shortage-of-funding situation and the threatened abolishment of USF's Ph.D. programs, Smith registered as a Florida lobbyist and traveled to Tallahassee to speak with Florida legislators, many of whom he had worked with and knew well. In talking with the legislators, Smith underscored that USF had already awarded some 4,600 graduate degrees, completed a new medical center, begun construction of a new College of Business Administration, and acquired land in Fort Meyers for a satellite campus. To put it in the vernacular, USF was on a roll and now was not the time either to cut programs and to decrease funding.

Of even greater concern to Smith (and to many of the USF students and faculty) was the possible abolishment of many of the University's Ph.D. programs. Students were anxious about a cut in programs that might affect their career plans. President Smith at an open forum was asked by a student what would happen if the State cut USF's Ph.D. programs. Smith acknowledged it might occur but cautioned it was not a time to panic. He told the *Tampa Times*:

"We haven't lost the battle yet," but added that if the Regents stripped USF of its doctoral programs, "it would weaken our academic quality, our ability to attract students and to keep distinguished professors, and our ability to conduct research to serve the community."

The proposal to abolish the doctorate programs was part of a larger plan supported by certain members of the Florida Legislature to make UF and FSU the only two major research universities in the state, thereby relegating USF and five other state universities to "regional status." For USF in particular—already well on its way to becoming a research institution—this would have a *major* negative impact on its growth and prestige. The USF faculty was not only displeased, many members considered the proposal elimination of the University's Ph.D. programs to be an insult. One faculty member, Dr. Glen Burdick (who with Smith had earlier co-chaired the USF Goals and Missions Committee) wrote Smith declaring: "The role of USF should be that the University develop and maintain doctorate and research programs in the arts, humanities, sciences, and professional fields."

The Legislature set a November 15th deadline for USF's official response to its "Role and Scope Proposal" that included the transfer of USF's Ph.D. programs. primarily to UF. With the assistance of James Redman and Guy Spicola (influential members of the Hillsborough County's legislative delegation), Smith drafted USF's official response (which was later referred to as "Smith's papers.") In addition to the written response, Smith, Redman, and Spicola "worked" the Legislature. Smith, moreover, put the issues squarely on the table of the Board of Regents.

The intense efforts paid off. The Legislature's Role and Scope Proposals were modified and the doctorate programs at USF were preserved. Today, the University of South Florida has become a Carnegie Foundation recognized major research university with the opportunities and prestige that accompany that designation.

In another matter regarding the future growth and reputation of USF, despite a severe economic downtown during his leadership at the University, Smith secured continuation of existing levels of funding for virtually all schools and programs. Moreover he was able to bring in additional monies for Ph.D. work in connection with all the state medical schools, including USF's. Finally, Smith procured a large capital outlay for expansion of USF's St. Petersburg campus.

Smith's successful efforts were especially welcomed and appreciated by USF faculty and administrators who believed that the prior pattern of allocation of funds by the Chancellor's office had favored UF and even FSU to the disadvantage of USF, though all three aspired to be recognized research universities. But Smith had changed the pattern, at least for the time being. He acknowledges that his efforts "served overall to improve University morale and confidence in my work." Indeed. Any initial reservations about Smith being a lawyer and not a professional educator, had evaporated.

Student Budget and Activity Fees

Cecil Mackey (Smith's predecessor as USF president), not long before his departure, had vetoed student government controls over student-activity fees and redirected the monies according to his own wishes. The upshot was that funds available for student affairs were at a lower level when Smith took over. Historian Peter Klingman notes that by doing so, Mackey "ignited a furor" with the officers of the USF student government, which "created a direct confrontation" between the administration and the student government organizations. Smith inherited both the problem and the consequent fermenting bad feelings. In due course, he was able to restore the student affairs budget and dissipate to a large degree the students' frustration. But it took time, open conferences, and budgetary action to steer around the crisis and under Smith's helm the University moved on.

But that was not the only financial problem Smith faced involving students. Another centered on the allocation of student-activity fees collected on the five separate USF campuses: Tampa, St. Petersburg, Lakeland, Fort Meyers, and Sarasota, the latter four being referred to as the "branch" or "satellite" campuses. Many from the outlying schools claimed that an unfair portion of student revenues was being allocated disproportionately to the main Tampa campus, to the detriment of students attending the branch campuses. The concerned student leaders from the branch campuses did not hesitate to let Smith know their disquietude.

In response, Smith invited student-government representatives from the campuses to come together and meet with him in Tampa. Those from the branch campuses, however, declined to do so, contending that the meeting should take place at a "neutral" location. But where? Smith came up with an innovative idea, one that seemingly would be difficult for any student-government leader to refuse—a moving beer wagon. Smith explains:

> When the student leaders refused to meet with me on the main campus, I borrowed Art Pepin's [the local Budweiser distributor] 'Budweiser Bus,' picked up the leaders at their campuses and drove in a wide circle while the matter was discussed, without resorting to the beer that was dispensed by faucet on the bus.

An article in the *St. Petersburg Times* the following day reported "an agreement was honed" during the bus excursion, noting: "Tampa students no longer will have any say over how the branch campuses spend their student activity fees.... It will be a matter between the students on each campus and the USF administration." The article noted that the amount of money that had been collected in one year on the branch campuses topped a quarter of a million dollars.

USF Sun Dome (Mass Seating Facility)

One of the more interesting decisions Smith had to make during his presidency was how to use a one-time infusion of $9 million for capital construction granted the University by the Board of Regents. The money could be used for many possible projects, including a performing arts center in downtown campus, a fine arts center on the USF campus, or a mass seating, multipurpose facility on the campus. Each choice had strong advocates.

Chester Ferguson of the Board of Regents advised Smith to allocate the money to build a downtown USF "performing arts center," which could be used to draw major shows and performances to the city. At that time there was no such venue in Tampa. Meanwhile, Harrison Covington, dean of the College of Fine Arts, lobbied for a "fine arts center" on the Tampa campus, a plan strongly supported, naturally, by the fine arts faculty. Though Dean Covington worked hard to convince Smith (a classmate from Plant City High School days) to use the funds for that purpose, others felt that what the University needed most was a large, mass-seating, multi-purpose facility that would accommodate thousands of people. USF did not even have a large gymnasium at that time.

After listening to the various arguments, Smith decided a mass-seating facility was the University's most pressing need. He met with architects and engineers and studied the projected costs of such a facility. Smith was surprised to learn that $9 million would not be sufficient if the building were to be an entirely solid structure including the roof. Hearing Santa Clara University in California had an "air-supported dome," in December 1976 Smith went to see it. His first impression was negative. Entering the structure building he noticed several buckets at various locations on the floor. Looking up he saw that the roof of the dome was leaking. Officials told him, however, that the problem was being fixed by doubling the strength of the roof's fabric.

After returning to USF, Smith went to the UF campus in Gainesville where the University was building an air-supported dome. Impressed, Smith told the *Tampa Tribune* the UF facility was "an improved version" but he had concerns about acoustics as well as the high energy costs. But, in balance, Smith realized that an air-supported dome would cost considerably less then an all steel-girded arena and if built properly, would be more cost effective. In the end, the Board of Regents agreed with Smith on the dome concept.

As a strong advocate for the mass-seating structure, Smith told the *Tampa Tribune*, that the new facility would not have the problems that seemed to plague the UF dome. Moreover, to assure that the USF facility could be built within budget, the planners had adopted several lower-cost alternatives, including seating costs and outside parking areas. USF in-house architect Mike Patterson worked closely with Smith, Dick Bowers (USF director of athletics), and others in developing the plans and construction budget for the facility. The original budget was set at $7 million with the $2 million extra to be used for a new College of Fine Arts rehearsal hall.

In late August 1977, only three weeks before Smith's presidency would end, the contractors' bids came in. To Smith's disappointment, the lowest bid was $2.1 million higher than the University had budgeted. The *Tampa Tribune's* sports Editor, Tom McEwen interviewed Smith the day after the bids were announced. Smith essentially had no comment. McEwen wrote: "It was clear by [Smith's] mood and tone he was disappointed. It was also clear that he would not accept the news as defeat for the projects." Not at all. Smith continued to lobby for the building to the end of his tenure at USF. Subsequently, the Regents approved the building. The structure stands today as the USF Sun Dome.

Inter-Campus Governance

Not unexpectedly, administrative tensions and disagreements among the administrators at the regional campuses and those on the main Tampa campus had been evolving, and continued to do so during Smith's presidency. Underlying the dispute was a fundamental question of whether the regional campuses should evolve as free-standing units, essentially self-governed, or if they should be under central authority. This question was especially critical when considering funding and academic issues. But those were long-range questions and there needed to be a short-term clarification of who was in charge. In February 1977, Smith was quoted in *The Oracle*:

> Until such time as the campuses are free-standing units, it shall be the responsibility of the Regional Campus Administrator to determine the programs or program elements to be supported and to allocate the funds necessary.

Smith emphasized that the regional campuses lacked sufficient resources to maintain separate accreditation of their programs. Accordingly, "the regional campuses," he said, "must rely upon the accreditation of the University and its colleges, and all the campus programs must comply with [unified] educational standards."

Thereafter, in July 1977, Smith released a white paper containing a detailed proposal designed to clarify the lines of authority between USF's main campus and branch campuses. He prefaced his recommendations by noting that troubles had arisen from "deficiencies in structure and planning, and a failure to follow established procedure and to communicate through established channels." Smith made it clear that the deans at the Tampa campus would be responsible for "academic accreditation and standards, program and course content, employment and assignment of faculty and adjuncts, and promotion and tenure...."

The Oracle reporters called Smith's proposals "a fair shake for everyone," adding that "interim President Smith is providing USF an opportunity to unite its four campuses into one big, happy university." Smith's proposal, they noted, included an appeal process should problems arise between regional and central administrators, one that would end up in the president's office. In addition, Smith's proposals gave branch campus faculty members wider opportunities to participate in departmental and college-wide events. They concluded their commentary by noting "it is Smith's opinion that current 'we and they' attitudes are detrimental to the concept of a single university."

First Amendment Issues

Smith has been involved in several matters involving free speech issues. Already mentioned was the tenured USF faculty member who advocated during the Vietnam War that people rebel against the U.S. government. But Smith's concern about protecting the First Amendment right of free speech was tested more than once during his presidency. At one point, the Florida Legislature entertained the idea of censoring certain classroom offerings in the public universities of the state. Smith led opposition to what he considered an encroachment on the right of free speech as well as the principle of academic freedom inherent in a institution of higher learning. The legislative initiative failed.

In another matter, members of the local media appeared to overlook the right of free speech when they criticized the University for allowing a "sexual attitude" workshop sponsored by a USF student organization to take place on campus. Smith allowed the seminar to take place, noting yet again that the law of the land was involved—guarantees of the U.S. Constitution and its Bill of Rights. On a somewhat similar issue, Smith was confronted with people within and without the University who wanted the school to cancel a scheduled adult movie on campus. The matter was subsequently resolved quickly when the movie proved to be unavailable.

"The Hardest Decision"

As his year as Interim President drew to a close, Smith learned that scores of students, faculty, and staff within the University wanted him to stay on and become the University's on-going president. The pressure to remain also came from outside the campus. In the Spring of 1977, members of the Board of Regents informed Smith that he could have the appointment as the USF president if he wanted to pursue it. In his initial reaction, he said, yes, he would like to be considered. Smith's indication prompted favorable reactions throughout the community. Comments and editorials supporting his remaining at USF appeared in the *Tampa Times*, *Tampa Tribune*, *La Gaceta*, *St. Petersburg Times*, and *Tampa Commerce*. The student paper, *The Oracle*, commented:

> William Reece Smith, Jr., [is] "an all-around guy".... More than a third of the faculty signed petitions urging him to stay on, and student leaders have voiced similar sentiments. During his seven months as acting [sic] president, he has proved to be open and fair with everyone— students, faculty, staff, and alumni. He's been highly visible, talking with just about anyone, almost anywhere, almost anytime.

The *Tampa Commerce* reported that Interim President Smith "was held in such high esteem, that a large percentage of faculty members signed a petition backing him to be president of USF."

But another road was beckoning. On the issue of whether he should seek to remain the USF president, Smith explains: "I vacillated. All deans and some 900 faculty and career service employees signed petitions urging me to accept. I was sorely tempted, but I was still active in ABA affairs and the timing was right for me to seek the ABA presidency." He withdrew his name from consideration for staying on at USF as its president. Today, he says, it was the "hardest decision of his life." He truly had been torn. Smith loved the challenges of running a major university and based on both inside and outside assessments, he had succeeded brilliantly.

His decision to withdraw from consideration disappointed many. As reported in *University of South Florida, The First Fifty Years 1956–2006*, USF Dean

Travis Northcutt lamented: "No person for a presidency in the history of a state university system would have had as much and as widespread support as he would have had." Mark Greenberg, principal author of *The First Fifty Years*, wrote: "Despite favorable reviews during his brief tenure, [Smith] declined consideration and stepped down in May 1977."

At the end of his USF interim-presidency, Smith was quoted in *USF Today* magazine: "I have a renewed appreciation for the University. My association with students has been pleasant and heartwarming [and] I have great respect for the mission and commitment of the faculty." Smith's accomplishments at USF were recognized and appreciated throughout the University, the greater Tampa Bay community, and Florida. The cities of Tampa, Clearwater, and Temple Terrace all sponsored public "Reece Smith Days." Meanwhile, various student organizations, as well as faculty, staff, and alumni groups, gave him plaques, testimonials, and declarations of appreciation for his leadership at the University of South Florida.

* * *

CHAPTER FIFTEEN

PRESIDENT-ELECT
OF THE ABA

Facing the prospect of seeking the presidency of either USF or the ABA, Smith comments philosophically: "Life is full of choices, and I occasionally wonder if I made the best one available to me when I left USF." But he has no regrets. And, surely, he would be successful whichever road he chose. In the end, Smith's decision to seek the presidency of the ABA—the nation's oldest, largest, and most prestigious organization of attorneys—and his hopes of what he could accomplish on behalf of the legal profession and the country's poor turned out to be prophetic.

The ABA: Founding and Mission

No national organization of lawyers existed in the country until January 1878, when Simeon E. Baldwin, a respected Connecticut lawyer and faculty member at the Yale Law School, introduced a motion before the state's bar association "that a committee be appointed to consider the propriety of organizing an association of American lawyers." Baldwin and his committee circulated a letter in July 1878, inviting recipients to meet at the Saratoga Springs Resort in upstate New York. In August, the invited lawyers assembled at Saratoga Springs. There they adopted a constitution for what would be a national bar association encompassing lawyers from every state. The group included prominent lawyers and judges as well as a few law professors from well-known law schools.

Simeon Baldwin and Lewis Delafield (president of the American Social Science Association) pushed the attendees at the Saratoga meeting to form a new national bar organization. Among other things, it could establish a set of recommended national and uniform standards for lawyers to be eligible for admission to practice law rather than leaving this matter entirely to variable and divergent state-by-state standards. Setting and enforcing educational standards remains one of the ABA's priority missions today, but its agenda has greatly expanded over the years.

Two-Year Campaign

Becoming president of the ABA does not happen quickly. After Smith returned to his law firm following his service as interim president of USF, he began to campaign in earnest for the position of president-elect of the ABA. He was fifty-one years old and five years had passed since his presidency of The Florida Bar had ended. Smith knew the ABA campaign would be long and demand all his energies. His main objective was to contact each of the fifty ABA state delegates and explain why he would be a good ABA president. The state delegates constituted the ABA committee to nominate candidates for the Association's presidency.

For Smith to win the nomination, he had to gain the support of a majority (twenty-six) of the state delegates. The formal nomination then was made by the House of Delegates at its mid-year meeting in February. At the time, Smith came up for election, the House of Delegates consisted of about 380 members. By tradition, the state delegates' nominee was elected unanimously by the House to the post of ABA president-elect. The president-elect then automatically became ABA president the following year. In essence, the process meant that once a candidate obtained firm commitments from at least twenty-six state delegates, the race was usually over and the later formal vote was *pro forma*. It was possible, however, to oppose the nominee by petition, always a concern to candidates who, like Smith, sought the presidency through commitments of state ABA delegates.

Smith began his campaign in June of 1977. After learning he had an opponent from New Jersey, he stepped up his activities, traveling as often as his law practice and available time permitted. He tried to meet individually with as many ABA state delegates as circumstances permitted. Robert Ervin from Tallahassee was the state delegate for Florida and Smith asked him to be his national campaign manager. He describes Erwin as a "shrewd and effective bar association politician who was of great assistance" in his campaign. Another of Smith's strong supporters was Russell Troutman, then president of The Florida Bar. Troutman wrote Ervin that he would cover as much territory as possible in support of Smith's campaign. Troutman also sent Smith a handwritten note:

> You should know I am supporting your cause because I know you love our profession, have worked unstintingly for it, [and] are extremely capable.... It is your devotion, your capability and the fact that you have inspired me that prompts my unbridled support. In return, I expect nothing.

Scores of other lawyers stepped up to support Smith's bid. National support came from seven former presidents of the ABA including Cody Fowler and Chesterfield Smith, both from Florida. Support throughout Florida was extensive and swift after Smith made known his intention to seek the presidency. Judges, lawyers, and friends sent letters of support. One was from Chief Judge Winston Arnow of the U.S. District Court for the Northern District of Florida who wrote: "I'm keeping my fingers crossed for you and hoping for full and complete success in your quest for the presidency of the ABA." A similar letter came from Judge C. Clyde Atkins, a jurist on the U.S. District Court for the Southern District of Florida. Atkins wrote: "You can certainly count of my spreading the word among friends." Smith's campaign was an extensive exercise in networking contacts. Having worked for years in the ABA, Smith met with national and state bar leaders around the country. His support was growing exponentially.

Smith needed to garnish as much support as he could because he was facing a formidable opponent—Adrian M. Foley, Jr., of Newark, New Jersey. Foley was a member of both the ABA Board of Governors and its House of Delegates, as well as a former president of the New Jersey State Bar Association. Like Smith, he was a Fellow of the American College of Trial Lawyers, and was an elected member of the American Law Institute.

Foley was a strong opponent not only due to his obvious qualifications and experience, but also because he was not from Florida. It was disadvantageous for Smith that two former ABA presidents had come from his state—Cody Fowler from Tampa and Chesterfield Smith from Lakeland. All things being equal, it was the practice of the ABA to select presidents over time from various regions of the country.

Smith wrote his friend John McCarthy "It appears that I am in the middle of a real horse race." As the campaign got underway, more supporters came forward. His friends assembled a steering committee to assist the campaign, including Chesterfield Smith, Robert Ervin, Earl Hadlow, Russell Troutman, Burton Young, Marshall Cassedy, and Fletcher Rush. On July 14, 1978, The Florida Bar formally endorsed Smith for the ABA presidency.

In short order Smith had written commitments of support from nineteen state delegates and believed seven others were on his side. Though gaining confidence in the outcome, Smith continued to campaign hard. Shortly thereafter, Smith and Foley spoke to the state delegates at the ABA mid-year meeting. Foley asked Smith if he could speak first since he had a golf date with the U.S. Attorney General. "Feeling Foley had greatly impressed the delegates with his governmental contacts," Smith recalls: "I, nevertheless, made my ususal little speech of my dedication to service in the public interest and to the legal profession."

Following the meeting, an article in the *American Lawyer* magazine appeared about the ABA race, noting that because the candidates' agendas appeared similar, an assessment of their respective characters would be significant:

> [T]he delegates see little difference in the two longtime ABA activists;
> whatever differences they may see they are not anxious to discuss be-
> cause their choices will be highly personal ones based more on con-
> tacts and character assessments than on the kinds of political and social
> issues that often highlight the resolution agenda at ABA conventions.

The article quoted one ABA delegate as saying: "We are looking for someone
with the character, stature and leadership to represent the profession to the
public.... We know [we have an] image problem. We think it's important to
have the right spokesman."

Smith continued campaigning and his efforts were reaping the desired result. By late fall 1978, he had garnered sufficient commitments to assure the
nomination. Doing the math, Foley withdrew from the race.

Smith went to the February 1979 ABA mid-year meetings in Atlanta with
forty written commitments in hand. Following deliberations, all fifty state delegates unanimously nominated him to become the head the ABA. Six months
later, on August 14, 1979, Smith was elected its President-Elect without opposition, the one-year term to begin immediately. (Incredibly, two days prior
to being elected ABA President-elect, Smith chaired a meeting of the National
Conference of Bar Presidents as *its* president.)

Following Smith's victory, he received scores of letters of congratulations
and responded to each one writing a personal note. The news media also responded to his achievement. Reporter Patrick McMahon of the *St. Petersburg
Times* wrote:

> Another of [Tampa's] pre-eminent lawyers will be officially chosen
> president elect of the American Bar Association. He has no opposition
> and automatically becomes president in 1980. He is William Reece
> Smith, Jr. Unlike folksy Chesterfield Smith, Reece Smith strikes a more
> urbane, almost patrician profile. He is soft spoken, articulate and a lit-
> tle stuffy.

Smith was not put off by the "little stuffy" comment, though those who
know him well would not agree with McMahon's assessment.

President-Elect

By assuming the position of President-Elect and subsequently President of
the ABA, Smith became its chief spokesperson. But as historian Klingman
notes, Smith was not only a spokesperson *for* the legal profession, he also was
a persistent speaker *to* that profession, urging lawyers to work for the public

interest and to intensify efforts to raise the ethical standards of the bench and bar. It was a never-ending, full-time task, necessitating constant study, preparation, meetings, and travel.

Upon becoming President-Elect, Smith began to promote the dominant theme he would pursue, especially after he became the ABA President the following year. Explaining that it was customary for "each ABA president to undertake some pet project," Smith said, "mine was to seek to increase involvement of state and local bar associations in organized legal aid activity." In an interview with Joy McIlwain of the *Tampa Tribune* Smith said the increased cost of legal services was one of the more serious problems facing the legal profession, emphasizing that among his goals as ABA President was to make legal services available to those who could not afford them.

Smith began his agenda as President-Elect, calling for increased private bar involvement in legal aid to supplement the services of the federally funded Legal Services Corporation (LSC), about which he harbored some doubts. Indeed, the relationship between the private bar and the LSC was anything but harmonious.

For years, the ABA had two committees that shared in common the goal of promoting *pro bono* legal services to the poor. One was the ABA Public Interest Practice Committee and the other was the ABA Commission on Legal Aid and Public Defenders. Both committees had existed for several years prior to Smith becoming ABA President-Elect. To some degree, members of both groups shared a belief that was then prevalent in the private bar—that LSC attorneys wanted to bring about social change more than handling the legal problems of the poor. Many lawyers referred to LSC attorneys as young "do-gooders." According to a Chicago lawyer, Ruth Ann Schmitt, "the LSC had a bad reputation in part because its lawyers tended to be dogmatic rather than diplomatic, and in part because they often sued local and state governmental agencies and individuals without any prior negotiations."

On the other side, many LSC lawyers assumed private lawyers were unqualified and largely unwilling to work for the poor. They were unable to do so, in the LSC's view, because they were not steeped in poverty law and spent little, if any, time working with clients having the legal problems of the poor. Moreover, it was claimed, they had little proclivity to do so because *pro bono* work would distract them from spending more time with their income-producing clients. Smith understood there was some basis for these concerns, being well aware the law practice increasingly was evolving into specialized disciplines and that so-called "poverty law" was becoming one of them.

Smith had become concerned about the mutual misapprehension between the role of the private bar and the government subsidized legal assistance lawyers, in particular the LSC. But he began to see the issues differently as he came to better understand the bases for the apprehension: First, the private bar's lack of knowledge about what publically funded legal service do; and second, the belief many public service lawyers clung to the notion that private lawyers' involvement in legal assistance to the poor would be both ineffective and inefficient. At the time Smith became ABA President-Elect, the LSC itself was facing challenges to its very existence. Smith overcame his own reservations about the LSC and worked for increased private bar involvement in furnishing legal services along with government supported programs, the largest of which by far was the federal LSC. But there was an immediate threat that the LSC might be eliminated altogether; Smith was worried. A trip to Puerto Rico intensified his concerns.

Speaking Out for Legal Aid

In December 1979, Smith received a letter from Howard Eisenberg, executive director of the National Legal Aid and Defender Association (NLADA). The NLADA was (and remains) the oldest and largest national, nonprofit organization of attorneys who represent indigents in court, either voluntarily or in paid capacities. Eisenberg wrote that he hoped the NLADA could work with the ABA to strengthen the delivery of legal services to the poor. He acknowledged that "misapprehension between the private bar on the one hand, and the public defenders and paid legal services lawyers on the other, concerning their respective roles existed." Subsequently, Smith was invited to the annual meeting of the NLADA in Puerto Rico, where he talked with delegates and learned about their concern over the ramifications of Congress cutting off funding for the LSC. Pitching his prepared speech to the side, Smith spoke spontaneously to the attendees, pledging that he would work with the ABA in opposing elimination of the LSC. He did so (as related in the following chapter.)

During the remainder of his year as President-Elect, Smith continued to give speeches. Among his various proficiencies, public speaking may be his best. Those who have heard him (including the author) says he captivates his listeners with lucid and insightful remarks, while making coherent and substantive points, all intermixed with humorous anecdotes. During the two years Smith served as President-Elect and President of the ABA, he made 217 speeches, including addressing all fifty state bar associations (a feat, he says, that had only been done once before by an ABA president).

In his last speech as ABA President (one he made in New Orleans in the Summer of 1981), Smith criticized the Reagan administration's attempt to abolish the LSC. He was well aware that an important proponent for its dismantlement was sitting a few feet away at the head table—George Herbert W. Bush, the Vice President of the United States, and a strong proponent for the LSC's demise. His critical remarks notwithstanding, Smith recalls Bush to be warm and charming. When ABA president, Smith met with Vice President Bush on other occasions.

In addition to meeting many of America's leaders, Smith traveled to every state to address lawyers and meet with bar and public officials. He also visited ten foreign countries. These meetings not only gave Smith the opportunity to inform listeners about what was happening within the ABA, it also afforded him forums to push for reforms and changes in the legal profession. His subjects were wide ranging but all dealt in some manner with improving the American legal system. The topics are listed below and reveal the matters that most concerned him:

- Encouraging lawyers to understand professionalism conceptually in the context of the public interest. Similarly, stressing the professional obligation of every attorney to assure that justice and legal services are available to all segments of society.
- Explaining the ABA's pilot Volunteer Lawyer Programs.
- Raising ethical standards applicable both to judges and lawyers.
- Stressing that professionalism demands good character as well as competency and commitment.
- Promoting merit selection of qualified and unbiased judges.
- Calling for judicial salaries to be raised and removing age barriers for appointment to the bench, both steps necessary to attract and retain qualified and competent jurists.
- Underscoring the dangers and risks of governmental encroachment on the practice of law, especially by the Federal Trade Commission and the United States Congress.
- Pointing out the benefits of an integrated bar, which encompasses every lawyer in a state and works with the state's highest court in setting high ethical standards for the profession and then enforces those standards through investigatory and disciplinary procedures.
- Supporting the recruitment of greater numbers of minorities (notably African-Americans and Hispanics) into law schools as well as into law practice and to become active in professional bar associations.
- Reminding lawyers that they have a continuing obligation to protect fundamental constitutional rights afforded all citizens.
- Emphasizing that women in far greater numbers must be recruited into the legal profession, and that barriers for their advancement must be removed.

- Arguing that women lawyers should be given greater responsibility and leadership positions within the organized bar (which Smith did when ABA President).
- Encouraging organized bars to set goals and engage in long-range planning for their implementation.
- Pointing out to the media the problems with TV coverage in courtrooms as adversely affecting the adjudicatory process and the public's understanding of the criminal justice system.
- Decrying increasing reliance on litigation to settle disputes rather than through negotiations or by utilizing, to a much greater degree, alternative methods of dispute resolution.
- Pressing the importance to restore the public's trust in the ideals and the prestige of the legal profession.
- Calling on lawyers and judges to upgrade the rules and procedures applicable to the criminal justice system both on the federal and state levels.
- Suggesting the need for the bar to regulate lawyer advertising to protect the public interest.
- Supporting Chief Justice of the United States Warren Burger's call for better trained lawyers in trial and appellate practice, as well as for law schools to focus more on skills training.
- Explaining why the federal Legal Services Corporation should not be abolished, or have its funding considerably cut back by Congress.
- Arguing that the ABA's Private Bar Involvement *pro bono* programs would work best in cooperation with the federal Legal Services Corporation.

Then there was a "special topic," one Smith chose at the last minute having been told by his host that the audience "would appreciate something different than the usual ABA-type speech." At the Virginia State Bar Association meeting, Smith discarded his prepared remarks and spoke on the value of a liberal education. "It was a hit," he recalls "summaries of my comments were published in several Virginia journals and sent to the president of each Virginia university and college."

During Smith's speech-making excursions, he had occasions to meet privately with dignitaries to discuss matters of mutual importance. These included Chief Justice Warren Burger (several meetings); Associate Justice Byron White; Attorney General Benjamin Civiletti; Oral Roberts (founder of Oral Roberts University); Peter Taylor, Lord Chief Justice of Great Britain; and Hillary Clinton, later U.S. senator and Secretary of State under President Barack Obama.

A Short Detour: International Diplomacy

When Smith was ABA President-Elect, then ABA President Leonard Janof-sky asked Smith to lead a group of ABA leaders to Taiwan. An invitation had come from the Republic of China via the Chinese Comparative Law Association. Prior to Smith's departure, Professor Ruth Bader Ginsburg (a law professor at Columbia University and later an associate justice of the U.S. Supreme Court) called him on behalf of Amnesty International. She asked him to urge the Taiwanese government to hold public trials rather than secret military trials of intellectuals and journalists arrested in connection with riots directed against the Taiwanese government in Kaohsiung. Smith agreed to try. In addition to planned talks with government officials, Smith had "clandestine meetings" in Taiwan with lawyers for accused intellectuals and journalists, along with representatives of the U.S. Institute of Taiwan (America's official representatives in the Republic of China in absence of formal diplomatic relations between the two countries.)

In Taiwan, Smith was taken to a military prison where the accused were incarcerated. There, government officials allowed him to observe—but not to speak with—each of the prisoners. The government wanted Smith to see for himself that they had not been tortured or killed in prison. But in later meetings with Taiwanese officials, he voiced concern about the imprisoned journalists and intellectuals and urged they be afforded public trials.

Subsequently, public trials of the accused were held, though Smith does not know whether his efforts affected the government's decision. In any event, Professor Ginsburg was appreciative of Smith's contribution, though the Taiwanese government apparently was not. "I was told during my visit," Smith says, "that I would be invited back to receive an honorary degree from a university that had moved to Taiwan with Chiang Kai-Shek, but I never received the invitation."

Regulation of Legal Profession

During his year as ABA President-Elect, Smith often spoke about governmental regulation of the legal profession. He acknowledged that the profession was subject to state regulation, especially under the rules of each state's highest court. In an article published in the *West Virginia State Bar Journal*, he noted: "The practice of law is regulated, in one form or another, by government. Mainly ... by state government through the courts, the legislature, or both." But, he pointed out, the control came from the courts and state legislatures, not from the federal government. What concerned Smith was the possibility of the federal government becoming more involved in regulating the profession.

Around this time, various proposals were being made by the Federal Trade Commission (FTC) that would give it wide authority to oversee the legal profession. Smith warned of the dangers of increased federal regulation: "Tampering with the current [state] system of regulating the profession would not serve the public interest." The oversight by each state's supreme court, he told his audience, "is the best way to maintain high standards," adding that the public interest is far better served by supreme court supervision than by schemes to either deregulate the profession or have more pervasive governmental regulation, especially if it came from Washington. Smith declared that "the profession is effectively policing itself."

Thus, Smith viewed with alarm the rumors that the FTC was investigating certain legal practices within the profession, including the operation of legal clinics. Concurrently, state legislatures were expressing an interest in increasing their regulation of lawyers. One was in Smith's home state. As reported in the *Tampa Times*, members of the Florida Legislature believed the legislative branch should regulate lawyers' conduct, rather than the judiciary and the Bar—a move, Smith believed would seriously weaken the profession.

Smith's concerns over legislative inroads on both the state and federal levels were shared by many members of the Bar and judiciary not only in Florida, but throughout the country. In time, calls for additional federal and state legislative intrusions into regulating lawyers fell, for the most part, by the wayside. Today, the primary regulation of attorneys remains a matter for the state and federal judiciaries and the states' organized bars, especially those that are integrated such as Florida.

For Smith, his year as ABA President-Elect had been an active one. He had crisscrossed the land—to borrow Woody Guthrie's lyrics—"from California to the New York Island, from the Redwood Forest to the Gulf Stream waters." He gave a speech at virtually every stop and met with public officials and with state and local bar leaders in the process. Spending time with attorneys around the country also afforded Smith opportunities to evaluate lawyers he might appoint as committee chairs when he became the ABA President.

By mid-Summer 1980, Smith had assembled his core team and was prepared to become head of the largest national organization of lawyers in the world. The 1980 annual ABA meeting was split between Honolulu, and Sydney, Australia. In Sydney, Smith became President of the American Bar Association in a ceremony attended by his wife, son, and father.

* * *

CHAPTER SIXTEEN

PRESIDENT OF THE ABA: PART ONE

Making Legal Aid More Accessible

In Smith's 1980 ABA inauguration address, he spoke of the need for the ABA to intensify its efforts to make available legal services to the poor and also talked about the association's shortcomings when it came to long-term planning. He believed the ABA staff should be involved in long-range planning, and that the membership would be better served if ABA presidents pursued a common long range plan that could be refined and modified over time. He knew the goals of the ABA presidents often were similar, but a tradition had evolved that each incoming president have a special agenda for the year. Smith felt that the long-range ABA's goals should take priority over those of a one-year duration, especially given that specific projects started by earlier presidents often were not completed during their term and, consequently, encumbered the ABA budget somewhat indefinitely.

Smith told his audience he understood that the official position of the ABA on issues might, from time to time, differ from his, and he was determined to avoid confusion by clearly distinguishing his own views from those of the organization. An example was the death penalty. When Smith became ABA President, the organization had no official position on the issue. He personally opposed capital punishment but made it clear to the media that the ABA had taken no position on it. On the other hand, at an ABA meeting in Dallas, Smith stated that though he personally was against the death penalty, he supported guidelines for its use: "If we're going to have the death penalty, then we ought to have humane standards." When asked why he was opposed to the death penalty personally, Smith declared that the death penalty "is counter to our aspirations for a more civilized, humane society."

Though Smith's predecessors typically came to the ABA presidency with specific, tailor-made agendas, he came to advance a long-standing existing objective of the ABA and one dear to him—the pressing need for increased legal services to the poor. The ABA's policy coincided with Smith's long held beliefs, and he welcomed the opportunity to further the private involvement of the bar in promoting practicing lawyers to furnish *pro bono* legal services—specifically, by the Association's setting up pilot programs in selected cities across the country. Linda Greenhouse in the *New York Times* wrote that the new President of the ABA hoped to "concentrate on long-range planning and on improved delivery of legal services to the poor."

During his term as the ABA President, Smith tried to educate politicians and the public of the magnitude of the inadequacy of legal aid services for the poor. In an address before the National Legal Aid and Defender's Association, he said: "In spite of the profession's continuing strong tradition of volunteer services to the poor, we have a long way to go." In an interview published in *U.S. News & World Report*, Smith noted that Americans do not have equal access to legal services. The article quoted Smith as saying that in response to the problem, "the ABA urges every lawyer to provide assistance to the disadvantaged on a pro bono basis," adding that the ABA supports "the Legal Services Corporation and the Public Defender Program" as well.

Abolishing the Legal Services Corporation

During President Lyndon Johnson's administration, the Office of Economic Opportunity (OEO) was established as part of what he called "the War on Poverty." Funding for the OEO came primarily from the Ford Foundation. Beginning in 1965, the OEO began to make direct grants to local legal aid organizations throughout the country. This was the first time money from the federal government supported the delivery of legal services to the poor. Then ABA President Lewis Powell, Jr., later an associate justice of the U.S. Supreme Court, supported the creation of a national legal services agency. In 1974, Congress passed the Legal Services Corporation Act, which established the Legal Services Corporation (LSC), a law signed by President Nixon.

At the twenty-fifth anniversary of the founding of the LSC, then First Lady Hillary Clinton (who years earlier had been chair of the LSC) told those assembled (including Smith) in the East Wing of the White House how the Corporation came about:

> [LSC] was born as a bipartisan cause in 1974 under President Nixon, and with Republicans and Democrats in both the House and Senate supporting it, and supporting it strongly. And many of you, through the years, stood for that bipartisan commitment.

President Clinton also spoke at the LSC anniversary reception. He reminded the attendees that former President Jimmy Carter had appointed his wife head of the Corporation in 1980 (the year Smith had become the ABA president). Clinton alluded to the struggle that the Corporation and the ABA had been dealing with for decades:

> For years now, some in Congress have tried to dismantle [LSC]. They have seen it as a political thing. I do not believe it is political to say a poor person should have the same right as a rich person. I do not believe it is political to say we have to bring the law into the real lives of all Americans. We have stood firm in the support of the Legal Services Corporation.

The efforts to dismantle the LSC reached its zenith in 1981. When Smith became ABA President in the summer of 1980, Hillary Clinton headed the LSC. A few months later, Ronald Reagan was elected President and took office in January 1981. Not long thereafter, Hillary Clinton was replaced as chair of the LSC, and the very existence of the Corporation LSC became threatened.

Historian Peter Klingman has reviewed the history of the battle to save the LSC and has studied in particular Smith's files pertaining to that dispute. Klingman adds this historical perspective to the debate:

> The political fight over the LSC sliced American history in two — the ambitious grand vision of Lyndon Johnson's Great Society that poverty could be eradicated, and the conservative counter movement that saw no reason to have faith in government's ability to solve deeper social problems.

Philosophies in Conflict

In 1980 when Ronald Reagan was campaigning for the U.S. presidency, the conservative Washington "think tank" — the Heritage Foundation — released a report, in anticipation of his victory, designed to influence the new administration's policies on federally-subsidized social programs. The report charged various federal agencies. including the LSC, of "fostering a particularly political ideology." The focus of the Foundation's report, though ideological, was couched in economic language. Example: "Until and unless balanced dialogue takes place over the very issue of what truly is in the interest of America's vulnerable and needy, conservative efforts to reform and reshape the federal budget are likely to fail." The report faulted the LSC for its size, complexity, philosophy, activities, and most of all, for its commitment to a liberal ideology, claiming that the LSC was "unabashedly, a government subsidized 'public interest' law mechanism which shares and sustains the ideological biases of that movement."

Klingman notes that several members of Congress were concerned about saving money in opposing the LSC while others were opposed to the perceived liberal philosophy of the Corporation and to certain activities alleged to be "abuses" of its mission. The abuses listed by the Congressional Republican Study Group included a charge that Florida Rural Legal Services, which had received a $1.96 million grant from LSC, supported a rent strike in Belle Grade, Florida, by tenants against landlords in public housing projects, as well as a charge against West Texas Legal Services, which had received a $3 million LSC grant in 1980, for representing Iranian students at Texas Tech University in overturning a denial of a parade permit to march past the home of the son of the Shah of Iran. The Republican Study Group also charged LSC attorneys with paying "more attention to class action suits" than to individual client needs. In a "fact sheet" distributed to members of Congress and released to the media, the Study Group cited a report from Orlando Legal Services that two class action suits had used up half of the agency's 1980 budget.

Republicans and conservative Democrats who were opposed the LSC pointed to the dramatic increase of the LSC budget from its founding in 1974 through 1981, an increase from an original $71.5 million appropriation to $321.3 million in the year Smith was ABA President. Conservative Republicans voiced fears that the LSC could not be "budged from its liberal directions." The Republican Study Group noted that though President Reagan controlled all the appointments to the Corporation's board, the localized control and nature of the Corporation's actual work throughout the country meant that "the weaknesses evident in the LSC will not be corrected simply by changing the [national] board."

Klingman comments that the disagreement over LSC's continued existence was "a national debate fought well beyond the halls of Congress." It roused the passions of lawyers, editorial boards, conservatives, liberals, congressmen, and senators. Meanwhile, ABA President Smith was receiving letters, both opposing and supporting his efforts to save the LSC. Moreover, the correspondence for and against the LSC was not divisible into Republicans and Democrats, or those having a liberal or conservative bias. Regardless of the thrust of the letters, Smith replied to each one, explaining his position and that of the ABA.

In Smith's home town, a local television station — WTVT — opposed the ABA in supporting continuation of the LSC, arguing that alternatives for providing legal services to the poor existed. Ray Dantzler, WTVT's Director of Public Affairs, said on the air that "good motives don't justify using [taxpayer's] money for activities they may not approve of," adding "there are other ways of assuring legal help … including a voucher system…." Smith responded, noting that the idea of vouchers would be "far more expensive" than continuation of the LSC and that, moreover, the LSC legal services program should be the foundation upon which voluntary, private lawyer *pro bono* programs should be based.

Smith repeatedly heard the charge, especially from lawyers representing municipal and local governments, that LSC-funded legal service agencies pushed "social issues" at the expense of resolving legal issues of the poor. In responding to one such complaint, Smith wrote:

> For ten years I served as City Attorney [for Tampa] and I have defended cases brought against the City by federally funded attorneys, including some related to the operation of our municipal court and our city jail. The cases aggravated me then but I cannot say that they were without merit, especially since I lost some of them.

Many opponents of the LSC wrote Smith expressing their belief that it was the private bar's obligation to provide legal services to the poor, not that of the federal government. In a reply to one such letter, Smith noted that the private bar had tried to respond to the legal needs of poor people through voluntary efforts for nearly seventy-five years, but that effort had been largely unsuccessful, given the numbers of economically disadvantaged Americans needing the services and given the comparatively fewer lawyers willing (or able) to donate professional skills and time on a *pro bono* basis. Though Smith believed it was every lawyer's professional obligation to be involved in *pro bono* legal services, many within the legal profession did not do so.

Announcement; Reaction

In early 1980, the social and political debates hit a wall of reality. The new administration made its intention clear—the LSC must go. Shortly after taking office, President Reagan and Attorney General Meese publically called for the dismantlement of the LSC as part of Reagan's promise to sharply cut the federal budget. The official announcement was made on March 10, 1981. Having anticipated the news, Smith (as ABA President) had earlier in March sent a statement to the media under the headline: "ABA President Calls for Continuation of Legal Services Corporation." The announcement proclaimed: "We are deeply disappointed by the President's reported recommendation to eliminate the Federal program providing legal service for the poor," adding, "we regret the President's decision." In his statement Smith declared that the administrations's plan "was unwise and not in the nations's best interest."

After the government's announcement was released, Smith held a press conference in Washington, D.C., where leaders of the California, Florida, Los Angeles, Maryland, Michigan, New York City, New York State, Pennsylvania, Philadelphia, and Wisconsin bars joined him. Smith and the ten other state and city bar leaders stood together in a show of unity in opposing the abolishment of the LSC. Speaking to the media, the bar representatives made it clear that they strongly disagreed with the Reagan administration's proposal to dismantle the LSC, thereby eliminating its public service programs.

Stuart Taylor, Jr., covered the Washington, D.C. press conference for the *New York Times*. Taylor quoted ABA President Smith who told the assembled media that the Reagan administration's plan "would undermine a commitment to 'equal justice under law,' and destroy a cost-effective $321 million program that has made real progress in meeting the needs of the poor…." The *New York Times* article continued:

> Mr. Smith said that he was planning a lobbying effort in Congress to help save the independent Legal Services Corporation, which … distributes Government funds for the nation's 5,000 legal aid lawyers. [Smith] predicted that 'most leaders of the organized bar would stand united in strong support of the corporation,' Republicans as well as Democrats.

An earlier story in the *Washington Post* quoted Smith as saying that the elimination of the LSC program "in the long run would cost our society far more than any immediate dollars we may save in the short run." In the administration's official announcement, the elimination of the LSC was coupled with a suggestion that President Reagan might support replacing the program with federal "block grants" awarded to states for "social services projects." But no monies would be directly allocated for legal services though, in theory, a state might seek funds under a block grant proposal where a portion of the grant could be used in that manner. But even in the best of circumstances, monies that the federal government might designate for state or local legal aid s agencies after the demise of the LSC would be a pittance in comparison with the $300 million LSC budget.

Administration leaders speaking in favor of killing the LSC program included not only President Reagan and Attorney General Meese, but also Vice-President George Bush. The battle lines were drawn. Historian Peter Klingman describes the economic, political, and philosophic clash that was unfolding:

On one side was the 'Reagan Revolution,' meaning a conservative program of reducing the size of the federal budget while adding tax cuts to stimulate a lagging economy. On the other were those like Reece Smith who believed in the positive good the LSC program had reaped for the American poor. The battlefield was the Congress of the United States.

At the outset of the Reagan administration, many (if not a majority) of Congressional Republicans were disinclined to authorize an appropriations bill to fund the LSC further. On the other hand, Congressional Democrats were vociferous in their opposition to the planned elimination of one of their party's key social programs, which had begun with President Lyndon Johnson's "war on poverty" and continued through President Carter's administration.

Outside Congress, the two sides mustered their forces and joined the battle. Arguing that the LSC must go was the Heritage Foundation and other conservative groups. Arguing that the plight of America's poor would worsen appreciably if the LSC was dismantled were various liberal leaning organizations and some considered middle of the road, including the ABA. But a more significant battle was to be fought in the halls of Congress. Smith understood the minds that had to be changed were those members of Congress who supported the administration's plan to abolish the LSC. Smith raised his trumpet, so to speak, and gave a clarion call.

Smith Leads March on Washington

After the Reagan administration announced its intention to do away with the LSC, Smith worked furiously in a lobbying campaign in an effort to defeat the administration's proposal. Near the end of March, he flew to the Capital to testify on behalf of saving the LSC before the House Judiciary Subcommittee on Courts, Civil Liberties and the Administration of Justice, chaired by Representative Kastenmeier, a Democrat from Wisconsin.

On another front, Smith convinced scores of private and public service lawyers to rearrange their schedules to travel to Washington to take part in the LSC lobbying effort on April 1, 1981. His efforts succeeded in gathering over one hundred bar leaders, representing some three hundred bar associations, "to march on Washington" and "to descend on Congress." They not only lobbied individual Congressmen, they also testified before Congressional panels.

The effort began with the ABA's breakfast for LCS supporters. Among those attending were House Representatives Rodino (D-New Jersey), chair of the

House Judiciary Committee and sponsor of a bill to continue funding the LCS for three years; Kastenmeiner (D-Wisconsin); Railsback (R-Illinois), ranking minority member of the House Judiciary Subcommittee on the Courts, Civil Liberties and Administration of Justice; and Senator DeConcini (D-Arizona), member of the Senate Judiciary Committee.

The bar leaders and LSC supporters divided into small groups to canvas the Hill. For three days they met with scores of members of Congress. Among those Smith personally met with was Senator Strom Thurmond of South Carolina. Smith recalls that Senator Thurmond's "welcome was less then warm until," Smith adds, "I told him I was a graduate of the University of South Carolina; though I did not win his vote, I believe he remained silent during the Senate debates."

Besides lobbying Congress, LSC supporters had a wider audience to address. Under Smith's guidance, the ABA's professional staff began to mobilize and co-ordinate the efforts of the nation's organized bar to lobby for the continuation of the LSC. A first concern was organizing an effective communications campaign. Heading that effort was Gail Alexander, head of the ABA's Division of Communications. She put together a national public relations program, writing to community leaders, well-known persons in the public's consciousness, and decision-makers who had indicated their support of the LSC, asking them all to communicate with their local members of Congress to support the LSC program.

In addition, Alexander and her staff solicited editorial boards and columnists around the nation, contacting them directly, sending them press packages, and inviting them to open media conferences to inform the public that the LSC was a vital component of the American justice system, one that was accessible to all citizens regardless of economic or social circumstances. She recommended that those in the news media maximize the message in news events involving law and the American system of justice such as "Law Day" (May 1), as "a good time to make a statement on the importance of the [LSC] Corporation in our democratic system."

Besides the public relations blitz, the ABA Standing Committee on Legal Aid and Indigent Defendants lent its strong support to the public education and lobbying effort to save LSC. Its chair, Jerome Shestack (whom Smith had appointed) testified before a task force of the House Budget Committee on March 16, 1981. Shestack told House Committee:

> For millions of the poor, the Legal Services Corporation provides access to our system of justice which they would otherwise be denied. Through this program, problems which might fester and grow and require public assistance and intervention are resolved through the traditional justice system.

He also noted the overhead of the LSC was "less than three percent," noting that "attorney salaries averaged $14,971 a year." The LSC programs, he said, have been "extremely innovative in using the services of non-lawyer paralegals, in developing standardized pleadings, in streamlining intake and interview procedures, and in otherwise increasing the cost-effectiveness of their operations."

Shestack prepared a report showing that an estimated 30 million poor people resided in the United States in 1980, far too many to have access to needed legal services if only to be furnished by private bar volunteers. The report noted that many of the legal disputes poor people had involved public officials and that it was unrealistic to expect those same officials to fund legal aid programs that might enable citizens to sue public officials. Finally, the report emphasized that only fifteen percent of all the cases that came into LSC offices around the country went to trial. This was especially significant because, in 1980, the ABA estimated that LSC offices handled approximately 1.5 million cases.

Smith and ABA Presidents Send Letter to Congress

Smith prepared a letter to be sent to all members of Congress, asking each to support the continuation of the LSC and its funding. The ABA staff sent the letter to all former ABA presidents from 1960 onward, asking each who was eligible, (i.e., not a member of the judiciary) to sign. Besides Smith, the signers (in order of their presidencies from 1960 through 1981) were: Whitney North Seymour, Edward Kuhn, Earl Morris, William Gossett, Bernard Segal, Leon Jaworski, Robert Meserve, Chesterfield Smith, James Fellers, Lawrence Walsh, Justin Stanley, William Spann, Jr., Shepherd Tate, and Leonard Janofsky. The ABA sent the letter to every member of Congress. The letter urged Congress to fund the LSC and explained why. It read in part:

> Convinced that our state and local governments cannot and will not step in to continue to assure the disadvantaged access to our judicial system, and satisfied that depriving them of such access would be unjust and unwise, we ask that you authorize the continuation of the Legal Services Corporation with adequate funding to perform its assigned tasks.

In response to the ABA media campaign, the federal Office of Management and Budget (OMB) released a paper of its counsel, David Horowitz. In it, Horowitz not only attacked the LSC, he also made complaints about the ABA and the private bar:

It is difficult to understand how a practicing bar whose gross annual income in 1977 exceeded $19 billion cannot substantially support a legal services program it admittedly is obligated to provide.... [The bar] exercises its responsibility by lobbying for federal funds rather than by doing it themselves.

Perhaps the most significant aspect of the communications and public relations effort of the ABA was an op-ed piece Smith himself provided for national distribution to the nation's media. Describing the proposal to abolish the LSC as "unsound, unwise and not in this nation's best interest," Smith quickly got to the heart of the matter:

The pledge of allegiance reads "with liberty and justice for all," not just for those who can afford it.... Access to the legal system is access to justice. And it is our collective responsibility to ensure that this fundamental right is protected for every American.... Elimination of [the LSC] program, which provides legal representation to millions of our nations's disadvantaged citizens, would, in the long run, cost this nation far more than any immediate dollars we may save.

Smith concluded his op-ed piece by declaring the ABA believes the LSC "deserves and needs the continued support of every citizen. It should be strengthened, not eliminated." His message promoting both private and public legal aid to the poor appeared in newspapers throughout the country. His views were acclaimed by a majority of the editorial responses to his article, while criticized by a few. The editorials came from the *Juneau Empire* in Alaska to the *Miami Herald* in Florida. Moreover, the political spectrum of support came from the conservative *Manchester Union Leader* in New Hampshire to the liberal *St. Petersburg Times* in Florida.

Meanwhile, Attorney General Meese continued the attack on the private bar in a commencement address at Widener University, chastising private attorneys for their reluctance to handle cases for the poor. He then turned to the ABA:

I frankly think the American Bar Association is abdicating its responsibility to encourage private practitioners of the law to contribute some of their time and some of their support to legal services. I think this is a very shortsighted and limited view of legal services that we have to tax the taxpayers to provide legal services to the poor.

The Attorney General was mistaken in his assertion that private lawyers were not serving the poor. Smith stressed that, in the short span of three years, over 2,000 legal clinics providing legal services to the poor had opened in the country.

After becoming ABA President, Smith led the expansion of its private-bar activation program (discussed in next chapter), including the establishment of prototype legal services offices in five American cities. In Smith's view, for Meese to state that the ABA was shortsighted and had a very limited view of legal services was outright wrong. Meese's charge that the ABA was "abdicating its responsibility" in failing to support the private bar's involvement in legal services to the poor was as well. Smith acknowledged private lawyers were not doing enough in rendering *pro bono* services, but the Reagan administration's contention that the private bar *alone* could solve the problem of legal services for the poor was unrealistic. Smith and others—including Hillary Rodham Clinton—pointed out that, even with the LSC existing programs, together with state and local private bar programs utilizing volunteer lawyers, the numbers of poor people being adequately served was small in comparison with the need. More was needed.

Arizona attorney John Robb wrote Smith that the LSC was unlikely to survive unless it was given both increased financial support and increased supervision from the organized bar. Robb suggested important policy making decisions required a strong supervisory role by the ABA through "substantial representation on the Board of Directors of the Legal Services Corporation." Robb suggested that Smith, as the ABA President, along with officials of the LSC, push members of Congress to authorize increased ABA oversight of the agency, which might increase Congressional support for continuing to fund the LSC program.

During this period, over 300 state, county, and municipal bar associations passed resolutions calling for the saving of the LSC. Many endorsements underscored Smith's point that efforts of the private bar to meet the need for legal services in voluntarily in a *pro bono* fashion had been woefully unsuccessful, especially in light of the great numbers in need of legal assistance.

In addition to support from the media and organized bar, more than fifty national organizations wrote letters to endorse the ABA position, including the League of Women Voters, the Children's Defense Fund, the AFL-CIO, the International Association of Machinists and Aerospace Workers, the National Council of Churches, the National Association of Counties, the American Civil Liberties Union, the United States Conference of Mayors, the League of United Latin American Citizens, the National Mental Health Association, and the National Farmers League. The pressure was mounting for LSC's survival, and Congress was responding.

By June 1981, the struggle to save the LSC was nearing closure. The fight had taken a large amount of Smith's time and effort during his presidency. At the August 1981 annual meeting of the ABA, Robert Raven, Chair of the ABA's Committee on Legal Aid and Indigent Defendants, passed out a memo to the delegates describing the LSC fight for survival. Raven noted that Smith had warned them the struggle "is not a race for the short winded." Raven continued:

> [T]he persistent and diligent actions of the organized bar has made an enormous difference and have been recognized and praised by the decision-makers, the press and the public. The bar has brought the issue to the point that we can begin to see the light at the end of the tunnel.

The LSC Is Saved

Although the LSC was on the road of being saved, in what form and with what level of support remained in doubt. The Reagan administration and Congress would exact a price, a very big price. LSC would have its funding drastically scaled back and would have Congressionally-imposed restrictions on the kinds of legal matters it could bring to court. That is exactly what happened.

In June 1981, members of House debated proposed H.B. 3480, a law that would authorize continuation of the LSC for two years, but at a funding level not to exceed $241 million—a significant reduction from LSC's then $300 million plus budget. Moreover, LSC lawyers would be prohibited from filing class action law suits, lobbying, and on handling suits in support of controversial social policies such as abortion or gay rights. Certainly, the legislation was not what Smith or the ABA favored, but it did enable the LSC to continue serving poor people in the delivery of needed legal services.

Concluding that the House bill probably was the best to be expected, Smith sent a widely distributed letter to Congress on June 10th, in which he acknowledged he did not favor all of the bill's provisions, but recognized it was "a responsible effort to prevent alleged abuses while ensuring the legal needs of the poor will be met." He also used the letter to counter arguments opposing passage of H.B. 3480, led by Attorney General Meese, who contented block grants should replace the LSC. Smith responded:

> The suggestion that block funds be used to meet this need is illusory. The Administration has recommended that none of the funds now provided for the LSC be used in calculating the block grant allotment to the states. This is a striking contrast to the 75% current funding approach used for most social service programs and is a clear signal to the states that this program has the lowest priority.

Following a long debate, the House passed H.B. 3480, but the danger to the LSC was not over as President Reagan threatened to veto the bill. Moreover, the Senate had its own ideas. A pending Senate bill—S.B. 1533—authorized the continued existence of LSC for three years, but at a funding level of only $100 million, a 70 percent reduction compared with the Corporation's 1981 budget. Such a drastic cut in Congressional funding was an enormous concern to those favoring a strong and effective LSC. Many believed that if the Senate measure became the law, the nation's legal services for the poor would take an enormous hit.

Yet, from the perspective of LSC proponents, it turned out the final resolution was not as bad as it could have been. In any event, the Corporation was going to survive, though its programs would be sharply reduced.

In the Fall of 1981, a compromise between the House and Senate bills was reached when the conferees agreed on the House prescribed appropriation of $241 million, still a significant reduction from the Corporation's current budget. Once it became clear that Congress was re-authorizing the LSC, President Ronald Reagan backed off his veto threat. At the end of the day, the Legal Services Corporation had been saved. After the LSC was saved by Congress, President Reagan effectively took over executive control by appointing board members sympathetic to the administration's views that LSC activities should be curtailed.

Later, Smith and Elizabeth Diane Clark, one of his administrative assistants at the ABA, co-authored a paper titled "The Quest for Equal Justice." In describing the history of legal services to the poor in America, they noted that the Reagan appointees to the LSC board put in place "reforms" that "placed restrictions" on the scope of legal services the Corporation's attorneys could engage in and "which put field programs under often unfriendly scrutiny." The authors continued:

> [O]ne salutary result of the attacks on the Corporation is that the private bar and the professional poverty law community came together in a common cause to shore up and defend legal services ... With the loss of [LSC] funds, voluntary legal aid became even more imperative. In response, the [ABA] committed a half million dollars to enhance private bar involvement in providing legal services to the poor.

In a speech two years after leaving the ABA presidency, Smith observed that, with the critical reduction in funding, "the Corporation programs—and, consequently the poor—suffered throughout the country." Overall, the LSC's programs lost an estimated 30 percent of their staff positions. The Chicago Legal Assistance Foundation alone "lost $1 million in funding and was forced to eliminate twenty-five attorney positions and to reduce staff in its neighborhood offices."

The sharply lower funding for the LSC created both a problem and an opportunity for Smith when he was drawing near the end of his presidency of the ABA. The problem was that funding derailment sharply reduced LSC's capability to furnish legal services to the poor at the levels that had evolved during the administration of President Carter. The opportunity was the increased awareness that the gap must be filled by bringing in thousands of private lawyers in what became known as private bar involvement projects—both sponsored by the ABA and through the LSC itself.

Regarding the Corporation's use of private attorneys, Smith found himself in the center of a debate over *the extent* to which LSC field grants should be directed to private attorneys as mandated by the Congressional funding resolution placing conditions on LSC grants. The question centered on what the percentage of congressionally appropriated LSC funds should be directed to private lawyers in order to fulfill the resolution's mandate that the private bar have a "substantial involvement in providing legal services to the poor."

The original proposal was to notify each LSC project director that 10% of the grant allocated to that project had to be used to pay private lawyers for their service contributions. But others within the Reagan administration and on the LSC board, as well as many within the organized bar itself, wanted the amount to be at least 15 to 20%, a proportion that would further cut back full time LSC project lawyers and staff. Smith and other supporters of the LSC believed this would diminish the overall level and quality of legal services to the poor in the United States. In time, the LSC settled on a 12.5% formula, directing that percentage of each basic grant be directed to stimulate private attorney involvement in LSC programs.

The drastic cut in LSC funding, though a major disappointment for Smith, ultimately did, in Smith's view, have some salutary effects. In a speech in 1983, he remarked:

> It sensitized the private bar to the fundamental importance of the federal program. It improved the bar's credibility within the Corporation circles. And it led to significant growth in the provision of *pro bono* legal services. Thus, in late 1981, the Corporation decided to allocate 10% of each basic field grant to private attorney involvement in support of local programmatic activity.

Smith's Role in Saving the LSC

Smith did not become President of the ABA to save the LSC, but he came with his long-held conviction that equal justice for all meant equal access for all to the American legal system. The poor need legal services as much, if not more, than those who have the means to pay. Justice demands they have access to America's justice system, especially because many of their difficulties under the law involve problems with government agencies and personnel. Over time Smith became convinced that the private bar alone could not handle the caseload of the country's disenfranchised. But throughout his career, he has never wavered in his belief in and support for *pro bono* volunteer legal services.

At the outset of his ABA presidency, Smith's primary goal was to develop greater private bar involvement in legal services to the poor. Still, he came to realize that the LSC also must be preserved. What caused him to see that the private bar and the LSC had to work together was recognition that the need for justice for the poor was far greater than the private sector could fulfill. In no way did this mean Smith became less promotive of volunteer *pro bono* services furnished by the private bar. To the contrary, with a better understanding of the breath of the problem involving access to legal services, Smith had no doubt that the private bar and the public LSC had to *work together*, that both private and public involvement and cooperation was indispensable if the goal of equal access to justice in America was to be realized.

The fight to save LSC took much of Smith's time while ABA President. Coming as it did at the apex of Smith's career-long commitment to promote equal justice to all the poor, historian Klingman believes the battle to save the LSC "defined Smith's presidency of the ABA," adding "it stretches the truth to claim that Reece single handedly 'saved the LSC,' [but] *it is the truth that he was the most vocal, most visible, most powerful lobbyist and advocate to take part in the fray. Few others could have pulled it off.*" [Emphasis added.]

In the Summer of 1981, Howard Eisenberg, Executive Director of the National Legal Aid and Defender Association, wrote Smith a thank-you letter. It reads in part:

> I anticipate that once the future of the Corporation is clear and the legislative fight ended, there will be many people claiming credit for the effort. There is no question in my mind, however, but that you are the single person most responsible for saving the LSC. While many have worked night and day to assure the continuation of the LSC, your moral leadership and persuasion, combined with your ability to activate the Bar, is what put us over the top.

Once again, Reece Smith—this time as President of the most prestigious organization of lawyers in the world—won another battle in his career-long efforts to make legal aid available for poor Americans by working for the survival of the LSC. But the story is not yet complete. The next chapter, among other issues, examines his work as ABA President in expanding the role of the private bar in furnishing *pro bono* volunteer legal assistance to those who are unable to pay.

* * *

CHAPTER SEVENTEEN

President of the ABA: Part Two

The ABA Private Bar Activation Project

In 1979, after becoming President-Elect of the ABA, Smith urged the LSC to make a $50,000 grant to the ABA to fund a "*Pro Bono* Activation Project." Smith had decided this would be his "ABA presidency's project." The grant was intended to encourage the ABA to promote and assist new *pro bono* projects to be developed through state and local bar organizations.

Smith's promotion of the ABA's *Pro Bono* Activation Program within the geographically scattered and politically diverse organization was a daunting undertaking, one that engendered resistance from several levels. Many ABA members opposed the Association's participation in any legal aid assistance to private bar programs, with or without LSC involvement. Moreover, some went further and sided with the Reagan Administration's desire to abolish the LSC. As to most members, Smith said: "Likely, the majority of the ABA members in 1980 was indifferent to the ABA's a *pro bono* activation project," adding, "it was of little concern to them one way or another."

Meanwhile, the active proponents for legal services, though dedicated to the cause, were divided on how best to go about meeting the need. Smith was well aware of the different points of view among LSC staff on the one hand, and ABA proponents of private bar *pro bono* legal services on the other, concerning what direction the legal services movement should take.

As ABA President, Smith understood that leadership, discussion, and vision were required to bring the entrenched and divergent viewpoints to a workable consensus. To this end, he invited persons of differing views to come to Chicago and thrash out the issues. In addition to LSC leaders, various officials and staff members of the ABA attended along with representatives of various interested groups, notably leaders of the National Legal Aid and Defenders Association (NLADA).

The guests came to Chicago with cautious expectations. Still, several of the LSC project directors felt they could not support Smith's proposal to institute a *Pro Bono* private involvement bar activation program. At least one person expressed a concern that, should the ABA be successful in its pilot activation programs, Congress might be less willing to continue funding the LSC budget at its current level. Should that happen, it would cause serious harm to the entire LSC organization and its national efforts.

The LSC representatives had other concerns as well. Many staff attorneys questioned the educational qualifications, levels of commitment, requisite skills, and degrees of knowledge regarding poverty law that volunteer *pro bono* lawyers representing poor clients would need to carry out their mission successfully. Some suggested that one reason volunteer lawyers might give a lower level of service was because *pro bono* representation would be a part-time undertaking, one not engendering the same commitment that lawyers directed toward their bread and butter paying clients. Consequently, the argument continued, private bar *pro bono* volunteers on the whole likely would expend less effort on non-paying clients than on those who paid for legal services and who, more likely, would continue to be clients of these lawyers.

Aware of these concerns, and expecting a somewhat cool reception from many of the LSC representatives with regard to the ABA Private Bar Activation Program, Smith decided to hold the conference not at the ABA headquarters, but at a location "removed" outside the ABA headquarters. He believed it would be more conducive for open, frank, and candid discussions. Smith accordingly held the meeting at the Hyatt Regency Hotel in Chicago.

The meeting convened on the morning of July 12, 1980. To the surprise of some of the proponents of greater involvement of private attorneys in *pro bono* work, LSC representatives stated that the Corporation did not oppose *any* increase of part-time volunteer lawyers rendering legal assistance to the poor. To the contrary: the LSC wanted to encourage private lawyers to become involved, but only if they did so under the agency's guidance. Harriet Ellis, an LSC official at the time, brought to the Chicago meeting a plan for disseminating information about a *pro bono* project to bar associations and other groups within the profession. Included was a manual LSC had drafted that was intended to assist private bar lawyers in efficiently providing legal assistance, with LSC acting as advisor.

For the most part, the discussions were frank, open, candid, and cordial. When it became Smith's turn to speak, he emphasized that he intended "to activate and stimulate" the private bar in getting more involved in furnishing *pro bono* legal aid services. Smith reminded the attendees there never would be enough money to meet all the needs of the poor, and that every lawyer, therefore, had a professional responsibility to volunteer time and effort for legal services to the less fortunate members of society. Smith made it clear that he certainly did not oppose LSC projects, but stressed the private bar "has a responsibility in providing legal services as well."

In line with this philosophy, President Smith pushed the further development of the ABA *Pro Bono* Activation Project. Prior to going on "the speaking circuit," he drafted "a personal letter" that accompanied the ABA manuals, which were sent to hundreds of recipients. In the letter, Smith enlisted the recipient's support for the Private Bar Activation Project. Among the organizations, groups, and private lawyers receiving Smith's letter were the NAACP Legal Defense Fund and various minority bar associations. These included the National Bar Association and the National Clients Council. Several organizations responded expressing interest in the Activation Project. They asked for assistance in various ways, ranging from advice on how to reduce costs of legal services, how to expand existing programs and implement new ones, and how to raise funds. Clearly, interest in the ABA *Pro Bono* Activation Project was growing.

Meanwhile, LSC planned to allocate a large sum of money for private attorney *pro bono* programs. Its solicitation for proposals indicated the LSC expected to fund twenty projects that would increase the level of legal services provided by private attorneys, and improve the quality of those services by enhancing the working relationship between the LSC's clients and the private bar. Not surprisingly, dissension arose over how the monies were to be allocated around the country and to what ends. Within the ABA itself, some advocated support for national conferences on delivering legal services to the poor, while others wanted to channel all the monies to local legal services agencies to assist in their funding needs.

Dan Bradley, President of LSC, wrote Smith: "This common effort must not be disrupted by divisive arguments over who gets the money." Bradley and the LSC wanted funds to be directed to local offices, pointing out that this approach had worked in the past and changing it would disrupt delivery systems already in place. On the other hand, Smith and other ABA officials favored a national focus, putting on regional conferences and sending "crisis intervention teams" to local problems in need or upon request, thereby expanding the project. After an exhausting and detailed analytic LSC study of various methods of providing legal services, the Corporation concluded that it should encourage the development of various creative approaches to the problem, and that the success of the effort "depends on the continued support and cooperation of the organized bar."

ABA Pilot *Pro Bono* Programs

Chicago lawyer Ruth Ann Schmitt, an executive at Chicago Volunteer Legal Services, was temporarily hired by the ABA to be its *Pro Bono* Activation Project Coordinator and to assist Smith in developing pilot activation programs. Understanding the competing views of providing legal services, she proposed a compromise that addressed the objectives of both the LSC and the ABA, one that envisioned creating a minimum of five (and ideally as many as fifteen) new *pro bono* projects within one year. These pilot programs would be in addition to continuing ABA regional programs, conferences, and assisting existing legal aid agencies.

Initially, it was assumed the ABA would seek funding for the new pilot projects from the LSC. But, of course, that would create "political problems" and raise the issues that existed between LSC staff and ABA officials. Instead, Schmitt suggested the seed money come from the ABA's General Fund. She estimated the budget for the ABA program for the 1980–81 fiscal year would require $140,000. Smith concurred in her judgment.

In September 1980, Smith asked the ABA's Board for the monies needed to implement the *pro bono* pilot programs. Smith noted with frankness the tensions that existed between the LSC and the ABA over funding. After outlining the history of the relationship, Smith emphasized these tensions had to be reduced by the ABA leadership through the ABA's private bar activation *pro bono* programs working together with LSC federal programs. He noted that many groups were ready and willing to participate in the effort, including the various groups forming the ABA's Consortium on Legal Services. These included the Association's Young Lawyer's Division and its Sections on Litigation and General Practice, as well as the *Pro Bono* Activation Project staff. Smith said that his proposal would be carried out "with full cooperation with these and other interested agencies."

Meanwhile, Ruth Ann Schmitt coordinated development of the proposed programs with help from bar associations throughout the country that had expressed interest in sponsoring *pro bono* private attorney projects. She hoped that as many as a dozen might become involved. Due to financial realities, however, the number would be more limited.

In late 1980, the ABA Board of Governors authorized $100,000 seed money to initiate five pilot *pro bono* projects in the cities of Austin, Baltimore, Duluth, Honolulu, and Portland. Each had been awarded a $20,000 ABA grant. The programs proved successful. Smith made it a point to travel to each of the five cities to acknowledge the success of their respective pilot program. He repeated his maxim to the lawyers and staff at the Austin program: "The legal profession does not exist for its members to get rich, it exists to serve."

But not all agreed with Smith's philosophy that lawyers individually, or the bar association collectively, had any responsibility to assure *pro bono* service. Some ABA members firmly opposed the use of their dues to fund the pilot projects. A Seattle lawyer opined the ABA should not underwrite *pro bono* legal services any more than businesses did so. "Why don't you write a letter to the banks," he asked Smith, "and ask them to give away their money to other people?" He ended by saying the ABA program was "nuts" and he was cancelling his ABA membership. Smith responded:

> Thank you for your letter.... As you point out, banks, airlines, and groceries do not give away that which they sell to the pubic. I do, however, think that ministers, doctors and lawyers are a bit different than businessmen. We are members of professions whose traditions include service to the less fortunate. I think we should honor those traditions and that it benefits us as well as the public to do so....

In 1996, Smith spoke at the fifteenth anniversary of the Hawaii Lawyers Care program that had started up as an ABA pilot program in 1981. Smith praised the leaders of the Hawaii group, especially the volunteer lawyers who had given, and continued to give, of their time and talents without compensation. He told his audience that when he became the ABA President in 1980, *pro bono* programs involving private lawyers were few and far between. In contrast, "today in 1996," Smith said, "the number of these programs is no longer fifty. It is around 950, and some 150,000 private lawyers are engaged throughout America in organized *pro bono* work." Describing the Hawaii Lawyers Care organization as a pioneer *pro bono* program, he said that it "has served as a model and challenge for the *pro bono* programs that later developed."

Not long following Smith's presidency, the ABA Private Bar Involvement Project came under the supervision of the ABA Consortium on Legal Services and the Public. Shortly after taking office, the ABA president who succeeded Smith appointed him as the Consortium's chair. Smith served for six years, during which he continued to meet bar officials and give speeches around the country on the necessity of providing *pro bono* legal services to the poor. While chair of the ABA Consortium, Smith each year prepared a report that described the development and growth the private bar's involvement in rendering legal services to economically disadvantaged citizens.

While ABA President, Smith oversaw the integration and cooperation of public and private lawyer involvement in the rendering of legal assistance to the poor. He attributes this success to "scores of dedicated men and women" both within and outside the ABA. One, mentioned earlier, was Ruth Ann Schmitt, the ABA *pro bono* coordinator during a portion of his presidency. Smith says this about her contribution: "Ruth Ann came to the ABA at a time of critical need and gave life and direction to our *pro bono publico* activities."

Pro Bono: Mandatory or Not?

Increasing the quality and availability of legal services to the poor was and remains a career-long occupation of Reece Smith. When President-Elect and then President of the ABA, Smith spoke out at every opportunity concerning a lawyer's *ethical* and *professional* obligation of public service, repeatedly declaring that voluntary *pro bono* work on behalf of the poor is an ethical responsibility of members of a learned profession.

Shortly after becoming ABA President, Smith told a reporter for the *Daily Oklahoman*: "Eliciting more *pro bono* work from the legal profession will be one of my top priorities." Speaking at an Anaheim, California conference on *pro bono* activity, he declared: "Meeting the legal needs of the poor is both a public and a professional responsibility.... Legal aid is not the domain either of full-time poverty lawyers or of the private bar. All are lawyers with an ethical duty to serve [and] all are needed. None [of us] should be excluded." In a media interview after becoming ABA President, Smith said: "As members of the legal profession and as members of a learned profession, we owe a higher duty than the average citizen, and one of these [is] the assurance that legal services and justice are available to all. It is my personal belief that all lawyers should be willing to give of their time for *pro bono* work ... [It] should be a commitment of every lawyer."

Smith repeatedly stated his belief that a person within a learned profession has the obligation to serve not only those who can pay for professional services, but also those who cannot. In an address as ABA President to Chicago Volunteer Legal Services Foundation in September 1981, he chastised lawyers who "do not care about their professional obligation to serve poor people." Some lawyers, Smith noted, may be excused because they are struggling to survive financially, but many "are simply too calloused or too busy or too thoughtless" to volunteer any portion of their professional services. He lamented that "far too many see a career in law solely as a money-making enterprise. In doing so, they disserve their country and their profession." Smith exclaimed: "We must put our money where our mouth is, or stop calling ourselves members of a learned professional ... though most lawyers would agree that public service is the hallmark of professionalism, all too many pay only lip service to that concept."

Whether the best way to accomplish this should be through mandating *pro bono* service, or by encouraging purely volunteer service on the basis of ethical and professional considerations, was a troublesome issue. In January 1980, the ABA's blue-ribbon Kutak Commission on the Evaluation of Professional Standards, circulated a discussion draft of its proposed Model Rules of Professional Conduct, which were intended to replace the existing ABA Code of Professional Responsibility. The Commission had begun its work in 1977, and was chaired by Robert J. Kutak, a distinguished Omaha attorney. The Kutak 1980 draft report engendered vigorous debate as soon as it was released, in part because of its proposed Rule 8.1, which would mandate a public interest service obligation for all practicing lawyers, a rule that has been described as one of the "most controversial features of the new rules."

But the national bar was not the only group to float the idea. The same month the Kutak draft was circulated, the President of the City Bar of New York appointed a committee to consider making *pro bono* service mandatory for lawyers practicing in the city. One member of the New York City Bar special committee, Steven Rosenfeld, cautioned that "serious controversy was to be expected."

A few months after the Kutak Commission released its proposed rules, Smith was sworn in as the ABA President and found himself in a firestorm. The issue of increasing *pro bono* representation of the poor through greater involvement of private bar attorneys was, of course, a top priority for Smith in his leadership of the ABA. But for the ABA to approve new rules declaring the service to be mandatory was further than he wished to go, both due to practical and philosophical concerns.

Smith disagreed with the initial recommendation of the Kutak Commission that *pro bono* be mandatory, partly because he considered it impractical to implement, and also because he believed a lawyer rendering public service to the poor was an *ethical* obligation resulting from membership in a learned profession, and that the compulsion to render service comes from the heart and soul of professionalism, not from some external edict. As he told law students at the University of Chicago: "I am not a strong advocate of mandatory *pro bono* because I don't think you can make people do things they don't want to do. Rather, we need to teach young persons coming into the profession that *pro bono* is part of their professional commitment."

In an article Smith wrote for *The Alabama Lawyer*, he urged law schools and law firms to teach young lawyers that *pro bono* work is part of the great tradition of professional responsibility within the American legal profession. In the article, he declared: "I regard *pro bono* work as part of the obligation of every learned profession, and I am still old-fashioned enough to think that I am a member of a learned profession." About the same time, he spoke at the annual meeting of the Georgia State Bar Association, telling his audience that if lawyers volunteer to help the poor "because they want to rather than because they have to, [the poor] will be better off."

During Smith's presidency, the Kutak Commission reversed its position on mandatory *pro bono* service. As reported in the January 1981 issue of the *American Bar Association Journal,* the chair of the ABA Commission on Evaluation of Professional Standards conceded that "the time for mandatory *pro bono* hasn't come." Instead, the Commission planned to rewrite its proposal to suggest that attorneys "should" render public interest legal service. In a December 1980 letter to local bar presidents, state chief justices, and the board of governors of the ABA, Kutak wrote:

> Many lawyers oppose the [mandatory] concept on practical, philo-
> sophical and political grounds, although they remain pledged as in-
> dividuals to the profession's long-standing commitment to the public
> service and to the legal assistance to the indigent.

The debate over whether *pro bono* legal services should be mandatory continued long after Smith's ABA presidency had ended, sometimes taking a different form. In 1989, a group of Florida lawyers—including Smith—petitioned the Court to change the rules governing The Florida Bar so as to recognize the right of litigants in civil cases to have the assistance of counsel, regardless of their economic circumstances. By signing the petition, Smith signaled that his stand years earlier against any form of mandatory *pro bono* had softened. The drafter of the petition was Talbot "Sandy" D'Alemberte, a prominent Florida lawyer (and later President of the ABA, Dean of Florida State University College of Law and, subsequently, President of the University).

D'Alemberte based the petition upon the judiciary's "the-rules-of-court" inherent power. He suggested that courts, "through their court rules, should become directly involved in solving the problem of legal services to the poor." The petition, however, was denied.

Though the idea of mandatory public service for lawyers seemed to be defeated, not so in the case of law students. Not long after Smith was ABA President, a few law schools began to incorporate a public service component into their curricula as a requirement for students for the J.D. degree. Tulane Law School in New Orleans may have been the first school to have done so, in the mid 1980s, followed by Valparaiso University Law School in Indiana in 1988. In 1996, the ABA amended its standards for approval applicable to American law schools "to encourage students to participate in *pro bono* activities and to provide opportunities for them to so."

Over the past two decades, the number of schools requiring that their students volunteer a certain minimum number of hours each year to public service has grown appreciably. Smith applauds this development and hopes the experience instills a greater sensitivity in law students for the poor and disadvantaged. He believes that *every* law student should learn about the legal profession's long tradition of providing volunteer *pro bono* legal assistance, and how that tradition has evolved and expanded. This is why, Smith points out, he has been teaching a law school course on professional responsibility and legal ethics in a Tampa area law school beginning in 1991 and continuing for nineteen years.

Lawyer Ethics and Professional Responsibility

In addition to tackling the issue of whether a lawyer's professional obligations should extend to mandatory *pro bono* services to the poor, the Kutak Commission's 1980 draft rules covering other controversial subjects. They included the extent and circumstances of a lawyer's duty to disclose a client's crime, fraud or perjury; a lawyer's ethical duties in connection with whistle-blowing; problems of lawyer neglect and discipline; and issues regarding the reporting of lawyer misconduct. These topics and others were debated throughout Smith's presidency, both within the ABA and among state and local bar associations.

Smith kept fully informed about the Kutak Commission's deliberations and differences of opinion regarding the language and meaning of the rules. He understood that the evolution and refinement of the professional rules for conduct is an on-going and desirable process. At an ABA workshop on disciplining lawyers for misconduct, Smith once said: "We must refine our discipline and enforcement ability [while] we must also refine the standards against which the conduct of lawyers is to be measured."

One of the problems debated during Smith's presidency was a proposed requirement that a lawyer disclose a client's crime, fraud, or perjury. The 1969 Disciplinary Rule 4-10(C) declared that "a lawyer *may* reveal ... the intention of his client to commit a crime and information necessary to *prevent the crime.*" On the other hand, one proposal read: "A lawyer who receives information that clearly establishes his client has [in the course of the lawyer's representation] perpetrated a fraud upon a person or tribunal shall promptly call upon the client to rectify the same, and if his client refuses or is unable to do so, he *shall reveal the fraud* to the affected tribunal or person."

Some were concerned that this requirement might seriously interfere with the lawyer-client privileged relationship, not only by undermining confidentiality but also by putting the lawyer in a potential adversary position to his or her clients as a result of competing obligations. Some lawyers suggested that a lawyer's duty to disclose prospective fraud or criminal act was absolute, while other lawyers argued an absolute obligation to reveal such matters was overly broad, suggesting it would always trump lawyers' other ethical obligations, including maintaining confidentiality.

When Smith was ABA President, the Commission attempted to fix the flaws in the old Model Rules by changing two concepts: first, by making it clear that a lawyer's obligation to disclose misconduct is not properly connected to the prohibition on assisting unlawful conduct and, second, by stating that the discretionary power to disclose information arises solely from the nature of the conduct and is not limited to the nature of the potential harm. The Commission's new proposed rule at that time provided:

> Confidentiality of Information:
> A lawyer *may* reveal such information to the extent the lawyer reasonably believes necessary.... to *prevent* the *client* from committing a *criminal or fraudulent act* that the lawyer reasonably believes is *likely* to result in *death or substantial bodily harm*, or in substantial injury to the financial interests or property of another. (Emphasis added.)

This reformulation of the rule was adopted and the proposal that a lawyer has absolute obligation to disclosure any knowledge or belief of potential criminal or fraudulent acts of a client did not prevail.

A related problem involved the Kutak Commission's 1981 revision of the "Whistle-Blowing" provision of the Model Rules, which limited the circumstances under which a lawyer may reveal information relating to the representation of an organization. The proposed change in the rules provided that a lawyer shall proceed as is reasonably necessary in the best interest of the organization, even in the face of improper conduct by an officer or employee. Upon failure of the highest authority of the organization to act, the lawyer *may* reveal information if the lawyer reasonably believes that the revelation is necessary for the best interests of the organization, and that the "highest authority in the organization has acted to further the personal or financial interests of members of that authority which are in conflict with the interests of the organization."

Perhaps the most important subject the Kutak Commission addressed was that of lawyer neglect. Smith described a lawyers' neglect of duty in representing clients as the "most pervasive lawyer discipline problem" facing the legal profession. The Commission's revised Rules 1.3 and 1.4 dealt expressly with the matter of lawyer neglect of duty. Under the Kutak proposals, lawyers must act with reasonable promptness and diligence, keeping his or her clients reasonably informed about their matters by periodically up-dating them and promptly complying with reasonable requests for information. Smith noted that the reformulated rules contained a "needed specificity to relieve a source of client dissatisfaction."

Smith also was concerned about the problem of reporting lawyer misconduct, especially when the government became involved. He always has been, and remains, an outspoken advocate for the legal profession's self regulation, fighting off periodic attempts from national, state, and local governments to intrude on the profession's responsibilities. In July 1981, Smith testified before Congress against proposed regulatory rules of the Federal Trade Commission (FTC) that would alter the existing self-regulating mechanisms of the profession, especially by limiting the role of the integrated state bars and the states' highest courts in overseeing the admission and discipline of their licensed attorneys. Smith especially was concerned when the FTC announced it was considering the regulation of professions that traditionally were self-regulated or state-regulated. He urged bar members to strengthen their own disciplinary systems, underscoring the importance of a peer review system, one in which attorneys "perceived to have professional shortcomings might be referred to a peer review board by judges, clients or colleagues." In a peer-guided system, Smith said,"lawyer incompetence should be dealt with in an instructional as well as disciplinary manner."

Regarding alleged lawyer misconduct and claims of incompetency, dishonesty, and neglect, Smith was adamant that the profession itself had to confront these issues directly. He understood the standards of professional conduct needed to require lawyers to report serious misconduct within the profession. He favored the Kutak Commission's proposed revision of Disciplinary Rule 1-103, which would require a lawyer to report information about any lawyer who it is believed has violated a rule that raises "a substantial question as to that lawyer's honesty, trustworthiness, or fitness as a lawyer." Smith agreed with the Commission's explanation of Rule 1-103: "[It] limits the reporting obligation to those offenses that a self-regulating profession must vigorously endeavor to prevent." Near the end of his presidency, he told ABA representatives that he hoped the Commission's recommendations would be adopted, stating it was important that "the profession adopt a holistic set of standards which provides direct, comprehensive and concise guidance to all lawyers."

Assessment of Smith's ABA Presidency

By the time Smith's presidency ended, he had accomplished many of the goals he had outlined during his inaugural address in Sydney, Australia one year earlier. These included increasing the legal profession's and public's awareness that the legal needs of poor people in America were not being a met; his energetic and successful efforts in helping to save the Legal Services Corporation (perhaps as best evidenced by assembling and leading the march of bar leaders across the country to Washington to lobby members of Congress to save the LSC); and his implementing private bar pilot *pro bono* programs across America to increase legal aid for the poor. By the time his presidency ended, Smith admits he "was a bit tired." Understandable. He had gone non-stop for twenty-four months.

Looking back, Smith is quick to point out that he was only one among many persons involved in the success of preserving and enhancing legal aid for the poor in America. True, but to this outsider (the author), it seems indisputable that Smith's character, commitment, and competence in pursuing the goal of a just America for all took several steps forward during his presidency of the ABA.

Smith likes to tell audiences a story he once heard about a man climbing the tower of a Rotterdam church in the Netherlands. As the man scaled the steps higher and higher, he noticed changes in his perspective, observing relics of the past while seeing the joys and sorrows of the city below. Higher up on the tower he becomes aware of the tranquility of the landscape below, allowing him a glimpse of a larger world, one very different from what he saw at ground level. His understanding of the community had changed. So too, Smith's own experience changed him during his two-year term as the ABA President-Elect and then ABA President. He saw the cultural and economic landscape differently and he, in turn, made a difference in that landscape. For one thing, he saw the poor people of the city more sharply than ever before and he made the world a little more knowledgeable about their plight.

Smith Receives the ABA's Highest Award: "The Gold Medal"

When Smith talks today about what has taken place since his presidency, he points to the exponential growth of legal assistance programs in America. This phenomena in no small measure is due to his vision, leadership, and drive during the two years he served as President-Elect and President. Thereafter, Smith has continued to work for the next twenty-seven years promoting the cause of legal aid for the poor and to speak out at every opportunity in support of *pro bono* and public funded legal aid programs.

For his service on behalf of the ABA and its interests, Smith received (and continues to receive) numerous awards and recognitions. The most significant may be the "ABA Gold Medal" bestowed on him on August 8, 1989, at the ABA annual meeting, when he was President of the International Bar Association. Then ABA President Robert Raven announced that Smith was being presented

"ABA's highest honor in recognition of his exceptionally distinguished service to the cause of American Jurisprudence." An article describing Smith's honor appeared in an issue of the *International Bar News*:

> ABA President Raven presented to IBA President Reece Smith the ABA gold medal to add to his Medal of Honor from the Florida Bar Foundation, the Herbert Harley Award from the American Judicature Society, the Distinguished Alumnus Award from the University of Florida, and the Algernon S. Sullivan Award from the University of South Carolina.... The award is conferred only in years in which the ABA Board of Governors determines that there is a leader of the legal profession who has rendered conspicuous service to the cause of American justice.

Because of Smith's efforts and successes in making legal services more accessible for the poor, he became known within the ABA and organized bar as "Mr. *Pro Bono*." In 1994, he received the ABA's prestigious "*Pro Bono Publico* Award." Scores of other awards and recognitions (listed in the appendix) followed. Two awards are particularly special to Smith. The Fellows of the ABA bestowed their 2007 annual award on "William Reece Smith, Jr., in recognition of distinguished service to the public and to the legal profession." Recipients have included U.S. Senators Howard Baker, Hillary Clinton, and Howell Heflin, along with Associate Justice Lewis Powell of the U.S. Supreme Court. That same year as well, Smith was honored by the ABA Young Lawyers Section of the ABA, in recognition for his "working to better the legal profession through the organized bar and promoting the rule of law and service in the spirit of *pro bono publico*."

It is not surprising that Smith has continued to champion *pro bono* legal services long after serving as ABA president. In an interview, he explained:

> I believe it is the obligation of every learned profession to employ its skills on behalf of those in need because I'm old fashioned enough to believe that we are still members of a learned profession rather than a business. In my opinion, real progress in assisting the poor in this country began only after the LSC came into existence. Nonetheless, public-funded programs are (and never can be) sufficient in themselves. To meet the needs of the poor, ... all lawyers have a duty to participate in one way or another in assisting the delivery of legal services to those who otherwise cannot afford them.

Even at this point, Smith's work for legal aid for the poor is not yet finished. Now, Smith embraces the world.

* * *

CHAPTER EIGHTEEN

PRESIDENT, INTERNATIONAL BAR ASSOCIATION

President: County, State, National, and World Associations

A published story in 1989 described Smith as the only American lawyer "ever to preside over" a local [Hillsborough] bar association, a state [Florida] bar association, a national [American] bar association, and the International Bar Association (IBA). Also of note, he is the only American to be *elected* president of the IBA in its sixty-two year history.

Established in London in 1947, the IBA describes itself as "the world's leading organization of international legal practitioners, bar associations and law societies." It was founded to provide an international forum where representatives of *bar associations* and *law societies* around the world could come together to engage in joint projects and hold educational conferences related to the work of the organized bars. As time went on, the IBA began to admit *individual attorney lawyers* into its ranks. As a result, its focus shifted more toward private international lawyers and providing them opportunities to meet and exchange information on substantive international law practice. By 2007, the IBA membership roll consisted of approximately 200 bar associations and law societies, and nearly 30,000 individual lawyers.

Challenges and Opportunities

Smith's participation began not long after his term as ABA President ended. In the Summer of 1981, one of Smith's friends at the ABA—Gibson Gayle of Houston, then ABA representative to the IBA Council—suggested Smith consider being Gayle's successor as ABA's representative on the IBA Council. Gayle explained that if Smith accepted the position, he would become a member of the IBA's governing board. Smith found the invitation attractive, knowing he would have opportunities to develop new and interesting friendships around the globe. Thus, Smith agreed to be the ABA representative.

For the next eight years, he regularly participated in IBA Council meetings, working with lawyers and bar officials from six continents: Africa, Asia, Australia, Europe, and both North and South America. He attended his first IBA Biennial Conference in New Delhi, India, in 1982.

In the mid-1980s, Smith was elected the IBA Secretary-General. As an IBA official, he traveled around the world giving speeches. His stops included Madrid, London and Johannesburg (the first of three trips to South Africa). Then, in 1986, Smith was elected the IBA Vice President, and worked closely with its then president, Kumar Shankerdass of India. As Vice President, Smith continued to speak at IBA meetings. At one stop—Lagos—he spoke on "world peace through law." Some Nigerian generals sitting in the front row, he recalls, appeared "less then enthusiastic about my plea."

During his travels, Smith became acquainted with various IBA members in many countries, several of whom urged him to seek the IBA presidency. It would be unconventional for an American to run for the office. A U.S. citizen *never had been elected* president of the IBA. (Though the first president of the organization was an American, he was appointed.) Smith decided he would try. The contacts he had made in countries around the world turned out to be decisive. In September 1988, Smith was elected for a two-year term as President of the IBA. The position required spending considerable time at IBA headquarters in London, one of his "favorite cities."

Responding to the Bifurcated Structure of the IBA

Smith's various roles as IBA President included overseeing the IBA's organizational structure, directing its staff, coordinating and attending meetings, and working with the ruling Council. Throughout, he traveled to meetings and conferences, at which he always was asked to speak. In addition, he worked with national and local bar representatives. His travel records while IBA President reveal he flew in excess of 300,000 miles.

Besides spending time traveling, Smith had to give attention to internal matters of the organization. At that time, the IBA was a bifurcated body, consisting of two competing sub-organizations—bar association members and individual members. Smith knew that tensions existed between the two categories of members. He was further aware that the bar association members' programs did not generate income near the amount produced by the lawyer sections, whose programs attracted large numbers of individual lawyers.

In response to this situation, Smith formed a committee to review the IBA's operations in light of its original purpose—the bringing together representatives of the world's organized bar associations and law societies. After study and consultations, the Committee to Enhance the IBA Mission and Goals, as it was called, issued a report that Smith took to the IBA Council. As a result, Smith and the Council concluded that the IBA should intensify its efforts to get the bar association members more involved in planning and participating in IBA programs around the world.

To that end, Smith put together a General Professional Program Committee and charged it with creating programs that would appeal to bar organization representatives. Topics considered included developing effective goal-oriented national and local bar associations, the role of national and local bar groups in promoting the rule of law, the regulation and discipline of lawyers, and the ways bar organizations could encourage and structure *pro bono* services for the benefit of the poor.

The latter topic was of special interest to Smith. The absence of effective *pro bono* legal aid was widespread throughout the world at that time, especially in undeveloped countries. But the problem existed in industrialized nations as well

In April 1990, Smith spoke to the Legal Aid Practitioners Group in Bristol, England. In his address, he mildly critiqued the English judicare model of legal aid as being an exclusive method of the delivery of legal services to the poor, an approach that seemed to ignore the concept of *pro bono* service as an obligation derived from the ethos of professionalism and the privilege of practicing law. He said: "Legal aid commenced in my country when, as a matter of tradition and professional obligation, individual lawyers voluntarily undertook to assist poor people without compensation." Smith called on the English bar to make legal service *pro bono publico* a part of the profession's undertaking in that country.

Later, Smith wrote an article, in which he responded to the British claim that compensating lawyers on a case-by-case method for legal aid work was more efficient than using volunteer lawyers. Smith noted that, given the overwhelming need of the poor for such services, many paid legal-aid lawyers apparently did not understand that *pro bono* legal service did not compete with paid legal services. Both paid and volunteer lawyers were needed. (This, of course, was the point Smith had made repeatedly while President of the ABA.) He added that many English lawyers perhaps were unaware that the American experience had shown that paid legal aid and volunteer legal aid systems could support each other's efforts.

In the years since Smith made these points, the English model of legal assistance has been modified to include *pro bono* activities promoted through local law societies. Over several decades, Smith kept in touch with a group of English lawyers who were interested in the *pro bono* programs in America and who were among those responsible in England for bringing about the change. Once again, his passion for assuring the poor had access to legal services bore fruit.

Reaching Out to "Third-World Countries"

As his work as IBA President went forward, Smith found that country bar associations and law societies differed widely. Many lacked structure and had *de minimis* financial resources. This was the case especially in the developing nations. Volunteer legal service programs for the poor—sponsored either by the bar or by the government—for the most part were non-existent in those countries.

Smith believed many lawyers perceived legal aid to the poor as "a source of personal income to be provided through government funding." The concept of *pro bono* volunteer and uncompensated legal services to the poor was virtually unknown.

Among the various initiatives and programs he pursued as IBA president, the most significant may have been overseeing the IBA out-reach to bar associations and law societies of "Third-World Countries." Smith was particularly interested in attempting to stimulate the growth of legal aid for the poor in these countries. But that turned out to be problematic due to three factors: lack of financial resources, non-existence of strong, well organized bar associations, and the absence among Third World lawyers of a tradition of *pro bono* service.

In order to get his messages out about the importance of strong national bar organizations and of responding to the need for *pro bono* legal service, Smith's air miles soared. In one trip he visited countries in Asia, South America, North America, and Europe, covering some 36,000 miles over sixty-seven hours of flying time. During his two years as IBA President, Smith visited Argentina, Australia, Austria, Bahrain, Bangladesh, Brazil, Canada, England, Finland, Germany, Ireland, Italy, Japan, Kenya, the Netherlands, New Zealand, Norway, Poland, Russia, Scotland, South Africa, and Zimbabwe. At each stop, he spoke at meetings of national and local bar associations and law societies as well as to unaffiliated lawyers. During his travels, he met privately with national presidents, governors general, cabinet officers, chief justices, and ambassadors.

Smith began his service as IBA President in Buenos Aires, Argentina. Next he went to New Delhi where he met with the country's Prime Minister, Rajiv

Ghandi. Smith was impressed with the quiet force of Ghandi's personality. Later, Smith took his first trip to an Arab country—Bahrain—where he met with the Emir of Bahrain, Sheik Isa bin Salman Al-Kalifa. Everyone called the Emir "His Highness." The Sheik was the senior member of the powerful Al-Kalifa family. He mentioned to Smith that he had once met the commanding general of the Central Command at MacDill Air Field in Tampa, Florida. Throughout their meeting, armed guards stood on either side of the head of the Al-Kalifa family.

While in Bahrain, Smith witnessed the Arabic and Islamic customs of the people. He attended an Arab breakfast consisting of unleavened bread, feta cheese, olives, tomatoes, onions, and a dish of warm beans. Walking in the city later, he observed women veiled and wearing robes. Smith heard the noon call to prayer cried out by a man standing atop the tower of a mosque.

When Smith addressed Bahrain's lawyers, government officials, and dignitaries, he spoke of the critical role a nation's lawyers and judges have in enforcing the rule of law. He also spoke of the benefits of a strong, organized bar, and praised the Bahrain Bar Society and its president, Hassan Radhi. The U.S. Ambassador to Bahrain was present and told Smith afterwards that his speech "was excellent," adding "you are a great credit to the United States."

It was time for Smith to move on—this time to the African continent. After a layover in Dubai, he flew to Nairobi, Kenya. Here he found the city very crowded. Smith took note of a van packed with hand-cuffed prisoner standing and herded together like cattle in a tight pen, peering outward while their freedomless hands clutched the steel rods of their enclosure. A more positive experience was meeting with Kenya's Chief Justice. Later, he met with the country's Attorney General and its Solicitor General as well.

In January 1989, Smith left Tampa on a strenuous trip to Dhaka, Bangladesh, taking fifty-one hours. Upon arrival in Dhaka, he was met by Ahmed Hussain, the President of the Bangladesh National Bar Association. The following day, Hussain drove Smith to the residence of the country's Chief Justice, a person Smith describes as a "small, older man who was cordial and had studied law at London University and was a member of Lincoln's Inn." Smith next met with the Attorney General, who was wearing morning clothes for an appearance before the Supreme Court of Bangladesh.

Smith also talked informally with approximately fifty members of the National Bar Association, learning about legal aid to the poor. He was told there were very few—perhaps thirty-five to fifty lawyers in the country—who volunteered free legal assistance, although there were approximately 1,000 lawyers in Dhaka.

Near the end of his stay, Smith gave a speech to several hundred people in a large hall. Poor lighting and a lack of a good voice amplification system made it extremely difficult for his remarks to be heard. To make matters worse, "constant talking was going on in the wing." Nonetheless, the national television covered the event and reported it on its evening news broadcast.

The following day, Smith participated in discussions in a standing-room only conference center. Several women took part in the presentations, including a law professor at the University of Dhaka who was working on a legal literacy project. Smith learned at the conference that law courses were taught in the Bengali language, though all legal judgments in the country were written in English, causing confusion for law students who could not read English. Upon leaving Bangladesh, Smith flew to Vienna to attend the European "Bar President's Conference," where he spoke as the IBA President.

Promoting Human Rights in South Africa

Smith was well aware that fundamental human and political rights were not constitutionally guaranteed in South Africa. But there was a prospect for change. In May of 1990, Smith flew to Durban to present the keynote speech at the Triennial Conference of the Association of Law Societies of South Africa. Smith called his address "Back to the Future." It dealt with the (then) state of the legal profession in South Africa and, most importantly, the significance of the country's adoption of a proposed bill of rights.

Prior to his address, Smith met with J. Pierre Olivier, a South Africa appellate judge who was on leave from the court in order to serve on the South African Law Commission. The Commission was working on a draft bill of rights for the country. Two widely differing proposals were being discussed. One called for a "group" bill of rights that would recognize the political and basic rights of all ethnic and racial groups. The other proposal envisioned a bill of "individual" rights like those set out in the Bill of Rights in the U.S. Constitution. In discussions with Judge Olivier, Smith suggested that the country adopt the individuals bill of rights concept rather than one of rights based on group membership. In notes about the meeting, Smith wrote: "Judge Olivier was inclined to do so, though [he said] this was the more difficult position for the Afrikaners to accept."

Smith believed that those who advocated group rights over individual rights wanted to preserve the country's tradition of apartheid in some manner. He knew that passage of an individuals bill of rights at that point in South Africa's history would be difficult. But the country was adopting a new constitution and the matter of human and political rights was of great concern, and justly so, given a country that had four racial components—Afrikaners, Whites,

Colored (like Ghandi), and Blacks—and had long segregated its people on a racial basis.

When Smith met Judge Olivier, Smith suggested that South Africa's courts should have the power to declare invalid legislative acts or executive orders that conflicted with the new constitution's bill of rights provisions—the power of judicial review as existed in the United States. Olivier did not directly respond to Smith's point but said to get an individual's bill of rights into a new constitution, proponents would have to change the political climate, altering the entrenched notions about racial and national divisions. The key to passage, Oliver said, was to educate the public about what the bill of rights would mean and how its enactment would enhance South Africa's image around the world.

A few days later when speaking at the Triennial Conference of the Association of Law Societies of South Africa, Smith spoke about the proposed bill of rights and shared his views about the benefits that would accrue to South Africa and to its legal profession if such a law was adopted. Following his address, Smith was interviewed by representatives of the country's media. In each interview, he focused on the country's need to included a declaration of individual human rights in its new constitution.

Smith also participated in a debate of lawyers, judges, and academicians over the country's adoption of a bill of rights. He was impressed with the insights of the discussants, especially Dean McQuoid-Mason of the University of Natal Law School. The Dean asked provocative questions about the effect of dissolving apartheid, how to redistribute wealth and property, and how the four South African racial divisions might be integrated into the country's legal education program. Regarding the latter point, Smith told McQuoid-Mason about America's Council on Legal Education Opportunities program, which encouraged minorities to apply to law school, and afforded introductory summer sessions to those admitted, thereby aiding in their transition from college to law school.

During his time in South Africa, Smith was invited to speak as the IBA President at the University of Witwatersrand in Johannesburg. There he met with the faculty and students and visited the University's legal aid clinic, which he found impressive. The clinic had been organized by Arthur Chaskalson, a courageous advocate who had defended Nelson Mandela in the apartheid dispute. After Mandela became President, he appointed Chaskalson to be Chief Justice of South Africa's Constitutional Court.

Before the end of his stay in South Africa, Smith had one last interesting experience. When he was at the Durban Airport before flying to Venice, he went to a barbershop and received what he calls a generic,"unisex" haircut. As the woman barber was clipping away, she recognized Smith from photograph in Durban's newspaper that morning. She told him that she knew that he had spoken on South Africa possibly adopting a bill of rights. Smiling at Smith, she exclaimed: "You're on our side"! Smith's note of the incident reads: "Since she had the scissors, I said 'yes,' but I still don't know what side she was on."

Smith considered this trip to South Africa (one of two he took there during his IBA presidency) productive. He was there at an historic time when the country was moving away from its apartheid system of racial and ethnic separations. During his last evening in South Africa, Smith and the country's Chief Justice listened to the editor of the *Johannesburg Times* talk of significant changes taking place in their country. But the fact remained, many—especially among the Afrikaners—were against change. It took great effort and leadership by courageous leaders, notably Nelson Mandela, to succeed in this endeavor.

Kenya's President Blocks IBA Conference

Not everything went as planned when Smith was President of the IBA, especially regarding a Biennial Conference planned for Nairobi, Kenya. The IBA staff had prepared a comprehensive agenda for the conference. The topics of the General Section Practice group's programs emphasized human rights and environmental protection, and included sessions on legal aid, *pro bono* litigation, speedy justice, family law issues, cultural property of nations, consumer protection, gender issues, and human rights. Jerome Shestack of the United States was to chair the human rights meetings that would focus on the African Charter, the development of global human rights, the death penalty, and representing political and other unpopular clients. On the printed program, Smith's words explained the IBA Nairobi conference would be the "first to be convened in an African country."

But there was a problem. The issue of human rights was a concern to the Kenyan government. While Smith was attending an IBA Council meeting in Venice, Italy, he was handed a fax advising that Kenya's Attorney General had cancelled the IBA conference due to a dispute within the host committee. An article in the *Kenya Times* reported that Kenya's President Moi had warned the state-sanctioned Law Society of Kenya (LSK) that the conference would be called off "if squabbles within the LSK were not stopped."

Smith was stunned and met with the Kenyan representatives attending the Vienna IBA meeting. He soon received another fax from Nairobi saying that Amos Wako, head of the Kenyan Host Committee and IBA conference leader, was en route to Venice to give Smith an explanation of the unexpected turn of events. Wako told Smith the "squabbling" began when some members of the Kenyan Law Society disputed the election of Fred Ojiambo as its chair.

But that story was a subterfuge. In reality, the Kenyan government feared that IBA members opposed to the government would speak out at the conference, declaring to the world that Moi's government was oppressing human rights (which it was). Moi's Attorney General had told Moi that the IBA's program included programs on human rights. Supposedly upon hearing this, Moi cancelled the conference and blamed the cancellation on alleged disarray within the Kenyan Law Society. The morning after Moi's action, the *International Herald Tribune* reported the IBA conference had been cancelled by Kenya in response to problems within the law society.

Back in Vienna, Wako urged Smith to fly to Nairobi as soon as possible to meet with government leaders. Smith said he would do so only if he were invited to Kenya by the government and could be assured that he would have a personal audience with Kenyan President Moi. If that could not be guaranteed, Smith said, the IBA would hold the IBA Biennial meeting elsewhere.

Within the IBA hierarchy, many officials agreed with Smith that unless his conditions were met, the meeting with the Kenyan President should not take place and the IBA conference should be shifted to another location. Others, on the other hand, wanted Smith to go to Nairobi, whether invited or not, and to persuade Kenyan authorities to reinstate the conference. Wanting further clarification, Smith called George Griffin in the U.S. Embassy in Nairobi. Griffin told Smith the "situation indeed was serious." Though many IBA Council members urged Smith to go on his own to Kenya, he steadfastly refused to do so, unless invited by the Kenyan government and assured of an audience with Moi. Smith emphasized Moi had to be told that the IBA human rights programs must remain if the conference was to take place in his country.

The following day, Wako told Smith that the Kenyan government had decided that it would invite the IBA President to come to Nairobi to meet with President Moi. A short time later, Kenya's Ambassador to Italy called Smith and confirmed the invitation. At a meeting of the IBA Council that morning, Smith told the members that he would go, but would not make any concessions to the Kenyan government. "We must," Smith said, "be able to pursue our program as planned, including the program on human rights."

Though the Council approved Smith's accepting Moi's invitation, not everybody was happy. Members of the Kenyan Host Committee were concerned over what they considered Smith's hard-line position, which they believed would make it difficult for Moi to change his mind.

Nonetheless, in late May 1990, Smith left Venice for Nairobi, along with IBA staff member Madeleine May (IBA's administrative head and executive secretary), Kenyan Law Society President Ojiambo, and IBA Kenyan Conference Chair Wako. They arrived in Kenya early on the morning of May 18. After a brief rest, Smith, Wako and May were driven in a government car to Nakuru where President Moi maintained a large country estate (the former home of the British High Commissioner when Kenya was a British Colony.) The presidential compound was surrounded by a wall and heavily guarded by soldiers. In the driveways were a number of Mercedes-Benz automobiles. Smith noticed several prisoners tending to the estate's extensive gardens.

Smith, May, and Wako were directed to a spacious hall where they were offered tea and coffee. On the wall (as was typical in public places throughout Kenya), was Moi's picture, under which was a plaque with his motto: "Love, Peace, and Unity." Following refreshments, Smith and his colleagues were escorted to the adjacent presidential residence and taken to a conference room furnished with chairs but no table. When President Moi entered the room carrying a large ivory baton, all were asked to stand. Smith remembers Moi as a powerfully built, erect man, one who "carried his years well." The ministers and the visitors—except one—called him "Your Excellency." The one exception was Smith who addressed him as "Mr. President."

Moi asked Wako to speak first. Then it became Smith's turn, and he spoke openly and candidly. Smith recalls:

> I told Moi the IBA was a responsible, internationally recognized organization; that we were surprised by the decision of his government to cancel without any prior notice; that if the decision were to be reversed, it must be understood that we would conduct our programs as planned and announced; that our members were responsible but must be free to speak and I could not control what they might say; that we must be assured that all IBA members—including South Africans—may attend.

Smith's outspokenness caused IBA executive Madeleine May to say afterwards: "you did not exhibit British diplomacy during your remarks." After Smith sat down, Moi spoke, declaring Kenyans were a proud people and he did not want international lawyers exposed to the "undignified squabbling" within the Kenyan Law Society. Then, without a hint—and to Smith's astonishment—Moi declared he was *not* cancelling the IBA conference after all, and that he welcomed all IBA members coming to his country.

After the meeting ended (and with his finest British-diplomatic style restored), Smith thanked President Moi for allowing the conference to go forward. Moi then led Smith outside on the grounds to meet with Kenyan television crews and reporters. The interview, Smith recalls, took place on steps leading up to a porch. Smith and other dignitaries stood on one step, then Moi climbed one step higher to appear taller (or so it seemed.)

Preparation for Kenya conference went well, but not for long. Three months after the meeting with Moi, demonstrators who opposed Kenya's one-party rule took to the streets in Nairobi and other parts of the country. When the police intervened, disturbances broke out and several of the demonstrators were killed. The events were reported around the world, as was the subsequent arrest and detention of scores of protestors. In response, the London IBA office received a flood of cancellations for the conference. Smith called the American Embassy in Kenya to inquire about the situation. He was told they could not assure the Nairobi disturbances would not recur during the scheduled IBA meetings.

Meanwhile, Kenyan Lee Muthoga, chair of the local host committee for the IBA Nairobi conference, was deeply concerned about ramifications of not holding the conference in his country. He called Smith and urged him *not* to cancel the conference, as did Kenyan host committee chair, Wako. Nonetheless, after meeting in London with IBA officials and advisors, Smith knew he had no choice but to cancel the conference. The Kenyan press, the country's Law Society, and the Moi government expressed displeasure over the IBA pull out. Muthoga, saddened by the chain of events, wrote an article in the Kenyan Law Society magazine explaining the background of the cancellation and saying "IBA president Smith and its officers were without a choice."

Following cancellation of the Nairobi conference, Smith and the IBA Council hurriedly rescheduled it to New York City. Much had to be done and it was. As a result, 2,500 IBA members attended the conference, including a delegation from Kenya headed by Amos Wako. He had earlier arranged to be on the agenda and, when his turn to speak came up, he told the delegates "President Smith had cancelled the Kenyan conference because of criminal elements on the streets of Nairobi," and then asked rhetorically: "Where did he go? He rescheduled the event in New York City." Laughter followed.

Historic Zimbabwe Meeting

The following year, the IBA held a meeting on the African continent in Harare, Zimbabwe, bringing together lawyers from around the world, including twelve African countries: Botswana, Ghana, Kenya, Malawi, Mozambique, Namibia, Nigeria, South Africa, Swaziland, Tanzania, Uganda, Zambia, and Zimbabwe (the host country). Organized by the IBA's "General Professional Programme Committee," the three-day conference was, in Smith's view, a significant step in getting African nations to work together as well as to become more involved with the IBA. In addition to the IBA, two U.S. organizations—the American Law Institute (ALI) and the ABA Committee on Continuing Professional Education—agreed to be co-sponsors. Paul Wolkin, executive director of the ALI, helped Smith structure the conference agenda. The meeting was co-chaired by Smith and by John Young, another IBA official. The meeting resulted in agreements for future cooperation among the African nation's law societies themselves, and with the IBA. As IBA President, Smith gave a speech titled: "Legal Aid and Advice Plans," saying:

> Successful implementation and perpetuation of legal aid and advice plans depend on one single factor more than all others. That factor is faith. We lawyers must believe strongly that the human condition is improved when poor persons have an understanding of the benefits to them of law and have reasonable access to the legal systems of the nations where they reside.

"Twinning" Developed Countries with Third-World Countries

Shortly after Smith became the IBA President, he proposed an innovative program to enable bar associations and law societies in developed countries to assist bar associations and law societies in developing countries. His idea was to integrate specific bars between developed and developing nations, whereby the more established bar groups would furnish programmatic assistance and other support to an emergent law society in a Third-World nation. He called his concept one of "twinning"—that is, bringing together two countries as if they were twins.

Smith invited a former IBA President, Thomas Federspiel, a Danish lawyer, to head a new committee to investigate the concept, explaining:

> I have in mind a group of sophisticated, experienced lawyers who would concentrate upon (1) identifying developed bars that might help developing bars that need help, and getting them together; (2) suggesting specific programs of assistance; and (3) identifying possible sources of funding. I have in mind a special committee that would fix goals and work to achieve them.... I am excited by its promise....

In his letter, Smith commented that the twinning program would be a major project of his presidency, telling the members it provided a "real opportunity to be of service to the legal profession and to advance the administration of justice."

In January 1989, Thomas Federspiel reported that the twinning project was going forward. Federspiel talked with officials of bar associations in Scotland, Australia, Canada, the Netherlands, Germany, New Zealand, and Ireland. He reported efforts to implement the program in his own country: The Danish Bar agreed to 'teach' the Danish legal aid system as a model of voluntary groups of local lawyers; the government consented to participate in the project, volunteering to add a course on 'teaching' how to treat criminals [in the criminal trial process]; and the Danish Center for Human Rights said it would add a course 'teaching' basic civil rights in the justice system.

About this same time, the British Commonwealth's Legal Secretariat was developing a similar scheme, assisted by the IBA Executive Director, Madeleine May. The aim was for a developed country's bar to gather, and then distribute, surplus legal materials to a law society in the developing countries of Asia and Africa. Once the program became know, requests began to pour into IBA's London headquarters.

But not all went as planned. Third-World requests for assistance went well beyond what the planners had envisioned. For example, the Uganda Law Society requested financial assistance to restore the country's collection of legal books and materials that had been lost in its 1980–85 civil war. Though a legitimate request, the IBA did not have the financial resources to fulfill the request. Similarly, other inquiries from law societies of developing countries sought funding for projects that would require large cash outlays. The requests spanned a wide gamut of projects, from paying judges higher salaries in one country to building a national law library building in another. A law society in Malawi notified the IBA that ninety percent of the country's legal practice was performed by expatriate lawyers, and the country needed its own legal education infrastructure. In a similar vein, the Paraguay law society wanted money to use as a loan guarantee for construction of new judicial facilities, while lawyers in Lesotho wanted financial assistance in publishing law reports.

The needs were real, but the funds sought were far in excess of IBA's ability to raise, let alone disburse. Still, a few programs implementing the twinning proposal developed. For example, the Law Society of Scotland joined with the Law Society of Kenya to work in cooperative ventures limited to technology matters. A Norwegian bar group joined with a law society in Nepal to jointly develop legal aid and legal literacy programs. Putting into effect joint plans did not come easily. The law society of the Netherlands attempted to link with its former colony, Indonesia, but the effort failed.

Meanwhile, in the United States, Virginia Russell—the ABA coordinator of international programs—spoke with Smith and learned about the linking of certain European law groups and those of developing countries. Smith and Russell discussed attempting to persuade state bar groups to get involved. Thereafter, Russell sent letters to all fifty state bars inviting each to participate in the international twinning project. Unfortunately, nothing of substance resulted.

Twinning was more problematic in its execution than Smith and the IBA committee had fathomed. The causes were many: international and internal politics; lack of organization and leadership in law societies in several Third-World countries; reluctance of many developed national bar associations (and state bars in the United States) to get involved; and, perhaps most significantly, an inability of partner nations to work out the funding arrangements necessary to implement their programs. Smith knew that funding had been the most important roadblock to the success of the project. Without sufficient financial support, the twinning project could not survive.

Discouraged but not daunted by the lack of success, Smith persevered in pursuing the twinning concept of bar linkages around the world. After his term as IBA President expired, he continued to encourage governments and law groups in developed and undeveloped countries to work together. As time went on, more did so. The project's goals may have been more aspirational than realistic at that time, but it was a step in the globalization of the international practice of law.

* * *

CHAPTER NINETEEN

TEACHING PROFESSIONAL RESPONSIBILITY

A moral character is the most effective means of persuasion.
                              —*Aristotle, The Art of Rhetoric*

Character, Competence, and Commitment

Reece Smith's philosophy of lawyering always has been based on three moral edicts: First: *Every* person deserves to have their basic rights protected, regardless of economic or social circumstances. Second: Lawyers are *privileged* professionals and as such have a responsibility to use their skills and knowledge for the betterment of all members of society. Third: In rendering legal services, lawyers must possess the virtues of *good character*, *competence*, and *commitment* to clients, the courts, and the public interest. Smith labels the three attributes of professionalism "The Three Cs." He elaborates:

Character
Character means encompassing and embracing and employing in both personal and professional life high moral principles and ethical values; adhering to those principles and values despite client demands and economic pressures; insisting on professional independence and retaining, as Elihu Root once suggested, "the ability to say no"; living and practicing with integrity; dealing honestly with clients and others and giving true value for our professional services; and being civil in our conduct toward courts and adversaries, recognizing that the professional lawyer can be both tough and courteous. The word "character" encompasses personal and moral virtues, including: integrity, honesty, subordination of self interest, civility, courtesy, collegiality, fairness, skilfulness, diligence, punctuality, and respectfulness, steadfastness in standing up for, and adhering to, high moral principles. Smith un-

derscores the oft-repeated declaration: "A nation without ideals cannot long survive and neither can our profession."

Competence

Competence means developing and employing the knowledge and skill required to serve clients effectively, diligently, and economically; being an adequate speaker and writer; having knowledge of public and professional affairs; and continuing to accumulate and effectively apply that knowledge to our practice.

In serving clients, Smith underscores that a lawyer must command the essential skills of lawyering, including advocating, drafting, and counseling. In exercising these skills, a lawyer's diligence and promptness are essential in effectively and economically representing her or his clients. Smith underscores another component of competence. For one thing, a lawyer must keep informed, always staying abreast with developments in his or her area(s) of practice as well as changes in the profession, while remaining attentive to public matters, and community issues.

Commitment

Commitment means accepting responsibility for the proper, effective functioning of our justice system and defending it when it deserves defending; seeking to reform the law to meet appropriate social needs; ensuring access to legal representation for all regardless of ability to pay; engaging in bar association work; and actively serving our community in public and private life for the common good.

Smith believes that commitment requires a focused attention to all components of the legal system: the law, clients, adversaries, judges and all officers of the court. This obligation includes supporting, defending, and improving the American system of justice. He emphasizes to law students that character, competence, and commitment is what it takes. "A lawyer," Smith says, "must be a good lawyer, not just a legal technician."

Teaching Legal Ethics and Professional Responsibility

Reece Smith in his multifarious roles has always taught 'the three Cs" of professionalism. His audiences have been wide ranging, including lawyers around the world, his colleagues in law practice, law students, and business and governmental leaders.

He first taught law as a visiting professor at the University of Florida College of Law after returning from Oxford in 1952. Two years later, he began teaching part time at Stetson University College of Law while working full time at his Tampa law firm. And more recently, over the last nineteen years Smith has served as a "distinguished professorial lecturer" at the Stetson Univerity College of Law campuses in Gulfport and Tampa, Florida, where, most semesters, he teaches a course in legal ethics and professional responsibility.

Smith's teaching has been a career-long undertaking, going far beyond the classroom. He has shared his passion for his professionalism with lawyers and students everywhere he goes. This book hopefully has demonstrated how Smith has attempted persistently to teach those about the ethical and moral bases of professional obligations, not only through his words, but more importantly, by his actions as a lawyer, civic leader, and educator. In reviewing the hundreds of Smith's speeches he made over the decades, there is one common thread: lawyers are professionals, and as such, they share a common *calling of service* to their clients, the legal system, the profession, and to all citizens of our nation, rich or poor. In teaching professional responsibility, Smith directs students to focus on the precise words of the rules and standards. He then posits problems which might or might not involve those rules, asking students to analyze how, in their opinion, the posited problem should be resolved before adding his own commentary.

The questions and class discussions notwithstanding, in the end Smith always stresses to his students that the rules, standards, and associated ethical principles of professional conduct must be understood and zealously followed. Not to do so jeopardizes a lawyer's privilege to practice law and casts aspersions on the lawyer's character. Smith gives examples of lawyers whose careers were ruined by carelessness and stupidity.

Early each semester, Smith asks students if the concepts of moral philosophy might be helpful in the study of legal ethics and professional responsibility. He suggests that, at a minimum, moral philosophy invites attention to basic premises of right and wrong. ? He asks: "Do lawyers have 'special duties,' do they think people 'have rights,' are they concerned about the best outcome to a situation"? And what actions will best serve the client, the rule of law, the integrity of the court system, and the ideals of the profession and professionalism? Like any truly inspiring teacher, Smith tries to get his students to think "beyond the words of the rules," and, by doing so, expands their perspectives and deeper understanding of professional ethics and professional responsibility. Smith maintains, however, that he does not spend much time on the deeper philosophical dimensions of professional responsibility, rather focusing more on the real-world situations in which every lawyer must fully comply with the promulgated codes of conduct.

His teaching style combines lectures with problems requiring students to interact in the discussions. Students over the years have given Smith generally excellent evaluations for his teaching, saying his examinations are "tough but fair." Most students voice a common response to his course in professional responsibility: they found it "more interesting" than they had expected.

A Philosophy of Service and Professionalism

It is instructive to observe how Smith conducts his first class in legal ethics and professional responsibility. He alerts students that legal ethics and professional responsibility are always priority matters they must be continually aware of in practicing law. His course syllabus notes that while the focus of the course centers on the Rules of Professional Conduct and Code of Judicial Conduct, the substance of professionalism goes much deeper. Smith emphasizes that the profession's codified rules set out what should be considered *minimum* standards of professional conduct. Are these rules and standards important? "Yes," Smith declares: "every lawyer must constantly adhere to them." But there is more. He points out that volunteer *pro bono* legal services has deep roots in American jurisprudence. Socially-beneficial traditions have grown out of shared normative values deeply felt.

Smith further suggests that a lawyer's professional responsibility extends "far beyond the standards and rules." At the core, one ought to have a "spirit of public service, which," Smith says, "that is fulfilled only by the able and honest representation of clients including those who cannot pay."

For the legal system to work, Smith teaches, it must work for all. He cautions students that some lawyers "appear to be interested primarily in only making money." Smith underscores that if all lawyers acted in such a selfish manner, the legal system would likely crumble. "Our livelihood," he emphasizes, "depends on the existence of an effective legal system," adding: "It is in our enlightened self interest to assure that the system works well." Smith continues:

> The public charges our profession with the responsibility of maintaining the legal system. And to make it work, we must assure the system is reasonably accessible and sensible. Law and the legal system respond to public as well as private needs.

Smith tells law students and lawyers that they have the power to assure the legal system is responsive to society's needs. To fulfil this mission, they must devote considerable time and talent to improving the legal profession. Many roads are available: enhancing the public's understanding of the substance and availability of the legal processes to resolve problems; participating in local, state, and national organized bar associations, and in the social, political, and economic activities of their communities. Lawyers should make available their training and consequent skills, knowledge, and competence for society as a whole.

Smith likes to end his first class each semester by raising the big picture. He tells students what he has been telling lawyers for decades: "professional responsibility involves not only complying with the Ethical Standards and Rules governing lawyers, and not only serving their clients well, it also means serving the profession, the legal system, and the communities in which we live."

"We Speak the Language of Liberty"

This biography of a consummate lawyer ends with Smith's own words from a speech he gave in Venice, Italy, on May 24, 1990, at the International Bar Association Conference for World Bar Leaders. Smith said:

> As lawyers, we must understand that we do not exist merely to make money and to live "the good life." We must remember always that we are members of an honorable, independent profession committed to the unselfish service to others.
>
> As lawyers, we protect the rights of persons and property and facilitate the flow of commerce. But our basic function is far more important. Above all, we serve both to secure through ordered government the collective interests of society's members and to protect the individual interests of those members from the excesses of government.
>
> Above all, we serve to assure freedom, peace and opportunity. Regardless of national affiliation, we lawyers speak a common language in the discharge of these basic responsibilities. *We speak the language of liberty.*

* * *

Selected List of Awards

ABA *Pro Bono Publico* Award, 1994.

ABA Young Lawyers Division, Annual Fellows Award, 2007.

African-American Heritage Award in Community Service, 1992.

Algernon Sydney Sullivan Award, University of South Carolina, 1987.

Alvin J. Arnett Award, National Clients Council, 1981.

Annual Brotherhood Award, Bay Area Chapter, National Conference of Christians and Jews, 1980.

Arthur von Briesen Award, National Legal Aid and Defender Association, 1980.

Award of Young Lawyers Section, The Florida Bar, as Most Outstanding Member, 1965.

B'nai B'rith (National) Humanitarian Award, 1977.

Bethune Cookman Student Government Appreciation Award, 1981.

Brotherhood Award, National Conference of Christians and Jews, 1980.

Champion of Higher Independent Education Award, State of Florida, 1990.

Citizens Award For Distinguished Community Service, City of Temple Terrace, 1977.

Citizenship Award, Civitan Club of Tampa, 1986.

Distinguished Alumnus Award, University of Florida, 1977.

Distinguished American Award, National Football Foundation and Hall of Fame (Tampa Chapter), 1977.

Distinguished Service Award, Stetson University College of Law, 2004.

First Recipient, Wm. Reece Smith, Jr. Public Service Award of Stetson University College of Law, 1990.

First Recipient, Wm. Reece Smith, Jr. Special Services to *Pro Bono* Award of National Association of *Pro Bono* Coordinators (NAPBCO), 1992.

Florida Bar Foundation Medal of Honor, 1981.

Florida Blue Key, University of Florida, 1949.

Florida Classic Host Committee Award, 1988.

Florida Jaycee Award for Outstanding Service in the Field of Good Government, 1965.

Frontiers of America Award for Distinguished Service, 1968.

Gold Medal, American Bar Association, 1989.

Herbert Goldberg Memorial Award, Hillsborough County Bar Association, 2002.

Herbert Harley Award, American Judicature Society, 1983.

Honored by LexisNexis and the International Bar Association (IBA) Young Lawyers' Committee through the establishment of the Wm. Reece Smith, Jr. Outstanding Young Lawyer of the Year Award, 2009.

Independent Colleges and Universities of Florida Award, 1990.

Inductee, Stetson University College of Law Hall of Fame, 2004.

Inductee, Tampa Bay Business Hall of Fame, 2007.

Outstanding Lawyer Award, Young Lawyers Section, The Florida Bar, 1980.

President's Award, Florida Association for Retarded Citizens, 1978.

President's Distinguished Community Service Award, Tampa Chamber of Commerce, 1984.

Professionalism Award of the American Inns of Court for the U.S. 11th Circuit, 2001.

Tampa Civitan Club, Outstanding Citizen of the Year Award, 1986.

Tampa Jaycee Distinguished Service Award as Outstanding Young Man, 1960.

University of Florida Law Center Association Trustees Award, 1981.

University of Florida Law Review Alumni Association, Alumnus of the Year Award, 1974.

Countries Visited

Argentina
Australia
Austria
Bahamas
Bahrain
Belgium
Belize
Bermuda
Bolivia
Brazil
Canada: All Providences
   except Northwest Territories
China (PRC)
Colombia
Cuba
Denmark
Dominican Republic
Ecuador
Finland
France
Germany
Greece
Haiti
Honduras
Hungary
India
Ireland
Italy
Jamaica
Japan
Kenya

Luxembourg
Malaysia
Mexico
Monaco
Morocco
Nepal
Netherlands
New Zealand
Nigeria
Norway
Panama
Paraguay
Peru
Poland
Portugal
Puerto Rico
Russia (USSR)
Samoa
Saudi Arabia
Senegal
Singapore
South Africa
Spain
Sweden
Switzerland
Taiwan
Turkey
United Arab Emirates (Dubai)
United Kingdom
United States: All fifty states
Vatican City

Yugoslavia
Zambia
Zimbabwe

Also:
British Virgin Islands
Cayman Islands
Hong Kong
Macau
U.S. Virgin Islands

BIBLIOGRAPHY

Books

David Alexander, *The American Scholarships in the History of the Rhodes Trust 1902–1999*, (Anthony Kenny editor, Oxford U. Press 2001).

The American Secretary of the Rhodes Trust, *Oxford and the Rhodes Scholarships* (Vienna, Virginia 2006).

14 Annuals of America, *1916–1928, World War and Prosperity* (Encyclopedia Britannica Inc., Chicago 1968).

Aristotle, *The Art of Rhetoric,* quoted in W. Ross Winterowd, *Rhetoric & Writing* (Allyn & Bacon, Inc., Boston 1965).

Frank Aydelotte, *The American Rhodes Scholar* (Princeton U. Press 1946).

Frank Aydelotte, *Rhodes Scholars Elect List for 1949* (American Secretary for the Rhodes Scholarship Trust 1949).

Frank Aydelotte, *The Vision of Cecil Rhodes* (Oxford U. Press, England 1946), (simultaneously published in the U.S. by Princeton U. Press).

Herbert Baker, *Cecil Rhodes* (Oxford U. Press, England 1934).

Best Lawyers in America (2008).

Book of Lists, Central Florida's Largest Law Firms, Ranked on Number of in-House Attorneys in Central Florida Office (2006).

Book of Lists, Law Firms Ranked by Number of Bay Area Lawyers (2007).

Quintilla Geer Bruton & David E. Bailey, Jr., *Plant City: Its Origin and History* (Valkyrie Press, St. Petersburg 1977).

Doyle Elam Carlton, Biographical Section, *Pioneer Florida,* Vol. 3 (Southern Publishing Co., Tampa 1959).

James C. Clark, *Delaying Tactics Hindered Florida School Integration, Quick Looks at Florida History* (Pineapple Press, Sarasota 2000).

James C. Clark, *Quick Looks at Florida's History* (Pineapple Press, Sarasota 2000).

David Colburn & Richard Sher, *Florida's Gubernatorial Politics in the Twentieth Century* (U. Press of Florida, Gainesville 1980).

James W. Covington & Debbie Lee Wavering, *The Mayors of Tampa: A Brief Administrative History* (U. of Tampa 1987).

Ed Cray, *Ramblin Man: The Life and Times of Woody Guthrie* (W.W. Norton & Co., 2004).

David Crockett, *Davy Crockett: His Own Story* (1834).

Robert Galloway Dixon, *States in the Federal System: Baker v. Carr* (5th ed. Aspen Pub. Co. 2005).

James A. Dooley & Alan W. Houseman, *Legal Services History,* National Legal Aid and Defender Association (1984).

Lord Elton, *The Rhodes Trust, 1903–1953* (Oxford U. Press, England 1955).

Charles Estes, *Estes Genealogies 1097–1893*, and Mary Folk Webb & Patrick Mann Estes, *Cary-Estes Genealogy* (1939).

Ralph Evans, *Register of Rhodes Scholars 1903–1955* (Oxford Trust 1996).

Charles Fontenay, *Estes Kefauver, A Biography* (U. Tenn. Press 1980).

Lawrence M. Friedman, *A History of American Law* (2nd ed., Sanford U. Press 1985).

Michael Gannon, *Florida: A Short History* (Rev. ed., U. Press of Florida, Gainesville 1993).

E.H. Gombrich, *The Story of Art.* (16 ed., Phaidon Press, London, 1996, repub. 2005).

George Marvin Green, Biographical Section, *Pioneer Florida* (Southern Publishing Co., Tampa 1959).

V.H.H. Green, *A History of Oxford University* (Batsford, England 1974).

Mark I. Greenberg, *University of South Florida: The First Fifty Years,1956–2006* (USF, Tampa 2006).

Richard L. Hansen, *The Supreme Court and Election Law from Baker v. Car to Bush v. Gore* (N.Y. U. Press 2006).

William C. Harvard & Loren Beth, *The Politics of Misrepresentation: Rural-Urban Conflict in the Florida Legislature* (Louisiana State U. Press, Baton Rouge 1962).

Roy A. Haynes, *The Success of Prohibition,* 60 Congressional Records, 2d Session, 2505–2507 (January 1927) reprinted in *The Annals of America* (Encyclopedia Britannica, Inc. Chicago, 1968).

William Hayter, *Oxford, The Golden Heart of Britain* (Thomas Pub., Oxford 1981).

Matthew P. Heinrich, *Davy Crockett: Not Just King of the Wild Frontier* (no date, out of print).

Christopher Hibbert, *The Encyclopedia of Oxford* (Macmillan, London 1988).

David M. Kennedy, *Freedom from Fear, The American People in Depression and War 1929–1945* (Oxford U. Press 1999).

Anthony Kenny, *The Rhodes Trust and Its Administration*, in *The History of the Rhodes Trust, 1902–1999* (Anthony Kennedy (editor), Oxford U. Press 2001).

Anthony K. Kronman, *The Lost Lawyer: Failing Ideals of the Legal Profession* (Harvard U. Press 1993).

Jethro K. Lieberman, *Milestones: 200 Years of American Law: Milestones in Our Legal History* (W.W. Norton & Co. 1978).

David Hayes Lowenstein, *Election Law: Cases and Materials* (3rd ed., Carolina Academic Press Durham 2004).

Giddings Earl Mabry, *Biographical Section, Pioneer Florida: Personal and Family Records*, Vol. III, 14 (Southern Publishing Co., Tampa 1959).

Mollie Z. Margolin, *Apportionment of State Legislatures; Action Taken by the U.S. Supreme Court in Baker v. Carr* (Library of Congress, Legislative Reference Service 1963).

James McDonald, *Rhodes, A Heritage* (Oxford U. Press, Oxford 1943).

James McDonald, *Rhodes, A Life* (Oxford U. Press, Oxford 1927).

George McKenna, *American Populism* (1974).

Marian C. McKenna, *Tapping Reeve and the Litchfield Law School* (Oceaba Publications 1986).

Bob Miller & Emma Dermen, *Leven-Cent Cotton* (1929) in *Songs of Work and Freedom* (Edith Fowke & Jose Glazer, eds.) reprinted in 14 *The Annals of America* (Encyclopedia Britannica, Inc., Chicago 1968).

William Mitchell, *Military Aviation and National Defense* (1925), reprinted in 14 *The Annals of America, 1916–1928 World War and Prosperity* (Encyclopedia Britannica, Inc., Chicago 1968).

The Oxford Companion to the Supreme Court of the United States, 2d ed. (Kermit L. Ha., ed., Oxford U. Press, Oxford 2005).

Oxford and the Rhodes Scholarships (Rhodes Trust, Vienna Virginia, July 2006).

Oxford University: What's Wi,at: The 1949–1949 Undergraduate Guide (Nuffield Press, Ltd., Oxford 1948).

Samuel Proctor, *The Prelude to the New History of Florida 1877–1919* (Michael Gannon, Ed., U. Press of Florida 1966).

Winona T. Read, *An Overview of Private Bar Delivery Systems, Legal Services Corporation* (1981) published by American Bar Association, *Involving Private Attorneys in the Delivery of Legal Services to the Poor: Models and Methods* (1982).

OK Reaves, *Biographical Section, Pioneer Florida*, Vol. 3 (Southern Publishing Co., Tampa 1959).

Alfred Z. Reed, *Training for the Public Profession of Law* (Charles Scribner's Sons 1921).

Deborah L. Rhode, *Pro Bono in Principal and in Practice* (Sanford U. Press 2005).

Deborah L. Rhode & Geoffrey C. Hazard, Jr., *Professional Responsibility and Regulation* (West 2002).

Robert L. Rotberg, *The Founder: Cecil Rhodes and the Pursuit of Power* (Oxford U. Press, N.Y. 1988).

Peter Sager, *Oxford and Cambridge, An Uncommon History* (Thames & Hudson, London, U.K. 1993).

Thomas J. Schaeper & Kathleen Schaeper, *Cowboys Into Gentleman, Rhodes Scholars, Oxford, and the Creation of an American Elite* (Berghahn Books, N.Y. 1997).

Arthur M. Schlesinger, Jr., *The Ages of Jackson* (1945).

Bernard G. Segal, *Living Gently Within the Law* (U. of Penn. Almanac, Feb. 1997).

Joseph A. Soares, *The Modernization of Oxford University* (Stanford U. Press 1999).

Robert Stevens, *Legal Education in America form the 1850s until the 1980s* (U. of North Carolina Press 1983).

Edward R. Sunderland, *History of the American Bar Association and its Work* (Harvard U. Press 1953).

Michael I. Swygert, *And, We Must Make Them Noble: A Contextual History of the Valparaiso University School of Law 1879–2004* (Carolina Academic Press, Durham 2004).

Michael I. Swygert & W. Gary Vause, *Florida First Law School: A History of Stetson University College of Law* (Carolina Academic Press, Durham 2006).

Lawrence Tribe, *American Constitutional History* (3rd ed., Foundation Press 2000).

Nancy Turner, *Ye Mystic Krewe of Gasparilla: 1904–1979* (The Cider Press, Inc., Tampa 1979).

U.S. News and World Report, reprinted on cover of E.H. Gombrich, *The Story of Art* (n.d.).

2007 Vault Guide to Top 100 Law Firms (Vault, Inc. 2007).

W.M. Wade, *Walks in Oxford* (Oxford U. Press 1817).

David Elmer Ward, Biographical Section, *Pioneer Florida* (Southern Publishing Co., Tampa 1959).

Michael Watts, *Christ Church Oxford* (Pitkin Pictures, London 1973).

Professional Journals

ABA President Visits Portland, Oregon State B.J. 16 (July 1981).

Development of Florida Legal Services, Inc., 48 Fla. B.J. 733 (Dec. 1974).

Diversity Scorecard, Minority L.J. (2006).

Thomas Eichelbaum, *The Profession: Standards and Independence,* New Zealand L.J. (Aug. 1990).

Bernard C. Gavit, *Indiana's Constitution and Admission to the Bar*, 16 ABA J. 595 (1930).

R. James Granelli, *Foley and Smith in Hot Race to Be ABA President-Elect*, N.Y. L. J. (Aug. 4, 1978).

Joel B. Grossman, *Federal Judicial Selection: The Work of the ABA Committee*, 8 Midwest Journal of Political Science 221 (Aug. 1964).

Peter D. Klingman, *Against Corruption: Suspensions and Removals*, Fla. Historical Quarterly.

Legal Forms and Work Sheets, Florida B.J. 380 (April 1959).

Rhonda McMillion, *The ABA's Lobbying Efforts Have Group Up Since Modest Start in 1957*, ABA J. 66 (April 2007).

William H. Neukom, *An Investment in Our Future*, ABA J. (April 2008).

Justice Sandra Day O'Connor, *Meeting the Demand for Pro Bono Services*, 2 B. U. Pub. Int. Law J. 1 (1992).

Roscoe Pound, *The Causes of Popular Dissatisfaction with the Administration of Justice*, J. of the Am. Judicature Society 45 (Aug. 1962).

James J. Robinson, *Admission to the Bar as Provided for in the Indiana Constitutional Convention of 1950*, 1 Indiana L.J. 209 (1926).

Warren A. Seavey, *The Association of American Law Schools in Retrospect*, 3 J. of Legal Ed. (1951).

Bernard Segal, *Non Partisan Selection of Judges*, 50 ABA J. 830 (Sept. 1964).

Scott Slonim, *Kutak Panel Report: No Mandatory Pro Bono*, 67 ABA J. 33 (1981).

Smith's Ascension Climaxes Career of Leadership in the ABA, National Law J. (Aug. 4, 1980).

Wm. Reece Smith, Jr., *Development of Florida Legal Services, Inc.*, Fla. B.J. (Dec. 1974).

Wm. Reece Smith, Jr., *Private Bar Involvement in Legal Services to the Poor*, 59 ABA. J. 12 (1985).

Wm. Reece Smith, Jr., *Professionalism? What's That?*, Fla. B.J. (May 1998).

Wm. Reece Smith Jr., *The 1980s—Building on a Firm Foundation*, West Virginia B.J. (Spring 1980).

Russell N. Sullivan, *The Professional Organizations and Legal Education*, 41 J. of Legal Ed. 401 (1952).

Times Seems Right for Prepaid Legal Services, Portland Oregon J. of Commerce (Jan. 27, 1981).

Glen R. Winters, *Judicial Selection and Tenure—The Missouri Plan*, 58 Illinois B.J. 510 (March 1960).

Law Reviews

R. Abel, *Law Without Politics: Legal Aid Under Advanced Capitalism*, 32 UCLA L. Rev. 474 (1985).

Adam M. Adams, *Bernard G. Segal*, 129 U. of Penn. L. Rev. 1023 (May 1981).

Paul D. Carrington, *The Revolutionary Idea of University Legal Education*, 31 William & Mary L. Rev. 527 (1990).

Talbot D'Alemberte, *The Role of the Courts in Providing Legal Services: A Proposal to Provide Legal Access for the Poor*, 17 Florida State U. L. Rev. 107 (1989).

Evan A. Davis, *The Meaning of Professional Independence*, 103 Col. L. Rev. 1280 (2003).

Harry T. Edwards, A Lawyers Duty to Serve the Public Good, 65 N.Y. U. L. Rev. 1148 (Oct. 1990).

Gregory A. Hearing, *Funding Legal Services for the Poor: Florida's IOTA Program— Now is the Time to Make it Mandatory*, 16 Fla. St. U. L. Rev. 337 (1988).

Esther F. Lardent, *Mandatory Pro Bono in Civil Cases: The Wrong Answer to the Right Question*, 49 Maryland L. Rev. 78 (1990).

Stephen T. Maher, *No Bono: The Efforts of the Supreme Court of Florida to Promote Availability of Legal Services*, 41 U. of Miami L. Rev. 973 (1987).

Lee Muthoga, *Why the I.B.A. Conference Was Moved from Nairobi*, 24 Nairobi L. Monthly 8 (Sept. 1990).

Steven B. Rosenfeld, *Mandatory Pro Bono: Historical and Constitutional Perspectives*, 2 Cardozo L. Rev. 255 (1981).

David L. Shapiro, *The Enigma of a Lawyer's Duty to Serve*, 55 N.Y.U.L. Rev. 735 (1980).

P. Siegel, *Interest on Lawyers' Trust Account Programs; Do They "Take Property" of the Client?* 36 U. Fla. L. Rev. 674 (1984).

Wm. R. Smith, Jr., *Constitutional Law: The Right of the Negro to Legal Education*, 1 U. Fl. L. Rev. 296 (Summer 1948).

Luther M. Swygert, *Should Indigent Civil Litigants in Federal Courts Have a Right to Appointed Counsel?*, 39 Wash. & Lee L. Rev. 1267 (1982).

Glen R. Winters, *The Merit Selection for Judicial Selection and Tenure—Its Historical Development*, 64 Duquesne L. Rev. 61 (Fall 1968).

Miscellaneous Reports

2006 Carlton Fields Annual Diversity Report (2006).

AALS Commission of *Pro Bono* and Public Service Opportunities in Law Schools, *Learning to Serve, A Summary of the Findings and Recommenda-*

tions of the Commission on Pro Bono and Public Service Opportunities in Law Schools, AALS (1999).

ABA Pro Bono Conference Anaheim, California (Jan. 1984).

ABA Standing Committee on Legal Aid and Indigent Defendants, *Support for the Legal Services Corporation* (Aug. 1981).

Larry Berkson, *A Merit Plan for Selecting Judges in Florida* (unpublished, n.d.).

Kenneth F. Boehm & Peter T. Flaherty, *Why the Legal Services Corporation Must Be Abolished*, The Heritage Foundation (Oct. 1995).

Conference Report, First Regional Conference of African Bar Associations 92–202, IBA (1991).

John Cooper, *Public Legal Services: A Comparative Study of Policy, Politics and Practice* (1983).

Marc Galanter & Thomas Palay, *Public Service Implications of Evolving Law Firm Size and Structure*, in *The Law Firm and the Public Good*, Robert A. Katzmann (editor), The Brookings Institution (1995).

Higher Education & Fl's Future, The Brumbaugh Report, Florida Board of Control, Council for the Study of Higher Education in Florida (1954).

Informational Report to the House of Delegates (ABA Feb. 18–19, 1985).

Informational Report to the House of Delegates (ABA Aug. 11–12, 1987).

International Bar Association Committee to Enhance IBA Mission and Goals (WRS, Jr. Archives 1990).

Mandate for Change, Heritage Foundation Report, 1st draft (WRS, Jr. Archives, Oct. 1980).

President's Report, *Annual Report*, Florida Legal Services, Inc. (1974).

President's Report, *Annual Report*, Florida Legal Services, Inc. (1975).

Charles E. Rounds, Jr., *IOLTA: Interest without Principle*, Cato Institute (Dec. 1997).

Legal Citations, Authorities, and Records

12 U.S.C. §36 and 81.

Art. III, §16(a) Florida Constitution (1968), subsequently amended and adopted 1998.

Art. V Florida Constitution §20 as amended (1972), subsequently amended and adopted 1998.

Baker v. Carr, 369 U.S. 186 (1962).

Brown v. Board of Education of Topeka, 347 U.S. 483 (1954).

Robert Butterworth, *Brief of Attorney General, in the Supreme Court of Florida, in re 2002 Joint Resolution of Apportionment*, Case No. SC02-194 (2002).

Colegrove v. Green, 328 U.S. 549 (1946).

Cone v. Florida Bar, 108 S. Ct. 268 (1987).

Cone v. Florida Bar, 626 F. Supp. 132 (M.D. Fla. 1985), *aff'd* 819 F.2d (11th Cir.) *cert. denied.,* 108 S. Ct. 268 (1987).

Cone v. Florida Bar, 819 F.2d 1002 (1987).

Dickinson v. First Nat. Bank in Plant City, Fl., 400 F.2d 548 (5th Cir. Sept. 12 1968).

First National Bank in Plant City, Florida v. Dickinson, 274 F. Supp. 449 (N.D. Fla. May 6, 1967).

First National Bank in Plant City, Florida v. Dickinson, 393 U.S. 1079 (Feb. 24, 1969) *aff'd First National Bank in Plant City, Florida v. Dickinson,* 396 U.S. 122 (Dec. 9, 1969) *reh. den.* by *First National Bank in Plant City, Florida v. Dickinson,* 396 U.S. 1047 (Jan. 19, 1970).

Record, Volume 1, *The First National Bank in Plant City, Florida, vs. Fred O. Dickinson, Jr., Comptroller of the State of Florida, ex officio Commissioner of Banking,* (legal files of Wm. Reece Smith, Jr., Archives).

First National Bank of Logan v. Walker Bank & Trust Co., 385 U.S. 252 (1969).

First National Bank of Plant City v. Dickinson, 396 U.S. 122 (1969).

Fisher v. Hurst, 68 Sup. Ct. 389 (1948).

Fla. Stat. 59.061(1)(a).

Fla. Stat. 659.06 (1)(a).

Florida Constitution, Article III, IV, V (Legislative, Executive & Judicial).

Florida East Coast Railroad v. U.S., 386 U.S. 544 (1967).

Florida Supreme Court Order for Clarification, May 28, 1974 in *Turner v. Judicial Qualifications Commission.*

In re Interest on Trust Accounts, 356 So.2d 799 (Fla. 1978).

In re Interest on Trust Accounts, 372 So.2d 67 (Fla. 1979).

In re Interest on the Trust Accounts, 402 So.2d 389 (Fla. 1981).

In re Interest on Trust Accounts, 538 So.2d 448 (Fla. 1989).

In re the Supreme Court of Florida, Petition for Provision of Legal Aid to the Poor (Amendment to the Rules Regulating The Florida Bar and the Rules of Judicial Administration); Petition for Rule Establishing Local Procedure to Meet Legal Needs (Aug. 8, 1989).

Mallard v. United States District Court for the Southern District of Iowa, 109 S. Ct. 1814 (1989).

Marbury v. Madison, 5 U.S. (1 Cranch) 137 (1803).

McLean Trucking Co. v. U.S., 321 U.S. 67 (1944).

National Bank Act, 68 Cong. Rec. 5815 (1927).

Plessy v. Ferguson, 163 U.S. 537 (1895).

Reynolds v. Sims, 377 U.S. 533 (1964).

Senate Judiciary Resolution, 52-D, 1971, adopted 1972.

Seaboard Air Line Railroad Co., 320 ICC 122 (1963).

Seaboard Air Line Railroad Co., 383 U.S. 154 (1965).

Shadwick v. Tampa, 250 So.2d 4 (1971).

Shadwick v. Tampa, 407 U.S. 345 (1972).

State of Florida v. Manatee County Port Authority, 169 So.2d 153 (Jan. 20, 1965).

State of Florida v. Manatee County Port Authority, 193 So.2d 162 (Dec. 14, 1966, *reh' den.* Jan. 23, 1967).

Shepherd v. Manatee County Port Authority, 193 So.2d 165 (Dec. 14, 1966, *reh' den* Jan. 23, 1967).

Statute of Henry VII, 1495m Hen. 12 (repealed 1883).

Swann v. Adams, 378 U.S. 553 (1964).

Swann v. Adams, 383 U.S. 210, 212 (1966).

Swann v. Adams, 385 U.S. 440 (1967).

Tampa Port Authority v. Manatee County Port Authority, 193 So 2d 165 (Dec. 14, 1966, *reh' den* Jan 23, 1967).

Texas v. Johnson, 491 U.S. 397 (1989).

Waters v. Wachovia Bank, 450 U.S. 1 (2007).

Wm. Reece Smith, Jr., Jurisdictional Statement in *Swann v. Adams* file (WRS, Jr. Archives 1963).

Wm. Reece Smith, Jr., RS Jr., Brief in Civil Action 1216, 3, U.S.D.C. North District of Florida (Nov. 23, 1966), on certiorari to the U.S. Supreme Court.

Wm. Reece Smith, Jr.'s Testimony, *Representation for Indigent Defendants in the Federal Courts*, Hearings Before Subcommittee of the Committee on the Judiciary House of

General Periodicals

A Report on IBA's First Regional Conference for Officials of African Bar Associations, IBA International Bar News (Feb.–March 1992).

A Talk with Reece Smith, The Phoenix (U. of Chicago Law School, Nov. 6, 1980).

ABA Chief Scores FTC, Urges Legal Aid for Poor, Richmond Times Dispatch (Nov. 21, 1980).

ABA Chief Voices Support for Prepaid Legal Plans, L.A. Daily Journal (Jan. 15, 1981).

ABA Honours IBA President, International Bar News (Nov./Dec. 1989).

ABA President Seeks Peer Review Support, N.J. State Bar Advocate (1981).

ABA President Speaks, Georgia State Bar News (March 1981).

Appeals Court Tosses $1.58 Billion Verdict Against Morgan Stanley, Florida Daily Business Journal (March 22, 2007).

Bar Opposed Reagan Plant to End Poverty Law Program, 17 ABA Washington Letter, American Bar Association (April 1, 1981).

Distinguished Alumnus Award Winner Reflects on His Carolina Experience, U. of South Carolina News 1 (Oct. 1991).

Florida First to Implement ABA Criminal Justice Rules, Broward Review (Feb. 27, 1973).

Florida Legal Elite, Florida Trend's Magazine (2006).

Former ABA Chief Urges Lawyers to Serve the Poor, Chicago Daily Law Bulletin (Sept. 25, 1981).

House Task Force Studies LSC, The ABA Challenged Critics of the Legal Services Corporation During Hearings Last Month, 17 ABA Washington Letter (April 1, 1981).

Candice Hughes, Donate Aid, Lawyers Told, Austin American-Statesman (Sept. 11, 1981).

Lacrosse Report, The Isis (Nov. 23, 1949).

Lawyers Giving Public A Raw Deal? U.S. News & World Report (Dec. 1, 1980).

Rhonda McMillion, *50-Year Dash,* ABA Journal, (April 2007).

Robert W. Meserve, The American Bar Association: A Brief History and Appreciation, The Newcomer Society (1973).

Kevin Rennie Meskill, Savvy and Timing, Courant (Nov. 4, 2007).

Prepaid Legal Plans Hailed by ABA Chief, Chicago Daily Law Bulletin (Jan. 8, 1981).

Prepaid Legal Plans Supported, Minneapolis Finance & Commerce Daily (Jan. 10, 1981).

State Commission Studies SUS, The Oracle (Nov. 19, 1980).

Wm. Reece Smith to Address Bar, Newsletter of the Orange County Bar Association (April 1966).

Wm. Reece Smith, Jr., Assistance to Local Organization Targeted; ABA President Stresses Pro Bono Activation Project, The API Account (May–June 1981).

Wm. Reece Smith, Jr., Legal Services for the Poor and Disadvantaged, The Alabama Lawyer (April 1981).

Wm. Reece Smith, Jr., Why the ABA Supports Prepaid Legal Plans, Risk Management (Aug. 1981).

Newspaper Stories and Editorials

ABA Chief Voices Support for Prepaid Legal Plans, L.A. Daily Journal (Jan. 15, 1981).

ABA Supports Prepaid Legal Services, Baltimore Record (Jan. 12, 1981).

Attorneys Debate *Trial Prejudicing,* St. Petersburg Times (June 19, 1965).

Ednam Bailey, *ABA President Targets the Changing Lawyer,* The Star Ledger (Nov. 6, 1980).

Fred Barbash, *End to Legal Aid Opposed by ABA Chief,* Washington Post, A6 (March 7, 1981).

Art Beauchamp, *Lawyer Juror Contact Limited,* St. Petersburg Times (Aug. 14, 1964).

Frank Bentayou, *Town-Gown Roles Explored by Smith,* Tampa Tribune (Sept. 5, 1976).

Brad Bole, *USF Gymnasium Gets Regents' Tentative Okay,* Tampa Tribune (Jan. 8, 1977).

Bar Chief Attacks Unruled Authority, St. Petersburg Times (June 11, 1973).

Bar Chief to Push More Free Legal Aid for Poor, Daily Oklahoman (Nov. 28, 1980).

Bar Installs Officers, Tampa Tribune (Jan. 19, 1963).

Can City Force Coast Line to Elevate Tracks, Tampa Tribune (June 1, 1964).

Charter Filed for Legal Aid to the Poor, St. Petersburg Times (Jan. 14, 1973).

Alan Cherry, *SG Leaders Won't Run Again,* The Oracle (Jan. 14, 1977).

Denton Cook Obituary, Tampa Tribune (2004).

Coronation of Queen, A Fine Event, Plant City Newspaper (March 1931).

Council to Move On Men's Clubs for Alleged Bias, Would Seek Admission of Women and Minorities, N.Y. Times (Jan. 23, 1980).

County Officials Ponder Court Changeover Problems, Tampa Times (Aug. 28, 1972).

Court Hears Ethics Plea, Tallahassee Democrat (June 5, 1973).

Herschel Cribb, Bill Bars Hospital Deficit, Tampa Tribune (n.d.).

Herschel Cribb, City Council Still Trying to Curb Night Door-to-Door Solicitors, Tampa Tribune (n.d.).

Herschel Cribb, Talking Doesn't Always Solve City's Problems, Tampa Tribune (n.d.1964).

Jay Cridlin, The World & Cup of Coffee: Tour of 35 Tampa Coffee Shops, St. Petersburg Times (Nov. 15, 2002).

Editorial, A Superior Guide for Florida's Judges, Tampa Tribune (June 16, 1973).

Editorial, Intent of the Law Was Abused, Tampa Tribune (Nov. 14, 1963).

Myrtle B. Faithful, County Borrows to Buy Land for Port, Bradenton Herald (May 6, 1966).

Myrtle B. Faithful, Economic Feasibility Ruled Out at Port Bond Hearing, Bradenton Herald (April 2, 1966).

Myrtle B. Faithful, Hearing on Port Manatee Bond Validation Ordered Continued After 3-Hour Argument, Bradenton Herald (March 26, 1966).

Myrtle B. Faithful, Judge Rules Rail Benefits 'No Concern', Bradenton Herald (April 5, 1966).

Myrtle B. Faithful, Legality of Port Bonds is Debated, Bradenton Herald (April 19, 1966).

Myrtle B. Faithful, Port Manatee Planner Faces 4-Hour Cross Examination, Tampa Attorney Quizzes Buckley, Bradenton Herald (April 2, 1966).

Myrtle B. Faithful, Port Manatee Project is Still Stalled, *Not Dead,* Bradenton Herald (July 17, 1966).

Myrtle B. Faithful, Port Opponents Seeks to Name Banks in Suit, Bradenton Herald (May 6, 1966).

Myrtle B. Faithful, Port's Bond Validation Hearing Slated Tomorrow, Bradenton Herald (March 25, 1966).

Myrtle B. Faithful, Tampa's Foes of Port Urged to Cease Fire, Bradenton Herald (May 6, 1966).

Florida Bar Approves Legal Services Corp., Daytona Beach Journal (Nov. 21, 1972).

David Frank, *Free Legal Referral Win's ABA Praise,* The Honolulu Adviser (July 11, 1981).

Rosemary Frawley, *Costs of Universities' Mass-Seating Facilities Up,* Tampa Tribune (June 14, 1977).

FTC Considers a New Position on State Rules, Los Angeles Times (July 16, 1981).

Good Hands for Tampa, Editorial, Tampa Tribune (Oct. 4, 1963).

Governor Reuben Askew Address to the Legislature, Tallahassee Democrat, (April 2, 1974).

Linda Greenhouse, *New President for Bar Group—William Reece Smith, Jr.,* N.Y. Times (Aug. 6, 1980).

Gary Haber, *Lykes Family Used Power to Help Shape City,* Tampa Tribune (July 25, 2004).

Ellen Hampton, *Bikeway May Become Reality,* The Oracle (May 12, 1977).

Ellen Hampton, *Interim President Gets Surprise Birthday Present,* The Oracle (Sept. 21, 1976).

Eric Hampton, *Reiterated "Open Door" Policy,* The Oracle (Sept. 30, 1976).

Leland Hawes, *USF Site, Names Stirred Struggles,* Tampa Tribune (Oct. 30, 1986).

Nora Jean Hill, 4 *Agencies Ask Out of Civil Service Merger,* Tampa Tribune (u.d.).

Winnie Hiu, *American Indian Finds Old Outlet in Youth Lacrosse,* N.Y. Times (National Edition, July 13, 2007).

House Kills Merit Plan for Judges, St. Petersburg Times (May 17, 1973).

Helen Huntley, *The Road Is a Little Smoother Now for New College of USF,* St. Petersburg Times (Nov. 29, 1976).

Implementers Mull Merger of Courts, Tampa Tribune (Jan. 29, 1972).

Tom Inglis, *'Tampans' Attack Port Manatee Again,* Tampa Times (April 2, 1966).

Tom Inglis, *Bond Issue Said Unconstitutional: Attorneys Battle Manatee Port,* Tampa Times (March 26, 1966).

Jim Jones, *Students Air PhD Plan Concerns,* The Oracle (Oct. 22, 1976).

Karen Lachenauer, *Reece Smith Takes USF Helm,* Tampa Times (Sept. 1, 1976).

Karen Lachenauer, *USF Opposition Mounts to Ph.D. Elimination,* Tampa Times (Oct. 15, 1976).

Law Day address in Tallahassee, New Article V Haled, Tallahassee Democrat (May 3, 1973).

D.G. Lawrence, *Bar Chief Lauds Report Critical of Fee Setting,* Orlando Sentinel (Dec. 5, 1972).

Legal ParaProfessionals Too? Florida Times Union (Aug. 2, 1972).

Ltr. to the Editor, Tampa Times (April 16, 1972).

William Mansfield, *Judicial Campaign Fund Bill Planned,* St. Petersburg Times (April 1, 1973).

John McCarthy, *City Attorney Gets JC Good Government Award,* Tampa Tribune (April 16, 1965).

Tom McEwen, *USF's Smith Will Wait To Comment,* Tampa Tribune (August 24, 1977).

Joy McIlwain, *Government Encroachment Hit By Lawyer,* Tampa Times (Jan. 7, 1980).

Joy McIlwain, *Reece Smith Expected to Get Bar Post,* Tampa Tribune (Aug. 14, 1979).

Patrick McMahon, *Reece Smith—Another American Bar Association President Will Come From Tampa,* St. Petersburg Times (Aug. 12, 1979).

Philip Morgan, *Retiring President Says It's More Attuned to the Public Interest,* Tampa Tribune (June 17, 1973).

New College Survival Is Forecast, Sarasota Journal (Nov. 29, 1976).

New Guidance Panel for State College Urged, Florida Times Union (Dec. 18, 1979).

New Redistricting Plan Proposed, Tampa Tribune (Jan. 29, 1963).

Kathleen Petersen & Cheryl Stine, *Regional Roles Defined,* The Oracle (July 6, 1977).

Pilot Plan for Cooperation, Orlando Sentinel (Dec. 6, 1972).

Reapportionment Case, Tampa Tribune (Nov. 5, 1962).

Reece Smith Interim President, The Oracle (Sept. 21, 1976).

Reece Smith, Jr. Acting as Tampa City Attorney & Attorney for Ms. Shepherd, Sarasota Herald Tribune (July 31, 1966).

Regents Appoint Smith to Serve as Interim President, USF Today (Fall 1976).

Regulation of Lawyers, Clearwater Sun (Oct. 9, 1979).

Right Priorities, Tampa Tribune (Sept. 16, 1976).

Tim Smart, *Higher Education Study Group Tackles Search for Quality,* St. Petersburg Times (Sept. 17, 1979).

Smith Heads Education Panel, Tampa Tribune (Aug. 1, 1979).

Smith Hosts Openline Today in Alpha Hall, The Oracle (Oct. 20, 1976).

Smith To Lobby for Funds, Tampa Tribune (Sept. 30, 1976).

Fred Smith, *Nuccio Continues City Hall Shakeup,* Tampa Tribune (Oct. 3, 1963).

Fred Smith, *Police Chief Problem,* Tampa Tribune (Nov. 17, 1963).

Wm. Reece Smith, Jr., *The View From the Top of the Tower,* St. Petersburg Times (June 14, 1981).

Cheryl Stine, *Plans Released to Clarify Campuses' Status,* The Oracle (Feb. 7, 1977).

Lee Strobel, *Battle Looms Over legal Aid for Poor,* Chicago Tribune (Feb. 10, 1981).

Patricia Sullivan, *Henry Zapruder: Advised Program Providing Legal Aid to Indigents,* Washington Post (Jan. 27, 2006).

Tampa Attorney Picked USF Interim President, Tampa Times (Aug. 21, 1976).

Tampa Bay News Notes, Tampa Tribune (Nov. 19, 1975).

Tampa Lawyer to Head USF, Tampa Tribune (August 21, 1976).

Tampa Lawyer to Serve as Chairman of Human Rights Group, Tampa Tribune (Jan. 17, 1976).

Stuart Taylor, Jr., *Bar Groups Support Funds for Legal Aid,* N.Y. Times (March 11, 1981).

Robert Thomas, Jr., *Bernard G. Segal Dies at 89; Lawyer for the Rich and Poor,* N.Y. Times (Jan. 5, 1997).

Top-Drawer Leaders? Tampa Tribune (Nov. 8, 1965).

Cherie Troped, Inside Tampa, La Gaceta (Aug. 27, 1976).

Bob Turner, *City Attorney Hits Civil Service Plan: Questions County-Wide Proposal, Tampa Times.*

Bob Turner, *Mayor, Council in Love Fest,* Tampa Times (Jan. 20, 1965).

Bob Turner, *New City Attorney, Comptroller Named,* Tampa Times (Oct. 2, 1963).

Bob Turner, *Nuccio Appointments Known for Achievements,* Tampa Times (Oct. 3, 1963).

Bob Turner, *Smith's Name Pops Up in Mayor's Race,* Tampa Times (June 22, 1967).

USF, Branches Solve a Problem "on Wheels," St. Petersburg Times (Jan. 19, 1977).

USF Commencement Ceremonies, Tampa Times (May 15, 1973).

USF Interim President, Tampa Tribune (Aug. 20, 1976).

Visiting Lawyers See Mock Trial, Birmingham Post Herald (Nov. 10, 1961).

Visiting Lawyers See Mock Trial, Washington Post (Aug. 31, 1960).

Paul Wilborn, *50 USF Demonstrators Gain Bike Path Approval,* Tampa Tribune (May 12, 1977).

Henry Zapruder; Advised Program Providing Legal Aid to Indigents, Washington Post (Jan. 27, 2006).

Correspondence

Ltr. from A. Clewis Howell to Wm. Reece Smith, Jr. (Sept. 2, 1976).

Ltr. from A. Skogly to Wm. Reece Smith, Jr. (August 11, 1995).

Ltr. from Bradley to Wm. Reece Smith, Jr. (July 17, 1980).

Ltr. from C. K. Allen to Wm. Reece Smith, Jr. (Jan. 31, 1949).

Ltr. from Clyde Atkins to Wm. Reece Smith, Jr. (Feb. 7, 1978).

Ltr. from Daniel Murphy to Wm. Reece Smith, Jr. (Sept. 1, 1976).

Ltr. from Dean Henry A. Fenn to Wm. Reece Smith, Jr. (May 12, 1952).

Ltr. from Earl Dayton Farr, Jr. to Wm. Reece Smith, Jr. (July 19, 1972).

Ltr. from Governor Reubin Askew to Wm. Reece Smith, Jr. (March 26, 1973).

Ltr. from Harriet Ellis to Wm. Reece Smith, Jr. (July 19, 1980).

Ltr. from Howard Eisenberg to Wm. Reece Smith, Jr. (Dec. 13, 1979).

Ltr. from Howard Eisenberg to Wm. Reece Smith, Jr. (July 30, 1981).

Ltr. from Irving F. Morse to Wm. Reece Smith, Jr. (Nov. 1, 1965).

Ltr. from Jane Barrett to Wm. Reece Smith, Jr. (Feb. 19, 1980).

Ltr. from John D. Robb to Wm. Reece Smith, Jr. (May 8, 1981).

Ltr. from Judge Winston Arnow to Wm. Reece Smith, Jr. (Feb. 8, 1978).

Ltr. from Len S. Vesro to Wm. Reece Smith, Jr. (May 9, 1949).

Ltr. from Patrick Emmanuel to Wm. Reece Smith, Jr. (July 12, 1972).

Ltr. from Prince Nicholas of Yugoslavia (handwritten) to Wm. Reece Smith, Jr. (May 28, 1951).

Ltr. from Rhodes House, Oxford University to Wm. Reece Smith, Jr. (1949).

Ltr. from Richard Gerstein to Wm. Reece Smith, Jr. (July 1, 1977).

Ltr. from Russell Troutman to Robert Ervin, copy to Wm. Reece Smith, Jr. (Aug. 8, 1977).

Ltr. from Russell Troutman to William Reece Smith, Jr. (Aug. 8, 1977).

Ltr. from Ruth Ann Schmitt to Wm. Reece Smith, Jr. (Sept. 5, 1980).

Ltr. from Thomas Federspiel to Wm. Reece Smith, Jr. (Jan. 20, 1989).

Ltr. from Wm. Reece Smith, Jr. to Dr. Robert L. Kirkpatrick (April 16, 1973).

Ltr. from Wm. Reece Smith, Jr. to Dr. Robert L. Kirkpatrick (May 5, 1975).

Ltr. from Wm. Reece Smith, Jr. to John M. Farrell, Esq. (May 2, 1975).

Ltr. from Wm. Reece Smith, Jr. to Mr. Hugh Smith (March 18, 1975).

Ltr. from Wm. Reece Smith, Jr. to Ms. Lee DeCesare (March 8, 1980).

Ltr. from Wm. Reece Smith, Jr. to Professor Manning J. Dauer (March 4, 1975).

Ltr. from Wm. Reece Smith, Jr. to Professor Robert L. Kirkpatrick (April 20, 1971).

Ltr. from Wm. Reece Smith, Jr. to Robert L. Kirkpatrick (July 8, 1980).

Ltr. from Wm. Reece Smith, Jr. to the Editor of the Tampa Tribune (Nov. 27, 1979).

Ltr. from Wm. Reece Smith, Jr. to Burton Loebl (Dec. 20, 1972).

Ltr. from Wm. Reece Smith, Jr. to George Allen (July 11, 1977).

Ltr. from Wm. Reece Smith, Jr. to J. Rex Farrior (June 19, 1977).
Ltr. from Wm. Reece Smith, Jr. to John McCarthy (July 27, 1977).
Ltr. from Wm. Reece Smith, Jr. to Members of United States Congress (June 10, 1981).
Ltr. from Wm. Reece Smith, Jr. to Paul Hannah (March 27, 1981).
Ltr. from Wm. Reece Smith, Jr. to Ray Dantzler, (March 24, 1981).
Ltr. from Wm. Reece Smith, Jr. to Richard Earle (Feb. 12, 1974).
Ltr. from Wm. Reece Smith, Jr. to William Warner (March 31, 1981).
Ltr. from Wm. Reece Smith, Jr. to Colleagues (with heading, IBA's New Committee on Twining") (May 1989).
Ltr. from Wm. Reece Smith, Jr. to Dan P. Danilov (Dec. 9, 1980).
Ltr. from Wm. Reece Smith, Jr. to Governor Reubin Askew (Feb. 19, 1973).
Ltr. from Wm. Reece Smith, Jr. to Ruth Ann Schmitt (Oct. 13, 1980).
Ltr. from Wm. Reece Smith, Jr. to Thomas Federspiel (Sept. 8, 1988).
Ltr. to William R. Gossett to Wm. Reece Smith, Jr. (Dec. 21, 1964).
Ltr. to Wm. Reece Smith, Jr. from Manning J. Dauer (Feb. 26, 1975).

Speeches

Wm. Reece Smith, Jr., *Access to Justice: The Legal Aid Experience in the United States,* Presentation to the Legal Aid Practitioners Group, Bristol, England (April 1990).
Peter R. Bonavich, Jr., *Address at ABA Pro Bono Conference in Honor of William Reece Smith, Jr., Baltimore, Maryland* (April 1993).
Wm. Reece Smith Jr., *Address to the Annual Meeting of the Virginia Bar Association, Williamsburg, Virginia* (1981).
Wm. Reece Smith, Jr., *Address to the Chicago Volunteer Legal Services Foundation, Chicago, Illinois* (Sept. 1981).
Wm. Reece Smith, Jr., *Address to Hawaii Lawyers Care, 1996 Awards Reception, Honolulu, Hawaii* (Nov. 1966).
Wm. Reece Smith, Jr., *Alternative Delivery Systems Speech, ABA Annual Meeting, New York City* (Aug. 1986).
Wm. Reece Smith, Jr., *Annual Meeting of the Chicago Volunteer Legal Services Foundation, Chicago, Illinois* (Sept. 1981).
Wm. Reece Smith, Jr., *Development and Implementation of Legal Aid and Advice Plans: Some Observations and Suggestions,* Regional Conference for Officials of African Bar Associations, Harare, Zimbabwe (1991).
Wm. Reece Smith, Jr., *Financing Civil Legal Aid: Observations Based on the U.S. Experience,* Strasbourg, France (Oct. 1989).

Wm. Reece Smith, Jr., *Florida Veterans Grand Reunion Speech, University of Florida College of Law* (April 1995).

Wm. Reece Smith, Jr., *Installation Ceremony of Sandra Warshaw Freedman as Mayor, City of Tampa* (July 1986).

Wm. Reece Smith, Jr., *Keynote Speech, Pro Bono Conference North Carolina Bar in Raleigh, North Carolina* (Nov. 1994).

Wm. Reece Smith, Jr., *Legal Aid and Advice Plans, IBA Seminar on the Role of Bar Associations in A Developing Country, Baden, Austria* (Sept. 1984).

Wm. Reece Smith, Jr., Legal Assistance Foundation of Chicago (Dec. 1983).

Wm. Reece Smith, Jr., *Legal Services to the Poor in the United States: The Quest for Equal Justice* (Archives of WRS, Jr.).

Wm. Reece Smith, Jr., *New Challenges to Legal Aid,* Speech at the ABA Pro Bono Conference, Baltimore, Maryland (April 1993).

Wm. Reece Smith, Jr., *Professional Responsibility in the 1990s, Speech at IBA Conference for World Bar Leaders, Venice, Italy* (may 1990).

Wm. Reece Smith, Jr., *The Proposed Model Rules of Conduct, Second Series, Address to the ABA Disciplinary Law Workshop,* Arlington, Va., (June 6, 1981).

Wm. Reece Smith, Jr., *Remarks, Annual ABA Meeting, Chicago Volunteer Legal Services Foundation* (Sept. 1981).

Wm. Reece Smith, Jr., *Speech to the Annual Luncheon of the Legal Assistance Foundation of Chicago* (Dec. 1983).

Wm. Reece Smith, Jr. *Speech at Dedication of Library Room at Plant City in honor of Mary Noel Estes Moody,* Plant City, Florida.

Wm. Reece Smith, Jr., *Speech, to National Legal Aid and Defendants Conference* (Feb 1984).

Wm. Reece Smith, Jr., *Speech Palm Beach Bar Association, Palm Beach Post* (March 1973).

Wm. Reece Smith, Jr., *Speech to Tampa General Hospital Patient Towers Opening Ceremonies* (May 1986).

Wm. Reece Smith, Jr., *USF Commencement Address* (June 1973).

Online Sources

25th Anniversary of Legal Services Corporation, The White House, Office of the Press Secretary, July 1999,
http://clinton4.nara.gov/WH/EOP/First_Lady/

About the Conservative Caucus, The Conservative Caucus,
http://www.conservativeusa.org/whoweare.htm (accessed Jan. 20, 2008).

About USF, University of South Florida Web Page
    http://www.usf.edu/About-USF/ (accessed (2008)).
Africa—Board Members, American Bar Association,
    http://www.abanet.org/rol/Africa/board_africa.html (accessed April 2,
    2008).
American Bar Association Committee on Federal Judiciary,
    http://www.answers.com/topic/america-bar-association (accessed Nov.
    27, 2007).
An Overview about the IBA (2008); website of the International Bar Associa-
    tion. http://www.ibanet.org (accessed April 2, 2008).
Reubin O'Donovan Askew, Wikipedia,
    http://en.wikipedia.org/wiki/Reubin_Askew (accessed Nov. 12, 2006).
Awards, Wm. Reece Smith, Jr. Esq., American Inns of Court, (2001),
    http://www.innsofcourt.org/Content/Default/aspx?Id=362 (accessed
    Nov. 14, 2006).
Biography of Arthur J. England, Jr., Greenberg Traurig,
    http://www.gtlaw.com/ people/biography/aspx?id+1701&detail=1 (ac-
    cessed Feb. 1, 2008).
Biography of Chester Ferguson, M.E. White American Inn of Court
    http://www.innsofcourt.org/Content/InnContent.aspx?Id=1316 (ac-
    cessed Nov. 12, 2006).
Carlton Fields, Attorneys at Law, Sylvia H. Walbolt, Carlton Fields website
    http://www.carltonfields.com/swalbolt.
Christ Church website: http://www.chch.ox.ac.uk/ (accessed on April 4, 2007).
Hillary Rodham Clinton, Remarks at Reception in Honor of the 25th An-
    niversary of Legal Services Corporation, The White House, July 29, 1999,
    http://clinton4.nara.gov/WH/EOP_Lady/thml/general speeches/1999
    (accessed Dec. 30, 2007).
Community Involvement & Pro Bono, Carlton Fields Website,
    http://www.carltonfields.com/aboutus/communityprobono/ (accessed
    on Jan. 1, 2009).
Hall of USF Presidents, University of South Florida Web Page (2009)
    http://usfweb2.usf.edu/History/presidents.html.
Human Rights Institute, International Bar Association.
    http://www.ibanet.com/humanrights/headpage.cfm (accessed April 2,
    2008).
IOLTA: Leadership for Equal Justice, What is IOLTA.ORG
    http://www.iolta.org.ioltahistory (accessed Nov. 11, 2006).
Kutak Commission Drafts, American Bar Association, Center for Professional
    Responsibility,

http://www.abanet.org/cpr/mrpc/kutak_commission.html (accessed March 24, 2008).

Legal Aid in Florida, Consumer Pamphlet: Legal Aid in Florida, http://www.floirdabar.org/tfb/TFBConsum.nsf/48e76203493b82ad85256 7090070. (accessed Nov. 18, 2006).

Thomas J. Meskill, Wikipedia, http://en.wikipedia.org/wiki/Thomas_J._Meskill, (accessed Nov. 27, 2007).

Philip Morgan, *Civil Rights Leaders are Rooted in Tampa's History,* The Tampa Tribune, http://www2.tbo.com/content/2008/jan/18/civil-rights-leaders-are-rooted-in-Tampas-history/life/ (accessed Jan. 4, 2009).

National Legal Aid & Defender Association, Wikipedia, http://en.wikipedia.org/wiki/National_Legal_Aid_&_Defender_Association (accessed Jan. 20, 2006).

Office of Cultural & Historical Programs, *A Brief History of Florida, Territorial Period,* State of Florida website: http://dhr.dos.state.fl.us/facts/history/summary/ (accessed 2004).

Peer Review Ratings—Explanation, Martindale Hubbell, http://www.martindale.com/ratings_explanation (accessed May 5, 2007).

Pro Bono & Public Service, American Bar Association, http://www.abanet.org/legalservices/probono/home.html (accessed Jan. 29, 2008).

Reflections on the John Allen Legacy, University of South Florida Web Page, http://usf.edu/History/allen_legacy.html (accessed 2009).

Revolt in Athens, Tennessee!, The Lawful Path, http://www.lawfulpath.com/ref/tnrevolt.shtml (accessed Jan. 19, 2006).

Wm. Reece Smith, Jr., International Academy of Trial Lawyers, http://www.iatl.net/profile.asp?id=628 (accessed Nov. 14, 2006).

Sylvia Walbolt, Carlton Fields Website, http://www.carltonfields.com/swalbolt/ (accessed Jan. 1, 2009).

Tampa Riots, Wikipedia (accessed Jan. 4, 2009).

Testimony of Norman Dorsen, Stokes Professor of Law, New York University Co-Chairman, Emergency Committee to Defend the First Amendment before the Subcommittee on the Constitution Committee on the Judiciary United States House of Representatives, American Civil Liberties Union, http://www.aclu.org/freespeech/flag/11152leg19970430.html (accessed Nov. 14, 2006).

The Florida Bar Foundation Leadership & Funding for Justice in Florida, http://www.flabarfndn.org accessed (Nov. 18, 2007).

The Florida Bar Foundation,
   http://www.flabarfndn.org (accessed Nov. 18, 2007).
University of Florida Foundation, Inc., Manning J. Dauer Eminent Scholar
   Chair in Political Science, Endowed Professors and Chairs, University of
   Florida Webpage,
   http://uff.ufl.edu/FacultyEndowments/Professorships (accessed March
   27, 2007).
USF: An Historical Perspective, University of South Florida Webpage (Jan. 1,
   2009).
   http://usfweb2.usf.edu/History/histpers.html.
What is CLEO? Council on Legal Education Opportunity,
   www://cleoscholars.com/all_aboutcleo/index.htm (accessed Nov. 11,
   2006).
Ybor City Historic District on Florida History website.
   http://www.floridahistory.org/westcoastfla/yborcity.htm (accessed Jan.
   22, 2007).

Brochures, Directories, Memoranda, Etc.

ABA Division of Legal Services, *Interest on Lawyers' Trust Accounts*, Directory
   of IOLTA Programs (Sept. 20, 2006).
Top Tribunal to Admit 27 Bay Area Lawyers (WRS Jr. Archives).
Brochure, *The University of Florida 1949 Commencement Convocation* (June 1949).
Brochure, *Oxford and The Rhodes Scholarships*, Office the American Secretary,
   The Rhodes Trust (July 2006).
Charter, *American Law Institute* (1923).
Hillary Clinton, *Remarks, 25th Anniversary of the Legal Service Corporation*
   East Wing, The White House, July 27, 1999).
William Clinton, Remarks, *25th Anniversary of the Legal Services Corporation*,
   East Wing, The White House, July 27, 1999).
Brochure, *What is a Scout? Frequently Asked Questions* (Lincoln College, Ox-
   ford U., 2005).
Memorandum, *ABA Pro Bono Activation Project* (July 10, 1980).
Articles of Incorporation of Florida Legal Services Inc.
Gail Alexander, ABA Division of Communications News Release: *Immediate,
   ABA President Recalls for Continuation of Legal Services Corporation* (March
   6, 1981).
Editorial, Legal Aid for the Poor, WTVT, Tampa, Florida (March 18, 1981).

IBA Travels, Compilation of Speeches and Article Titles (WRS, Jr. Actives, Sept. 1988–Sept. 1990).

The Worshipful Company of Grocers, Invitation to Wm. Reece Smith, Jr. (Oxford, June 2, 1950).

IOLTA Programs, *IOLTA Update* (Winter 1987).

Judicial Qualifications Commission, along with Correspondence and Notes (WRS, Jr. Archives).

Lawyers' Statement on Bush Administration's Torture Memos to President George W. Bush, Vice President Richard B. Cheney, Secretary of Defense Donald Rumsfeld, Attorney General John Ashcroft and Members of Congress (Wm. Reece Smith, Jr. is one of the signatories).

Brochure, *Legal Services Corporation Solicitation for Services* (1980).

Memorandum to ABA Board of Governors from Wm. Reece Smith, Jr., (Sept. 22, 1980).

Memorandum from Richard Earle to Wm. Reece Smith, Jr., (Nov. 2, 1973).

Memorandum from Ruth Ann Schmitt to Wm. Reece Smith, Jr. (Dec. 15, 1980).

Merit Selection and Retention, Media Resources, Bar Papers, The Florida Bar 1 (Sept. 2004).

President William Clinton, *Remarks at the 25th Anniversary Reception of the Legal Services Corporation,* The East Room of the White House (July 29, 1999).

Republican Study Committee Fact Sheet (1981).

Robert Katzmann, *Themes in Context,* in *The Law Firm and the Public Good* (Katzmann, ed.) The Brookings Institution (1995).

Robert Raven, *Memorandum, Legal Services Corporation* (Aug. 24, 1981).

Second Generation Firm Founders, Staff Matters (In-house publication of Carlton Fields, March, 2006).

Wm. Reece Smith, Jr., *Class Syllabus and Outline, Legal Ethics and Professional Responsibility, Stetson University College of Law* (2008).

Selected Correspondence and Materials on the Legal Services Corporation, (WRS, Jr. Archives 1980–1981).

Sylvia E. Walbolt Interview by Michael I. Swygert, (St. Petersburg, Fl., Dec. 11, 2007).

Wm. Reece Smith, Jr., *The Twenty Club Constitution* (Oxford U. 1935).

Wm. Reece Smith, Jr., *Travel Notes: Around the World Trip (New Zealand, Poland, The Netherlands, England)* (WRS, Jr. Archives, 1990).

Wm. Reece Smith, Jr., *Travel Notes: Trip to Bahrain and Kenya* (WRS, Jr. Archives, 1989).

Wm. Reece Smith, Jr., *Travel Notes: Trip to Dhaka, Bangladesh and European President's Conference, Vienna, Austria* (WRS, Jr. Archives, 1989).

Wm. Reece Smith, Jr., *Travel Notes: Trip to Norway, Meeting of Norwegian Bar Association* (WRS, Jr. Archives, 1990).

Peter Klingman, *William Reece Smith, Jr., Unpublished Manuscript* (WRS, Jr. Archives, 2002).

Wm. Reece Smith, Jr., *Historical Profiles of Carlton, Fields, Ward, Emmanuel, Smith & Cutler* (unpublished manuscript) (May 1992).

Wm. Reece Smith, Jr., *Profile: Edward Cutler,* Hillsborough County Bar Association (Feb. 2000).

Wm. Reece Smith, Jr., *Travel Notes, South Africa-Italy-Kenya* (WRS, Jr. Archives, 1990).

Wm. Reece Smith, Jr. & E. Diane Clark, *Legal Services to the Poor in the United States: The Quest for Equal Justice* (unpublished letter, June 30, 1996).

Wm. Reece Smith, Jr., *Personal Notes,* USF Interim-Presidency.

Wm. Reece Smith, Jr., *Three Score & Ten, an Epic Ode to Dan Lockwood McGurk by His Only Friend* (Unpublished letter, June 30, 1996).

Index of Names

Byron, Lord: 13, 152
Cahn, Herbert: 34
Caldwell, Millard: 71
Camp, William: 75
Carlisle, Russell: 126, 127
Carlton, Doyle Elam: 57, 211
Carlton, Gov. Doyle: 55, 57, 60, 81, 211
Carroll, Lewis: 37
Carswell, Harold: 72, 76
Carter, President Jimmy: 157, 161
Cassidy, Marshall: 125
Cecil, Lord David: 39
Chambers, Martin: 92
Chaskalson, Arthur: 191
Cheney, R.L.: 88
Childs, Barney: 34
Christopher, Warren: 39
Civiletti, Benjamin: 152
Clark, Elizabeth Diane: 167
Clark, James: 33, 59, 211
Clark, Thomas: 63
Clark, Wesley: 33
Clarke, Alec: 42
Clendinen, James: 121
Clinton, Hillary Rodham: 152, 156, 165, 183, 228
Clinton, President William: 9, 33, 156, 230, 231
Collins, Gov. Leroy: 125
Cook, Denton: 21, 51, 221
Coolidge, President Calvin: 11
Covington, Harrison: 139
Cowdrey, Lord: 45
Cowen, Sir Zelman: 39
Crandall, Clifford: 27
Cribb, Herschel: 82, 221
Criser, Marshall: 131, 132
Crockett, Davy: 10, 212

Crosby, Harold: 27
Culverhouse, Gay: (photos)
Cutler, Edward: 64, 126, 127, 232
D'Alemberte, Talbot "Sammy": 178
Daniels, Sam: 104, 105
Dantzler, Ray: 158, 226
Darrow, Clarence: 11
Dauer, Manning: 71, 74, 225, 226, 230
Dawson, Warren: 95, 96
Day, James: 27
DeConcini, Dennis: 162
Delafield, Lewis: 145
Deloney, Dexter: 27
Dickerson, Darby: xiii, (photos)
Dickinson, Fred, Jr.,: 75, 218
Disney, Walt: 57
Dixon, Howard: 125
Dodgson, Charles: 37
Douglas, Alec: 37
Doyle, Paul: 125
Drew, E. Harris: 69
Drew, John Rubin: 41
Dunlap, Davidson: 55
Earle, Richard: 104, 226, 231
Richard Earle, Jr.: 104, 226, 231
Eden, Sir Anthony: 37
Edward VII: 37
Edwards, Harry: 216
Eisenberg, Howard: 150, 169, 225
Eisenhower, President Dwight David: 43, 59, 110
Eliot, George: 12, 13
Elizabeth, H.R.H. Princess: 45
Elizabeth, H.R.H. Queen: 45
Ellis, Harriet: 172, 225
Elton, Lord: 32, 212
Emmanuel, Michel: 54
Emmanuel, Patrick: 225